Lecture Notes in Computer Science 538

Edited by G. Goos and J. Hartmanis

M. Kojima N. Megiddo
T. Noma A. Yoshise

A Unified Approach to Interior Point Algorithms for Linear Complementarity Problems

Springer-Verlag
Berlin Heidelberg New York
London Paris Tokyo
Hong Kong Barcelona
Budapest

Authors

Masakazu Kojima
Department of Information Sciences, Tokyo Institute of Technology
Oh-Okayama, Meguro, Tokyo 152, Japan

Nimrod Megiddo
Department K53/802, IBM Almaden Research Center
650 Harry Road, San Jose, CA 95120, USA
and
School of Mathematical Sciences, Tel Aviv University
Tel Aviv, Israel

Toshihito Noma
Department of Systems Science, Tokyo Institute of Technology
Oh-Okayama, Meguro, Tokyo 152, Japan

Akiko Yoshise
Institute of Socio-Economic Planning, University of Tsukuba
Tsukuba, Ibaraki 305, Japan

This work relates to the U. S. Department of Navy Grant N00014-87-C-0820 issued by the Office of Naval Research. The United States Government has royalty-free license throughout the world in all copyrightable material contained herein.

CR Subject Classification (1991): G.1.6

ISBN 3-540-54509-3 Springer-Verlag Berlin Heidelberg New York
ISBN 0-387-54509-3 Springer-Verlag New York Berlin Heidelberg

Typesetting: Camera ready by author
Printing and binding: Druckhaus Beltz, Hemsbach/Bergstr.
45/3140-543210 - Printed on acid-free paper

Preface

The recent remarkable developments of interior point algorithms began in 1984 with Karmarkar's polynomial-time interior point algorithm for linear programs using a logarithmic potential function and a projective transformation. The progress has been made so rapidly and extensively that it seems difficult to get a comprehensive view over the entire field of interior point algorithms. Indeed, numerous interior point algorithms have been proposed for various mathematical programming problems, including linear programming, convex quadratic programming and convex programming. Many computational experiments have also been reported together with various techniques for improving their practical computational efficiency. One way of summarizing the entire field would be to write a survey paper picking up some of the important results and stating their relationships. We will use a different approach because we are more interested in the common basic ideas behind the interior point algorithms developed so far than the individual algorithms and their relationships. Of course, it would be impossible to establish a common theory covering the entire field of interior point algorithms. We restrict ourselves to a certain subclass of interior point algorithms, and present a unified and basic theory for it. Even so, our theory involves many of the important notions that have been playing essential roles in this field.

We are concerned with the linear complementarity problem (LCP) with an $n \times n$ matrix $\boldsymbol{M}$ and an n-dimensional vector $\boldsymbol{q}$: Find an $(\boldsymbol{x}, \boldsymbol{y}) \geq \boldsymbol{0}$ such that $\boldsymbol{y} = \boldsymbol{M}\boldsymbol{x} + \boldsymbol{q}$ and $x_i y_i = 0$ $(i = 1, 2, \ldots, n)$. Recently, Kojima, Mizuno and Yoshise proposed an $O(\sqrt{n}L)$ iteration potential reduction algorithm for the LCP with an $n \times n$ positive semi-definite matrix $\boldsymbol{M}$. They showed a close relationship of their algorithm to the path-following algorithms given and studied in the papers by Megiddo and Kojima-Mizuno-Yoshise, and suggested a unified approach to both the path-following and the potential reduction algorithms for solving positive semi-definite LCPs. The purpose of this paper is to carry out an extensive and intensive study of their unified approach. We extend it to LCPs with P_0-matrices, and then propose a large class of potential reduction algorithms based on it. The distinctive features of our potential reduction algorithms are:

(a) Move in a Newton direction towards the path of centers.
(b) Choose a new point along the direction in a Horn neighborhood of the path of centers such that a sufficient reduction is attained in a potential function.

An algorithm in the class may be interpreted as a constrained potential reduction algorithm. If we take a narrow neighborhood, the algorithm behaves like a path-following algorithm. We may take the whole interior of the feasible region of the LCP for the neighborhood. The latter case covers not only the usual potential reduction algorithms but also a damped Newton method for the LCP starting from an interior feasible solution. The class of P_0-matrices includes various important matrices such as positive semi-definite matrices, P-matrices, P_*-matrices introduced in this paper, and column sufficient matrices. Under the assumption that the matrix M associated with the LCP is one of these matrices, we investigate the global convergence, the globally linear convergence and the polynomial-time convergence of potential reduction algorithms in the class.

Unfortunately the LCP is not as popular as linear programs. So it should be emphasized that the LCP serves as a mathematical model for a primal-dual pair of linear programs. More precisely, the optimality conditions (or the duality theorem) for a symmetric primal-dual pair of linear programs can be stated in terms of the LCP with a skew-symmetric matrix. Thus, if we focus our attention on the LCP induced from linear programs, the potential reduction algorithms given in this paper work as primal-dual interior point algorithms. We could start with either of a symmetric primal-dual pair of linear programs or a nonsymmetric primal-dual pair of linear programs, i.e., a pair of the standard form linear program and its dual, when we discuss primal-dual interior point algorithms. Most of the discussion there, however, could be extended to a larger class of LCPs. In fact, our unified approach originated from a primal-dual interior point algorithm for the standard form linear program and its dual. It was then modified and extended to the LCP with a positive semi-definite matrix, which has an important application in convex quadratic programs. Another advantage of dealing with the LCP rather than a primal-dual pair of linear programs is simplicity of notation and symbols. That is, the description of a class of interior point algorithms for the LCP is much simpler than the description of the corresponding class of primal-dual interior point algorithms for linear programs.

Most of this research was done while three of the authors, Kojima, Noma and Yoshise, were visiting at the IBM Almaden Research Center in the summer of 1989. Partial support from the Office of Naval Research under Contract N00014-87-C-0820 is acknowledged. The authors would like to thank Professor Richard W. Cottle, who brought their attention to the class of sufficient matrices. Without his suggestion, they could not have extended the unified approach to LCPs with column sufficient matrices. The authors are grateful to Professor Irvin J. Lustig. When he visited the IBM Almaden Research Center, they had a fruitful discussion with him on the global convergence of primal-dual affine scaling algorithms, which motivated them to include an affine scaling algorithm in their unified approach. As mentioned above, the unified approach was originally suggested by Kojima, Mizuno and Yoshise. The authors are indebted to Professor Shinji Mizuno from whom they have gotten many interesting ideas on interior point algorithms. Akiko Yoshise would like to thank her supervisor Professor Masao Mori for his warm encouragement throughout her study on interior point algorithms.

Contents

1. Introduction

Karmarkar [28] proposed a polynomial-time interior point algorithm for linear programming which uses a logarithmic potential function and projective transformations. Many interior point algorithms have been developed since then for various problems including linear programming ([1, 4, 10, 18, 22, 23, 24, 34, 49, 53, 57, 58, 59, 68, 69, 71, 72, 74, 76, 77], etc.), convex quadratic programming, ([20, 27, 46, 54], etc.), convex programming ([17, 26, 55, 65], etc.), linear complementarity problems ([13, 31, 35, 36, 42, 47, 48, 50, 51, 78, 79], etc.) and nonlinear complementarity problems ([30, 32, 33]). We should also refer to the interior point algorithm given by Dikin [11] in 1967 for linear programs, which was later rediscovered as an affine scaling version ([3, 76], etc.) of Karmarkar's algorithm. According to their main mathematical tools, these interior point algorithms are often called:

- Potential Reduction Algorithms.
- Path-Following Algorithms.
- Barrier Function Algorithms.
- Affine Scaling Algorithms.
- Projective Scaling Algorithms.

We mention the articles [21, 70] for readers who are interested in survey of interior point algorithms.

We are concerned with the linear complementarity problem (abbreviated by LCP): Given an $n \times n$ matrix M and a vector $q \in R^n$, find an $(x, y) \in R^{2n}$ such that

$$y = Mx + q, \ (x, y) \geq 0 \ \text{and} \ x_i y_i = 0 \ (i \in N), \tag{1.1}$$

where R^n denotes the n-dimensional Euclidean space and $N = \{1, 2, \ldots, n\}$.

Recently, Kojima, Mizuno and Yoshise [36] proposed an $O(\sqrt{n}L)$ iteration potential reduction algorithm, and showed a close relation of the algorithm to the path-following algorithms given in the papers Megiddo [42], Kojima, Mizuno and Yoshise [34, 35] and Kojima, Megiddo and Noma [29]. They suggested a unified interior point method (abbreviated by the UIP method) for both the path-following and potential reduction algorithms that solve linear complementarity problems with positive semi-definite matrices.

The purpose of this paper is to make an intensive and extensive study of their UIP method. It is known that a general LCP is NP-complete (Chung [8]). We will assume throughout the paper that the matrix M is in the class P_0 of matrices with all the principal minors nonnegative. Even under this assumption, the LCP (1.1) is rich and deep enough to explore. Indeed, the class of linear complementarity problems with P_0 matrices contains not only several important classes of linear complementarity problems such as ones with skew-symmetric matrices, ones with positive semi-definite matrices and ones with P-matrices, but also NP-complete linear complementarity problems (see Section 3.4).

One of the important aspects of the interior point algorithms developed for linear programs and convex quadratic programs is the space (the primal space, the dual space or the primal-dual space) on which the algorithms work. Some generate either a sequence of primal interior feasible solutions or a sequence of dual interior feasible solutions. Others generate sequences in both primal and dual spaces but update them separately at each iteration, and some other ones (Kojima, Mizuno and Yoshise [34], Monteiro and Adler [53], etc.), which we call primal-dual interior point algorithms, generate a sequence of pairs of primal and dual interior feasible solutions.

Consider the primal-dual pair of convex quadratic programs:

$$\text{P : Minimize } \boldsymbol{c}^T\boldsymbol{u} + \frac{1}{2}\boldsymbol{u}^T Q\boldsymbol{u} \text{ subject to } A\boldsymbol{u} \geq \boldsymbol{b},\ \boldsymbol{u} \geq \boldsymbol{0}.$$

$$\text{D : Maximize } \boldsymbol{b}^T\boldsymbol{v} - \frac{1}{2}\boldsymbol{u}^T Q\boldsymbol{u} \text{ subject to } A^T\boldsymbol{v} - Q\boldsymbol{u} \leq \boldsymbol{c},\ \boldsymbol{v} \geq \boldsymbol{0}.$$

Here Q is a symmetric positive semi-definite matrix. If we take $Q = O$ (the zero matrix) above, we have a symmetric primal-dual pair of linear programs. We can state the primal problem P and its dual D together as an LCP (1.1) with the positive semi-definite matrix M and the vector $\boldsymbol{q}$ defined by

$$M = \begin{pmatrix} Q & -A^T \\ A & O \end{pmatrix}, \quad \boldsymbol{q} = \begin{pmatrix} \boldsymbol{c} \\ -\boldsymbol{b} \end{pmatrix}.$$

Thus the LCP can be regarded as a mathematical model for the primal-dual pair of convex quadratic problems and linear programs. The UIP method serves as a primal-dual interior point algorithm if we focus our attention to LCPs arising from linear programming and convex quadratic programming. In fact, the UIP method is closely related to or includes as special cases many interior point algorithms (Kojima, Mizuno and Yoshise [34], Monteiro and Adler [53, 54], etc.) which work on the primal and dual spaces simultaneously. The global and the polynomial-time convergence results which will be established in this paper could be applied to a wider class of primal-dual interior point algorithms.

The reader may be interested in an application of the UIP method to the standard form linear program

$$\text{P}' : \text{Minimize } \boldsymbol{c}^T\boldsymbol{u} \text{ subject to } A\boldsymbol{u} = \boldsymbol{b},\ \boldsymbol{u} \geq \boldsymbol{0}.$$

The primal-dual interior point algorithm (Kojima, Mizuno and Yoshise [34]) referred to above was described as a method for the standard form linear program P′ and its dual. In this case, a necessary and sufficient condition for $\boldsymbol{u}$ to be a minimal solution of the problem P′ turns out to be

$$A\boldsymbol{u} - \boldsymbol{b} = \boldsymbol{0},\ \ \boldsymbol{u} \geq \boldsymbol{0},\ \ \boldsymbol{c} - A^T\boldsymbol{v} \geq \boldsymbol{0} \text{ and } \boldsymbol{u}^T(\boldsymbol{c} - A^T\boldsymbol{v}) = 0 \quad \text{for some } \boldsymbol{v}.$$

The above system is not exactly a linear complementarity problem, but we could easily modify the UIP method to handle it. Some necessary modifications were presented in the paper Kojima, Mizuno and Yoshise [36]. The details are omitted in this paper .

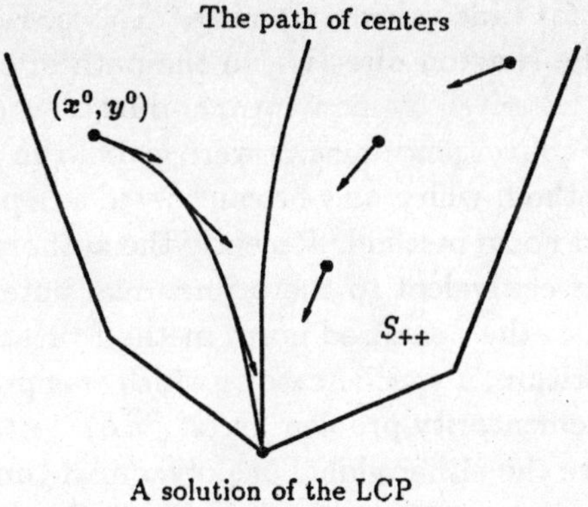

Figure 1: The path of centers and Newton directions to points on it.

To outline the UIP method, we begin by a smooth version of the method. We will define a vector field, induced by the Newton directions towards the path of centers, on the set S_{++} of all the interior feasible solutions of the LCP (1.1). The path of centers, which is sometimes called the central trajectory, has served as an important mathematical tool in the design of path-following algorithms. It was proposed by Sonnevend [65, 66], implemented for the first time in the polynomial-time interior point algorithm for linear programs by Renegar [57], and then extended by Megiddo [42] to the primal-dual setting and the linear complementarity problems. The path of centers also has a close relation to the logarithmic barrier function (Frish [19], Fiacco and McCormick [14]). See Appendix A of Kojima, Mizuno and Yoshise [35]. The vector field over the set S_{++} defines a system of differential equations such that each solution forms a trajectory (smooth curve) through each point $(x^0, y^0) \in S_{++}$ toward a solution of the LCP. See Figure 1. Furthermore, the Newton directions turn out to be descent directions of the potential function and the value of the potential function tends to $-\infty$ as a point (x, y) approaches a solution of the LCP along each trajectory.

The potential reduction algorithm [36] can be obtained from the smooth version of the UIP method if we appropriately specify a step size at each $(x, y) \in S_{++}$ to numerically integrate the vector field by using the first order method for differential equations. If in addition we choose an initial point sufficiently close to the path of centers and a suitably small step size at each iteration, the potential reduction algorithm works as the path-following algorithm [35]. Further details of the smooth version of the UIP method will be described in Section 4.3.

We should mention the works [67, 68, 69] by Tanabe. His centered Newton method, which was developed for linear programs, complementarity problems and systems of equations, and the polynomial-time primal-dual interior point algorithm for linear programs by Kojima, Mizuno and Yoshise [34] were independently proposed at the Symposium on "New Method for Linear Programming," Tokyo, February 1987. They share a basic idea of utilizing the Newton direction to the path of centers in the primal-dual space. This idea has been inherited by many primal-dual interior point algorithms developed so far. Although no convergence results were given, the centered Newton method includes a guiding cone method, which may be considered as a primal-dual path-following algorithm, and a penalized norm method. Recently the authors were notified by Tanabe that his penalized norm is equivalent to the primal-dual potential function introduced by Todd and Ye [72], and so the penalized norm method turned out to be equivalent to a potential reduction algorithm, a special case of which was proved to solve the positive semi-definite linear complementarity problem in $O(\sqrt{n}L)$ iterations by Kojima, Mizuno and Yoshise [36]. To ensure the either global or polynomial-time convergence of the UIP method, we will propose to choose a new point along a Newton direction in a "horn" neighborhood of the path of centers, which Tanabe called a guiding cone, at each iteration so that a sufficient reduction is attained in the primal-dual potential function. This specialization of the UIP method may be regarded as a combination of the path-following algorithm [35] and the potential reduction algorithm [36] as well as a combination of the guiding cone method and the penalized norm method since the penalized norm and the primal-dual potential function are equivalent. As we have seen above, Tanabe's centered Newton method and our UIP method stand on the common basis, and both aim at giving a unified view over a large class of interior point algorithms. We can say, however, that our analysis is different from his. In particular, we will place main emphasis on the global and the polynomial-time convergence of the UIP method applied to larger classes of linear complementarity problems.

We should also mention that this paper never aims at giving a unified view over all the interior point algorithms. Specifically, the UIP method does not cover

(i) interior point algorithms (Dikin [11], Karmarkar [28], Renegar [57], etc.) which work on either primal or dual space but not simultaneously,
(ii) the $O(\sqrt{n}L)$ iteration potential reduction algorithm given by Ye [77] for linear programs (see also Freund [18]),
(iii) the first potential reduction algorithm given by Kojima, Megiddo and Ye [31] for the LCP with P_0-matrices (see also Ye [78, 79]).

There has already been great success in interior point algorithms for solving linear programs ([7, 38, 63, 64]) and many computational experiments have been reported ([1, 7, 38, 41, 44, 45, 52]). Among others, we mention an efficient implementation of the primal-dual interior point algorithm on the OB1 system [41]. Recently Marsten, Subramanian, Saltzman, Lustig and Shanno [38] reported remarkable computational results on the OB1 primal-dual interior point code applied to linear programming problems with about 3000–200,000 variables on the supercomputer Cray Y-MP[1]. The classical application of convex quadratic programming is the portfolio selection theory [39]. It would be interesting to study the applicability of interior point algorithms to this practical problem. As we have stated, a primal-dual pair of convex quadratic programs can be put into an LCP with

[1]Cray and Cray Y-MP are federally registered trademarks of Cray Research, Inc.

a positive semi-definite matrix to which we can apply the UIP method. Although some computational results on interior point algorithms for solving convex quadratic programs were reported ([17, 51]), few codes are available to the public. Theoretical aspects of extensions of interior point algorithms to general convex programs and nonlinear complementarity problems have been studied in many papers ([17, 26, 29, 32, 33, 55, 65]). A practically efficient implementation of such extensions is a future theme in the field of interior point algorithms which is still growing and expanding rapidly.

Section 2 is devoted to a summary of the paper where we present necessary assumptions, the basic idea of the UIP method, the UIP method itself and global and polynomial-time convergence results for some special cases of the UIP method including potential reduction algorithms, path-following algorithms and a damped Newton method to the LCP starting from an interior feasible solution. This section might serve as a digest version of the paper for the readers who don't want to go into the detailed mathematics of the UIP method.

Throughout the paper we assume that the matrix M associated with the LCP is a P_0-matrix. In Section 3, we investigate the class of P_0-matrices from the point of view of the LCP. We introduce some subclasses of P_0-matrices and show their relations. We also give an example of NP-complete linear complementarity problems with P_0-matrices.

In Section 4, we state basic lemmas and theorems concerning the UIP method. Specifically, the existence of the path of centers is shown, and the smooth version of the UIP method is presented in detail. Some of the results established there are interesting in their own right, and some others will be utilized in the succeeding discussions.

Section 5 provides some materials related to the computational complexity. We show some methods for preparing initial interior points from which the UIP method starts, theoretical stopping criteria and some inequalities which will hold at each iteration of the UIP method under certain assumptions. Among these materials, methods for preparing initial points are important not only for evaluating the theoretical computational complexity but also for designing practically efficient implementations of the UIP method.

In Section 6, we present in detail main convergence results whose special cases are outlined in Section 2.4. Their proofs are given in Section 7.

In Appendix we list the symbols and notation used in the paper for the convenience of the readers.

2. Summary

This section summarizes the main results of this paper . In Section 2.1, we state some classes of linear complementarity problems to which we apply the unified interior point method (abbreviated by the UIP method). Section 2.2 explains the UIP method. Section 2.3 gives some assumptions that will be necessary when we discuss the theoretical computational complexity of the UIP method. Section 2.4 presents a large class of potential reduction algorithms as special cases of the UIP method, and their global and polynomial-time convergence properties.

2.1. Linear Complementarity Problems That Can Be Processed by the Unified Interior Point Method

Let R^n_+ and R^n_{++} denote the nonnegative orthant and the positive orthant of the n-dimensional Euclidean space R^n, respectively;

$$\begin{aligned} R^n_+ &= \{x \in R^n : x \geq 0\}, \\ R^n_{++} &= \{x \in R^n : x > 0\}. \end{aligned}$$

We call an (x, y) a feasible solution of the LCP (1.1) if it satisfies the first two conditions

$$y = Mx + q, \ (x, y) \geq 0,$$

of (1.1), and an interior feasible solution if

$$y = Mx + q, \ (x, y) > 0.$$

We use the symbols S_+, S_{++} and S_{cp} to denote the feasible region (i.e., the set of all the feasible solutions) of the LCP (1.1), its interior (i.e., the set of all the interior feasible solutions of the LCP) and the solution set of the LCP, respectively;

$$\begin{aligned} S_+ &= \{(x, y) \in R^{2n}_+ : y = Mx + q\}, \\ S_{++} &= \{(x, y) \in R^{2n}_{++} : y = Mx + q\}, \\ S_{cp} &= \{(x, y) \in S_+ : x_i y_i = 0 \ (i \in N)\}. \end{aligned}$$

It will be convenient in the succeeding discussions to consider the quadratic programming problem

$$\text{QP} : \text{Minimize } x^T y \text{ subject to } (x, y) \in S_+. \tag{2.1}$$

The LCP is equivalent to the QP in the sense that (x, y) is a solution of the LCP if and only if it is a minimum solution of the QP with the objective value zero. We will describe the UIP method in Section 2.2, and then derive a class of potential reduction algorithms in Section 2.4 as its special cases. If the condition below is satisfied, each algorithm in the class has a global convergence property. That is, each algorithm generates a bounded sequence $\{(\boldsymbol{x}^k, \boldsymbol{y}^k)\} \subset S_{++}$ such that $\lim_{k\to\infty} \boldsymbol{x}^{kT}\boldsymbol{y}^k = 0$; hence the sequence has at least one accumulation point, which is a solution of the LCP.

Condition 2.1.

(i) The matrix M belongs to the class P_0 of matrices with all the principal minors nonnegative.
(ii) A point $(\boldsymbol{x}^1, \boldsymbol{y}^1)$ which lies in the interior S_{++} of the feasible region S_+ is known.
(iii) The level set $S_+^t = \{(\boldsymbol{x}, \boldsymbol{y}) \in S_+ : \boldsymbol{x}^T\boldsymbol{y} \le t\}$ of the objective function of the QP (2.1) is bounded for every $t \ge 0$.

This condition was originally introduced in the paper Kojima, Megiddo and Noma [29]. We need requirement (i) to guarantee the existence and uniqueness of a solution to a system of linear equations for the search directions at each iteration of the UIP method. See Lemma 4.1. The class P_0 contains the following classes of matrices.

SS : the class of skew-symmetric matrices, i.e., matrices M satisfying $\boldsymbol{\xi}^T M \boldsymbol{\xi} = 0$ for every $\boldsymbol{\xi} \in R^n$.
PSD : the class of positive semi-definite matrices, i.e., matrices M satisfying $\boldsymbol{\xi}^T M \boldsymbol{\xi} \ge 0$ for every $\boldsymbol{\xi} \in R^n$.
P : the class of matrices with all the principal minors positive.
$P_*(\kappa)$: the class of matrices M satisfying

$$(1+4\kappa) \sum_{i \in I_+(\xi)} \xi_i [M\boldsymbol{\xi}]_i + \sum_{i \in I_-(\xi)} \xi_i [M\boldsymbol{\xi}]_i \ge 0 \quad \text{for every } \boldsymbol{\xi} \in R^n,$$

where $[M\boldsymbol{\xi}]_i$ denotes the i-th component of the vector $M\boldsymbol{\xi}$,

$$I_+(\boldsymbol{\xi}) = \{i \in N : \xi_i [M\boldsymbol{\xi}]_i > 0\}, \quad I_-(\boldsymbol{\xi}) = \{i \in N : \xi_i [M\boldsymbol{\xi}]_i < 0\},$$

and κ is a nonnegative number. Note that the index sets $I_+(\boldsymbol{\xi})$ and $I_-(\boldsymbol{\xi})$ depend on not only $\boldsymbol{\xi} \in R^n$ but also the matrix M.
P_* : the union of all the $P_*(\kappa)$ $(\kappa \ge 0)$.
CS : the class of column sufficient matrices (Cottle, Pang and Venkateswaran [9]), i.e., matrices M such that $\xi_i [M\boldsymbol{\xi}]_i \le 0$ $(i \in N)$ always implies $\xi_i [M\boldsymbol{\xi}]_i = 0$ $(i \in N)$.

Here $N = \{1, 2, \ldots, n\}$. Figure 2 illustrates the relations of these classes of matrices, which will be proved in Section 3.2. Let Q be a symmetric positive semi-definite matrix. As stated in Section 1, the primal-dual pair of convex quadratic programs

$$\text{P : Minimize } \boldsymbol{c}^T\boldsymbol{u} + \frac{1}{2}\boldsymbol{u}^T Q \boldsymbol{u} \text{ subject to } A\boldsymbol{u} \ge \boldsymbol{b},\ \boldsymbol{u} \ge 0,$$

$$\text{D : Maximize } \boldsymbol{b}^T\boldsymbol{v} - \frac{1}{2}\boldsymbol{u}^T Q \boldsymbol{u} \text{ subject to } A^T\boldsymbol{v} - Q\boldsymbol{u} \le \boldsymbol{c},\ \boldsymbol{v} \ge 0$$

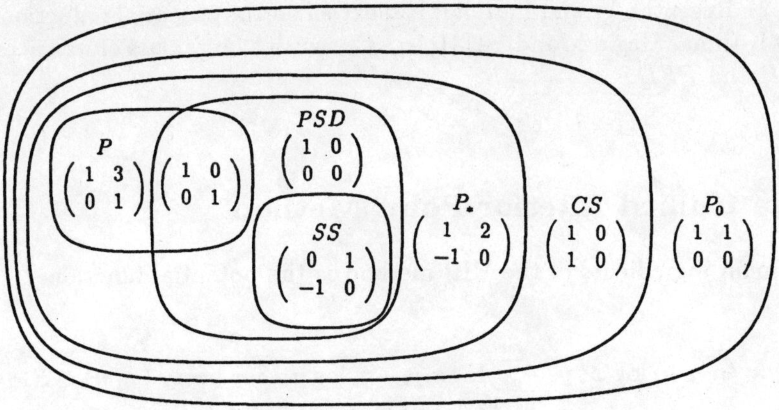

Figure 2: Relations and examples of the classes of matrices.

can be put together into the LCP (1.1) with the positive semi-definite matrix M and the vector q such that

$$M = \begin{pmatrix} Q & -A^T \\ A & O \end{pmatrix}, \quad q = \begin{pmatrix} c \\ -b \end{pmatrix}.$$

If in addition $Q = O$, P and D above turn out to be a symmetric primal-dual pair of linear programs. In this case, the matrix M is skew-symmetric.

The second requirement (ii) of Condition 2.1 offers an initial point $(x^1, y^1) \in S_{++}$ to start the UIP method, and the third one (iii) ensures the boundedness of the sequence $\{(x^k, y^k)\} \subset S_{++}$ generated by the UIP method.

Given an LCP with an $n \times n$ P_0-matrix M and a vector $q \in R^n$, (ii) and (iii) of Condition 2.1 are not generally satisfied. Suppose that the matrix M is in the class CS of column sufficient matrices. In Section 5.1 we will show how to transform the LCP into an artificial linear complementarity problem LCP′ with a $2n \times 2n$ matrix M' and a vector $q' \in R^{2n}$ such that

(a) the LCP′ satisfies Condition 2.1; hence the UIP method computes a solution (x', y') of the LCP′,

(b) we either obtain a solution of the LCP by deleting the artificial components from the solution (x', y') of the LCP′ or conclude that the LCP has no solution.

Therefore we can say that the UIP method solves the LCP if the matrix M is in the class CS.

Remark 2.2. Recently, Ye and Pardalos [82] extended the potential reduction algorithm proposed by Kojima, Megiddo and Ye [31] to LCPs with a large class of matrices including the classes P and PSD.

2.2. The Unified Interior Point Method

One of the main ingredients of the UIP method is the potential function $f : S_{++} \to R$ defined by

$$f(\boldsymbol{x},\boldsymbol{y}) = (n+\nu)\log \boldsymbol{x}^T\boldsymbol{y} - \sum_{i=1}^{n} \log x_i y_i - n\log n \quad \text{for every } (\boldsymbol{x},\boldsymbol{y}) \in S_{++}. \tag{2.2}$$

Here $\nu > 0$ is a parameter. This type of potential function has been utilized for linear programs in the papers Freund [18], Gonzaga [23], Todd and Ye [72], Ye [77], etc., and for linear complementarity problems in the papers Kojima, Megiddo and Ye [31], Kojima, Mizuno and Yoshise [36], Ye [78, 79]. The penalized norm given by Tanabe [68, 69] is equivalent to the potential function (2.2).

Associated with the quadratic programming problem QP (2.1) into which we converted the LCP (1.1) in Section 2.1, we consider the potential minimization problem:

$$\text{Minimize } \; f(\boldsymbol{x},\boldsymbol{y}) \; \text{ subject to } \; (\boldsymbol{x},\boldsymbol{y}) \in S_{++}.$$

We notice that the first term $(n+\nu)\log \boldsymbol{x}^T\boldsymbol{y}$ of the potential function f comes from the objective function $\boldsymbol{x}^T\boldsymbol{y}$ of the QP. The second term $-\sum_{i=1}^{n} \log x_i y_i$ works as a (logarithmic) barrier function (Frish [19], Fiacco and McCormick [14]) which prevents a point $(\boldsymbol{x},\boldsymbol{y}) \in S_{++}$ from approaching the boundary of the feasible region S_+ of the QP. The third constant term $-n\log n$ will be utilized below.

We will rewrite the potential function f as follows:

$$\begin{aligned} f(\boldsymbol{x},\boldsymbol{y}) &= \nu f_{cp}(\boldsymbol{x},\boldsymbol{y}) + f_{cen}(\boldsymbol{x},\boldsymbol{y}), \qquad (2.3)\\ f_{cp}(\boldsymbol{x},\boldsymbol{y}) &= \log \boldsymbol{x}^T\boldsymbol{y}, \\ f_{cen}(\boldsymbol{x},\boldsymbol{y}) &= n\log \boldsymbol{x}^T\boldsymbol{y} - \sum_{i=1}^{n}\log x_i y_i - n\log n \\ &= \sum_{i=1}^{n} \log \frac{\boldsymbol{x}^T\boldsymbol{y}/n}{x_i y_i} \\ &= n\log \frac{\boldsymbol{x}^T\boldsymbol{y}/n}{(\prod_{i=1}^{n} x_i y_i)^{1/n}}. \end{aligned}$$

The term $\dfrac{\boldsymbol{x}^T\boldsymbol{y}/n}{(\prod_{i=1}^{n} x_i y_i)^{1/n}}$ in the last equality corresponds to the ratio of the arithmetic mean and the geometric mean of n positive numbers $x_1y_1, x_2y_2, \ldots, x_ny_n$. Hence

$$f_{cen}(\boldsymbol{x},\boldsymbol{y}) \geq 0 \quad \text{for every } (\boldsymbol{x},\boldsymbol{y}) \in S_{++}. \tag{2.4}$$

It follows that

$$f(\boldsymbol{x},\boldsymbol{y}) \geq \nu f_{cp}(\boldsymbol{x},\boldsymbol{y}) = \nu \log \boldsymbol{x}^T\boldsymbol{y} \quad \text{for every } (\boldsymbol{x},\boldsymbol{y}) \in S_{++}. \tag{2.5}$$

Thus we may regard each $(\boldsymbol{x},\boldsymbol{y}) \in S_{++}$ as an approximate solution of the LCP if the potential function value $f(\boldsymbol{x},\boldsymbol{y})$ is sufficiently small.

The potential function f will serve as a merit function to choose the step lengths in the algorithms derived from the UIP method. It will also play an essential role in establishing either the global or the polynomial-time convergence of the algorithms. It should be noted that $\boldsymbol{x}^T\boldsymbol{y}$ may converge to zero even when $f(\boldsymbol{x},\boldsymbol{y})$ is bounded from below. In fact, we can easily see from (2.3) that $\boldsymbol{x}^T\boldsymbol{y}$ converges to zero as $f_{cen}(\boldsymbol{x},\boldsymbol{y})$ diverges to $+\infty$ whenever $f(\boldsymbol{x},\boldsymbol{y})$ is bounded from above. Hence, if we consider a bounded sequence $\{(\boldsymbol{x}^k,\boldsymbol{y}^k)\} \subset S_{++}$ satisfying the potential reduction property

$$f(\boldsymbol{x}^{k+1},\boldsymbol{y}^{k+1}) \leq f(\boldsymbol{x}^k,\boldsymbol{y}^k) \quad (k = 1,2,\dots),$$

there are three possible cases:

(a) $\lim_{k\to\infty} f(\boldsymbol{x}^k,\boldsymbol{y}^k) = -\infty$.

(b) $\lim_{k\to\infty} f(\boldsymbol{x}^k,\boldsymbol{y}^k) > -\infty$ and $\lim_{k\to\infty} f_{cen}(\boldsymbol{x}^k,\boldsymbol{y}^k) = +\infty$.

(c) $\lim_{k\to\infty} f(\boldsymbol{x}^k,\boldsymbol{y}^k) > -\infty$ and either the sequence $\{f_{cen}(\boldsymbol{x}^k,\boldsymbol{y}^k)\}$ itself is bounded or it contains a bounded subsequence.

We are interested in the cases (a) and (b) where we have $\lim_{k\to\infty} \boldsymbol{x}^{k^T}\boldsymbol{y}^k = 0$.

The other main ingredient of the UIP method is the path of centers or the central trajectory for the LCP (Megiddo [42], Kojima, Mizuno and Yoshise [35]). It is defined by

$$S_{cen} = \{(\boldsymbol{x},\boldsymbol{y}) \in S_{++} : \boldsymbol{X}\boldsymbol{y} = t\boldsymbol{e} \quad \text{for some } t > 0\}, \tag{2.6}$$

where $\boldsymbol{e}$ denotes the n-dimensional vector of ones and $\boldsymbol{X} = \operatorname{diag} \boldsymbol{x}$ the $n \times n$ diagonal matrix with the coordinates of a vector $\boldsymbol{x} \in R^n$.

Under certain assumptions, the path of centers S_{cen} forms a 1-dimensional smooth curve which leads to a solution of the LCP. See Figure 3. This fact was proved by McLinden [40] for the positive semi-definite case (see also Megiddo [42] and Kojima, Mizuno and Yoshise [35]), and by Kojima, Megiddo and Noma [29] under Condition 2.1. It provides a basic idea of the path-following algorithms (Megiddo [42], Kojima, Mizuno and Yoshise [34, 35], Monteiro and Adler [53, 54], etc.).

The path of centers S_{cen} can be rewritten using the function f_{cen}, the second term of the representation (2.3) of the potential function f. It is easily seen that in the inequality (2.4) the equality holds if and only if $(\boldsymbol{x},\boldsymbol{y}) \in S_{++}$ satisfies $\boldsymbol{X}\boldsymbol{y} = t\boldsymbol{e}$ for some $t > 0$, i.e., $(\boldsymbol{x},\boldsymbol{y}) \in S_{cen}$. Hence

$$S_{cen} = \{(\boldsymbol{x},\boldsymbol{y}) \in S_{++} : f_{cen}(\boldsymbol{x},\boldsymbol{y}) = 0\}. \tag{2.7}$$

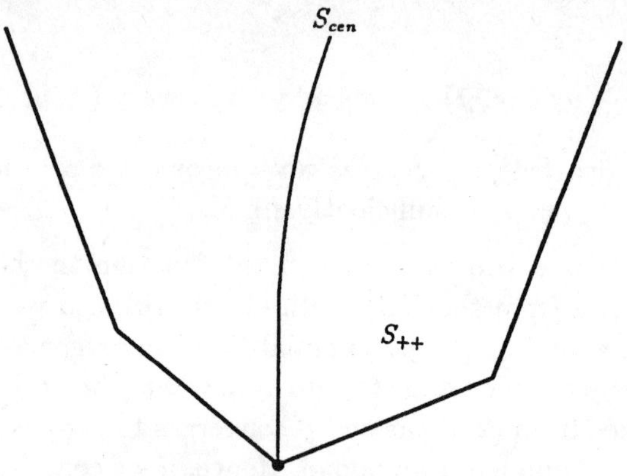

Figure 3: The path of centers leading to a solution of the LCP.

Now we shall show how to choose a search direction at each iteration of the UIP method described below. Let $0 \leq \beta \leq 1$. To each $(\boldsymbol{x}, \boldsymbol{y}) \in S_{++}$, we assign a vector $(d\boldsymbol{x}, d\boldsymbol{y}) \in R^{2n}$ such that

$$\begin{pmatrix} Y & X \\ -M & I \end{pmatrix} \begin{pmatrix} d\boldsymbol{x} \\ d\boldsymbol{y} \end{pmatrix} = \begin{pmatrix} \beta \dfrac{\boldsymbol{x}^T \boldsymbol{y}}{n} e - X\boldsymbol{y} \\ \boldsymbol{0} \end{pmatrix}. \tag{2.8}$$

Here $\boldsymbol{Y} = \text{diag}\, \boldsymbol{y}$ denotes the $n \times n$ diagonal matrix with the coordinates of the vector $\boldsymbol{y} \in R^n$. The coefficient matrix on the left hand side above is nonsingular whenever the matrix M is in the class P_0 (Lemma 4.1), and the coefficient matrix as well as the right hand side is smooth in $(\boldsymbol{x}, \boldsymbol{y}) \in S_{++}$, so that the set of all the $(d\boldsymbol{x}, d\boldsymbol{y})$'s forms a smooth vector field over the set S_{++} of all the interior feasible solutions of the LCP.

The direction vector $(d\boldsymbol{x}, d\boldsymbol{y})$ assigned to each $(\boldsymbol{x}, \boldsymbol{y}) \in S_{++}$ turns out to be the Newton direction at $(\boldsymbol{x}, \boldsymbol{y})$ for approximating a point $(\boldsymbol{x}', \boldsymbol{y}')$ on the path of centers S_{cen} such that

$$\boldsymbol{X}'\boldsymbol{y}' = \beta \frac{\boldsymbol{x}^T \boldsymbol{y}}{n} e \text{ and } \boldsymbol{y}' = M\boldsymbol{x}' + \boldsymbol{q}, \tag{2.9}$$

where $\boldsymbol{X}' = \text{diag}\, \boldsymbol{x}'$ denotes the $n \times n$ diagonal matrix with the coordinates of the vector $\boldsymbol{x}' \in R^n$. In other words, $(\boldsymbol{x}, \boldsymbol{y}) + (d\boldsymbol{x}, d\boldsymbol{y})$ corresponds to the point generated by one Newton iteration to the system (2.9) of equations at $(\boldsymbol{x}, \boldsymbol{y})$. The system (2.9) involves the parameter $\beta \in [0, 1]$. Figures 4, 5 and 6 illustrate three different cases $\beta = 1$, $\beta = 0$ and $0 < \beta < 1$, respectively.

In Figures 4, 5 and 6, the point $(\boldsymbol{x}', \boldsymbol{y}')$ on the path of centers S_{cen} denotes the solution of the system of equations (2.9). If we take $\beta = 1$ as in Figure 4, the point $(\boldsymbol{x}', \boldsymbol{y}')$ corresponds to the point $(\hat{\boldsymbol{x}}, \hat{\boldsymbol{y}})$ which minimizes the Euclidean distance $\|\boldsymbol{X}\boldsymbol{y} - \hat{\boldsymbol{X}}\hat{\boldsymbol{y}}\|$

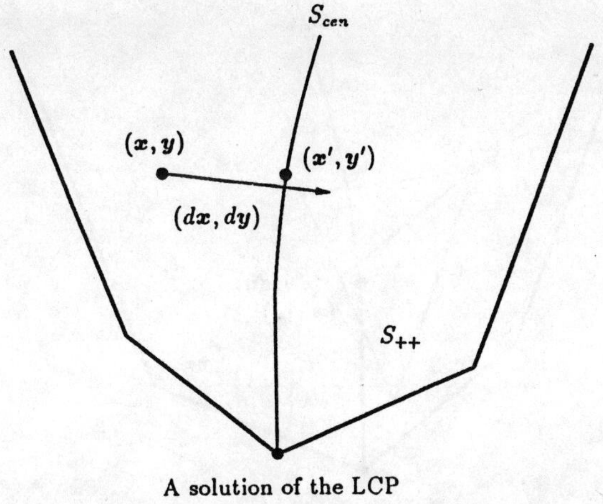

Figure 4: The direction vector (dx, dy) with $\beta = 1$.

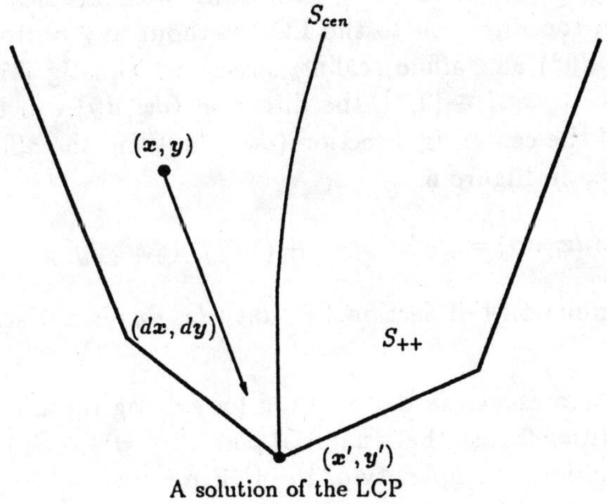

Figure 5: The direction vector (dx, dy) with $\beta = 0$.

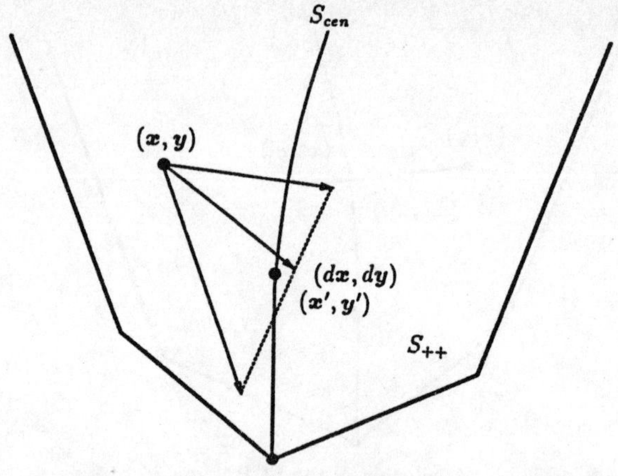

Figure 6: The direction vector (dx, dy) with $0 < \beta < 1$.

from the current point (x, y) to a point $(\hat{x}, \hat{y})$ on the path of centers. Thus the direction $(dx, dy) = (dx^c, dy^c)$ may be regarded as a "centering force" or "centering direction" in this case. On the other hand, if we take $\beta = 0$ as in Figure 5, the system (2.9) together with the nonnegativity condition on (x', y') coincides with the LCP (1.1) itself. Hence (dx, dy) gives the Newton direction to the LCP without any centering force. We will call $(dx, dy) = (dx^a, dy^a)$ an "affine scaling direction" (Lustig [37]) in this case. In general cases where we take $\beta \in [0, 1]$, the direction (dx, dy) can be represented as a convex combination of the centering direction (dx^c, dy^c) and the affine scaling direction (dx^a, dy^a) as illustrated in Figure 6:

$$(dx, dy) = \beta(dx^c, dy^c) + (1 - \beta)(dx^a, dy^a). \tag{2.10}$$

It will be shown in Lemma 4.14 of Section 4.3 that (dx, dy) is a descent direction of the potential function f.

Now we are ready to present the UIP method for solving the LCP (1.1). Recall that we have assumed Condition 2.1, so that an initial point $(x^1, y^1) \in S_{++}$ is available. When we discuss the computational complexity of the UIP method, we impose the additional assumption that the value of the potential function f at the initial point (x^1, y^1) is not greater than a given constant. (See Condition 2.3 in Section 2.3.) We will show how to prepare such an initial point in Section 5.1.

The Unified Interior Point (UIP) Method.

Step 1: Let $k = 1$ and $\epsilon > 0$.

Step 2: Let $(\boldsymbol{x}, \boldsymbol{y}) = (\boldsymbol{x}^k, \boldsymbol{y}^k)$. Stop if the inequality $\boldsymbol{x}^T\boldsymbol{y} \leq \epsilon$ is satisfied.
Step 3: Let $\beta = \beta_k \in [0, 1]$. Solve the system (2.8) of equations to get the search direction $(d\boldsymbol{x}, d\boldsymbol{y})$.
Step 4: Choose a step size parameter $\theta = \theta_k \geq 0$ so that

$$(\boldsymbol{x}, \boldsymbol{y}) + \theta(d\boldsymbol{x}, d\boldsymbol{y}) \in S_{++} \cup S_{cp}.$$

Define the new point $(\bar{\boldsymbol{x}}, \bar{\boldsymbol{y}})$ by

$$(\bar{\boldsymbol{x}}, \bar{\boldsymbol{y}}) = (\boldsymbol{x}, \boldsymbol{y}) + \theta(d\boldsymbol{x}, d\boldsymbol{y}).$$

Step 5: Let $(\boldsymbol{x}^{k+1}, \boldsymbol{y}^{k+1}) = (\bar{\boldsymbol{x}}, \bar{\boldsymbol{y}})$. Replace k by $k+1$, and go to Step 2.

The stopping criterion in Step 2 trivially covers the case that $(\boldsymbol{x}, \boldsymbol{y}) \in S_{cp}$, i.e., we have reached a solution $(\boldsymbol{x}, \boldsymbol{y})$ of the LCP (1.1). In practice, one can expect to obtain a sufficiently approximate solution of the LCP when the method stops providing that $\epsilon > 0$ is small enough. Theoretically, we choose $\epsilon = 2^{-2L}$ so that we can compute a solution of the LCP from the terminal point $(\boldsymbol{x}, \boldsymbol{y}) \in S_{++}$ of the UIP method as stated in the next section, Section 2.3.

The UIP method involves two different parameters $\beta \in [0, 1]$ and $\theta \geq 0$. The parameter β together with the current point $(\boldsymbol{x}, \boldsymbol{y}) = (\boldsymbol{x}^k, \boldsymbol{y}^k)$ determines the direction $(d\boldsymbol{x}, d\boldsymbol{y})$ toward which the new iterate $(\bar{\boldsymbol{x}}, \bar{\boldsymbol{y}}) = (\boldsymbol{x}^{k+1}, \boldsymbol{y}^{k+1})$ will be generated, while the parameter $\theta \geq 0$ controls the step length. In Section 6, we will explore flexible choices of these two parameters which ensure the global convergence (in certain case in polynomial time) of the generated sequence $\{(\boldsymbol{x}^k, \boldsymbol{y}^k)\}$. A summary is presented in Section 2.4.

2.3. Assumptions Which Are Necessary for Evaluating the Computational Complexity

For a meaningful evaluation of the computational complexity of the UIP method, we have to define the size of the input. The common definition (1.1) requires that all the entries of the matrix M and the vector $\boldsymbol{q}$ be rational. The rationality assumption is also necessary to guarantee that the LCP will have a solution with rational coordinates in the cases under consideration, which could be computed in a finite number of arithmetic operations. For simplicity, we further assume that all the entries of the matrix M and the vector $\boldsymbol{q}$ are integral when we discuss the computational complexity of the UIP method. We then define the size L of the LCP as follows:

$$\begin{aligned} L &= \sum_{i=1}^{n}\sum_{j=1}^{n} \{\lceil \log_2(|m_{ij}|+1) \rceil + 1\} + \sum_{i=1}^{n} \{\lceil \log_2(|q_i|+1) \rceil + 1\} + 2\lceil \log_2(n+1) \rceil, \\ &= \sum_{i=1}^{n}\sum_{j=1}^{n} \lceil \log_2(|m_{ij}|+1) \rceil + \sum_{i=1}^{n} \lceil \log_2(|q_i|+1) \rceil + 2\lceil \log_2(n+1) \rceil + n(n+1), \end{aligned}$$

where $M = (m_{ij})$ and $q = (q_1, q_2, \ldots, q_n)^T$, and $\lceil z \rceil$ denotes the smallest integer not less than $z \in R$. It is known (see Appendix B of Kojima, Mizuno and Yoshise [35]) that if an approximate solution $(\hat{x}, \hat{y}) \in S_+$ of the LCP satisfies

$$\hat{x}^T \hat{y} \leq 2^{-2L}, \tag{2.11}$$

then there exists a solution (x^*, y^*) of the LCP such that

$$\begin{aligned} x_i^* &= 0 \quad \text{if} \quad \hat{x}_i \leq 2^{-L}, \\ y_j^* &= 0 \quad \text{if} \quad \hat{y}_j \leq 2^{-L}. \end{aligned}$$

Furthermore, we can compute such a solution (x^*, y^*) in $O(n^3)$ arithmetic operations by using this information. Thus we may identify any $(\hat{x}, \hat{y}) \in S_+$ satisfying (2.11) with a solution of the LCP, so that the inequality (2.11) gives a theoretical stopping criterion for the UIP method.

We have stated in Section 2.1 that if the LCP satisfies Condition 2.1 then the algorithm which we will present in Section 2.4 as a special case of the UIP method generates a bounded sequence $\{(x^k, y^k)\}$ such that $\lim_{k\to\infty} {x^k}^T y^k = 0$. In this case, we can stop the UIP method after some finite number of iterations when

$${x^k}^T y^k \leq 2^{-2L}$$

holds and get a solution of the LCP. In other words, it is sufficient to choose $\epsilon = 2^{-2L}$ in Step 1 of the UIP method if our main concern is the theoretical computational complexity of the UIP method. Practically, however, it might be too complicated to compute with the number 2^{-2L} because it is too small.

When we discuss the computational complexity of the UIP method in the succeeding sections, we will often assume the following condition.

Condition 2.3.

(i) All the entries of the matrix M and the vector q are integral.
(ii) The matrix M belongs to the class P_*, i.e., to the class $P_*(\kappa)$ for some nonnegative number κ.
(iii) A point $(x^1, y^1) \in S_{++}$ with $f_{cp}(x^1, y^1) = O(L)$ and $f_{cen}(x^1, y^1) \leq \alpha$ is known, where $\alpha > 0$ is a given constant.

Condition 2.3 implies Condition 2.1 (Lemma 4.5). Hence the potential reduction algorithm which will be presented in Section 2.4 solves the LCP (1.1) under Condition 2.3. In Section 5.1, we will show a method of transforming a given LCP satisfying only (i) and (ii) of Condition 2.3 into an equivalent artificial linear complementarity problem satisfying (i), (ii) and (iii) simultaneously.

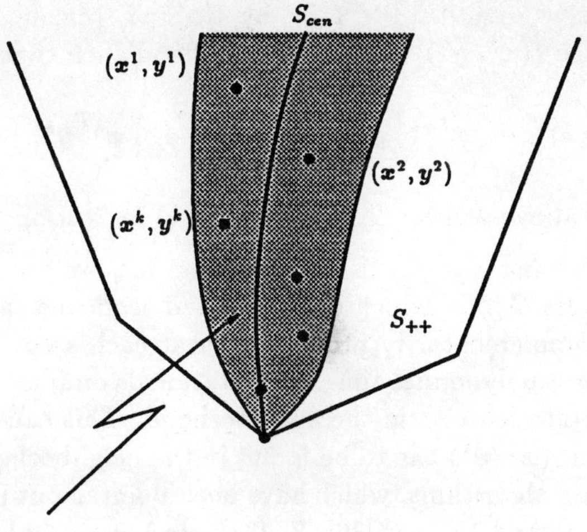

Figure 7: A horn neighborhood of the path of centers and a sequence generated by a path-following algorithm.

2.4. A Class of Globally Convergent Potential Reduction Algorithms

A common basic idea behind the path-following algorithms (Ding and Li [13], Gonzaga [22], Kojima, Mizuno and Yoshise [34, 35], Megiddo [42], Monteiro and Adler [53, 54], Renegar [57], Vaidya [74], Todd and Ye [72], etc.) developed so far is to trace the path of centers numerically. For the LCP (1.1), it has been defined as

$$S_{cen} = \{(\boldsymbol{x}, \boldsymbol{y}) \in S_{++} : \boldsymbol{X}\boldsymbol{y} = t\boldsymbol{e} \ \text{ for some } t > 0\},$$

which forms a nonlinear curve leading to a solution of the LCP under Condition 2.1. More precisely, a path-following algorithm generates a sequence $\{(\boldsymbol{x}^k, \boldsymbol{y}^k)\}$ in "a horn neighborhood" of the path of centers S_{cen} such that $\lim_{k\to\infty} {\boldsymbol{x}^k}^T \boldsymbol{y}^k = 0$. See Figure 7. There are several ways of defining a neighborhood of S_{cen} (Kojima, Mizuno and Yoshise [34, 35], Tanabe [67, 68, 69]), which we will present in Section 4.2.

We can state many of the path-following algorithms developed so far as special cases of the UIP method. This includes Ding and Li [13], Kojima, Mizuno and Yoshise [34, 35], Monteiro and Adler [53, 54] and Todd and Ye [72]. Specifically, if we take

$$\left\{(\boldsymbol{x}, \boldsymbol{y}) \in S_{++} : \left\| \boldsymbol{X}\boldsymbol{y} - \frac{\boldsymbol{x}^T\boldsymbol{y}}{n}\boldsymbol{e} \right\| \leq \alpha \frac{\boldsymbol{x}^T\boldsymbol{y}}{n} \right\}$$

with $\alpha \in (0, 0.2]$ as a neighborhood of S_{cen}, $\beta_k = 1 - \delta/\sqrt{n}$, ($\delta = \alpha/(1-\alpha)$) and $\theta_k = 1$ in the UIP method, we will have the $O(n^{3.5}L)$ polynomial-time path-following algorithm given for the positive semi-definite LCP by Kojima, Mizuno and Yoshise [35], which generates a sequence $\{(\boldsymbol{x}^k, \boldsymbol{y}^k)\}$ in the neighborhood such that

$$\boldsymbol{x}^{k+1^T} \boldsymbol{y}^{k+1} \leq \left(1 - \frac{\delta}{2\sqrt{n}}\right) \boldsymbol{x}^{k^T} \boldsymbol{y}^k.$$

The neighborhood above will be denoted by $N_\chi(\alpha)$ in Section 4.2.

In the path-following algorithms developed so far, we take a narrow neighborhood of the path of centers S_{cen} in which the generated sequence can run to gain a constant reduction in the complementarity product $\boldsymbol{x}^T\boldsymbol{y}$ at each step. Although such a narrow neighborhood ensures polynomial-time computational complexity, it enforces a short step so that the new iterate remains in the neighborhood. This causes a difficulty in practice since an initial point $(\boldsymbol{x}^1, \boldsymbol{y}^1)$ has to be found in the neighborhood. These disadvantages of the path-following algorithms, which have been pointed out in many papers (Gonzaga [24], Kojima, Mizuno and Yoshise [36], Ye [77], etc.), seem to be obstacles to developing a practically efficient path-following algorithm with the same polynomial-time computational complexity as the theoretical algorithms (Ding and Li [13], Kojima, Mizuno and Yoshise [34, 35], Monteiro and Adler [53, 54], etc.). Some modifications and improvements have been proposed to overcome these difficulties (Mizuno, Yoshise and Kikuchi [51], Mizuno and Todd [50]).

Let $\alpha > 0$. We employ a neighborhood of the path of centers

$$N_{cen}(\alpha) = \{(\boldsymbol{x}, \boldsymbol{y}) \in S_{++} : f_{cen}(\boldsymbol{x}, \boldsymbol{y}) \leq \alpha\}$$

given by Tanabe [67, 68, 69]. When $\alpha = +\infty$, we define $N_{cen}(+\infty) = S_{++}$. Recall that S_{cen} can be represented as in (2.7), i.e.,

$$S_{cen} = \{(\boldsymbol{x}, \boldsymbol{y}) \in S_{++} : f_{cen}(\boldsymbol{x}, \boldsymbol{y}) = 0\}.$$

Hence the path of centers S_{cen} itself coincides with the set $N_{cen}(0)$. Since the mapping f_{cen} is continuous, the subset $\{(\boldsymbol{x}, \boldsymbol{y}) \in S_{++} : f_{cen}(\boldsymbol{x}, \boldsymbol{y}) < \alpha\}$ of $N_{cen}(\alpha)$, which contains S_{cen}, is open relative to S_{++} for each $\alpha > 0$.

A potential reduction algorithm described below may be viewed as a path-following algorithm in the sense that it specifies a neighborhood $N_{cen}(\alpha_{bd})$ of the path of centers S_{cen} with $0 < \alpha_{bd} < +\infty$ or $\alpha_{bd} = +\infty$ as an admissible region in which it generates a sequence $\{(\boldsymbol{x}^k, \boldsymbol{y}^k)\} \subset S_{++}$ such that $\lim_{k\to\infty} \boldsymbol{x}^{k^T} \boldsymbol{y}^k = 0$. Its main features are:

(i) We can take a wider neighborhood $N_{cen}(\alpha_{bd})$ of the path of centers S_{cen} which contains any given point in S_{++}. Specifically, we can take $N_{cen}(+\infty) = S_{++}$ in which case it works as a potential reduction algorithm.

(ii) Each iteration decreases the potential function f but not necessarily the complementarity product $\boldsymbol{x}^T\boldsymbol{y}$.

We may take a narrow neighborhood of S_{cen} so that it will behave like a path-following algorithm. However, when we take a wider neighborhood of S_{cen}, it seems natural to regard it as a modification of a potential reduction algorithm. Thus we will have much flexibility in designing a practically efficient interior point algorithm for solving the LCP.

Given a neighborhood $N_{cen}(\alpha_{bd})$ with an arbitrary $\alpha_{bd} > 0$ or $= +\infty$ and an initial point $(\boldsymbol{x}^1, \boldsymbol{y}^1) \in N_{cen}(\alpha_{bd})$, we want to choose the direction parameter β and the step size parameter θ at each iteration so that the UIP method generates a sequence $\{(\boldsymbol{x}^k, \boldsymbol{y}^k)\} \subset N_{cen}(\alpha_{bd})$ such that $\lim_{k\to\infty} \boldsymbol{x}^{k^T} \boldsymbol{y}^k = 0$. To confine the generated sequence $\{(\boldsymbol{x}^k, \boldsymbol{y}^k)\}$ to the neighborhood $N_{cen}(\alpha_{bd})$, we need to move toward the center by taking a larger $\beta \leq 1$ if we are close to the boundary of $N_{cen}(\alpha_{bd})$. On the other hand, if we are far from the boundary of $N_{cen}(\alpha_{bd})$ or if we are close to the path of centers S_{cen}, we can take a smaller $\beta \geq 0$ to get more reduction in $\boldsymbol{x}^T\boldsymbol{y}$. To embody this idea, we introduce parameters α_{cen}, α_1, β_{cen} and β_{bd} such that

$$\left.\begin{array}{l} 0 < \alpha_{cen} \leq \alpha_1 < \alpha_{bd} < +\infty \quad \text{or} \\ 0 < \alpha_{cen} \leq \alpha_1 \leq \alpha_{bd} = +\infty, \\ 0 \leq \beta_{cen} < 1, \quad 0 < \beta_{bd} \leq 1, \end{array}\right\} \tag{2.12}$$

and then choose the direction parameter β at each iteration such that

$$\left.\begin{array}{ll} 0 \leq \beta \leq \beta_{cen} & \text{if } f_{cen}(\boldsymbol{x}, \boldsymbol{y}) < \alpha_{cen}, \\ 0 \leq \beta \leq 1 & \text{if } \alpha_{cen} \leq f_{cen}(\boldsymbol{x}, \boldsymbol{y}) \leq \alpha_1, \\ \beta_{bd} \leq \beta \leq 1 & \text{if } \alpha_1 < f_{cen}(\boldsymbol{x}, \boldsymbol{y}). \end{array}\right\} \tag{2.13}$$

Remark 2.4. The idea of taking a larger direction parameter $\beta \leq 1$ to approach the path of centers if the current point is far from the path of centers was proposed by Barnes, Chopra and Jensen [4] where a polynomial-time version of the affine scaling algorithm was presented. Based on a similar idea, Ye [80] also proposed a method for controlling the search direction parameter both for his potential reduction algorithm [81] and for the potential reduction algorithm [36].

Suppose now that we have computed the direction vector $(d\boldsymbol{x}, d\boldsymbol{y})$ for some direction parameter $\beta = \beta_k$ satisfying (2.13) at the k-th iteration. We will utilize the potential function $f = \nu f_{cp} + f_{cen}$ as a merit function for choosing the other parameter $\theta = \theta_k$, which determines the step length. Since the current point $(\boldsymbol{x}, \boldsymbol{y})$ lies in the interior S_{++} of the feasible region S_+ and the direction $(d\boldsymbol{x}, d\boldsymbol{y})$ satisfies the Newton equation (2.8), we see that

$$\boldsymbol{y} + \theta d\boldsymbol{y} = \boldsymbol{M}(\boldsymbol{x} + \theta d\boldsymbol{x}) + \boldsymbol{q} \quad \text{for every } \theta \geq 0.$$

Ideally we want to choose the step size parameter $\theta = \theta^* > 0$ which minimizes

$$f((\boldsymbol{x}, \boldsymbol{y}) + \theta(d\boldsymbol{x}, d\boldsymbol{y}))$$

subject to

$$(\boldsymbol{x}, \boldsymbol{y}) + \theta(d\boldsymbol{x}, d\boldsymbol{y}) \in N_{cen}(\alpha_{bd}) \cup S_{cp},$$

or equivalently

$$f_{cen}((\boldsymbol{x}, \boldsymbol{y}) + \theta(d\boldsymbol{x}, d\boldsymbol{y})) \leq \alpha_{bd} \quad \text{or} \quad (\boldsymbol{x}, \boldsymbol{y}) + \theta(d\boldsymbol{x}, d\boldsymbol{y}) \in S_{cp}.$$

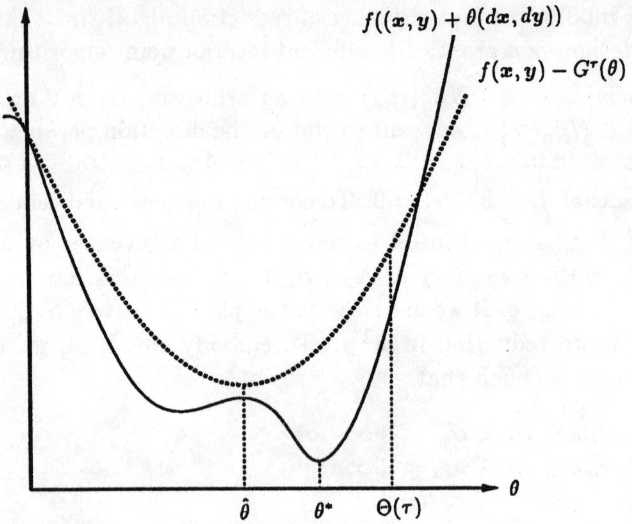

Figure 8: The quadratic function $f(x,y) - G^{\tau}(\theta)$ which bounds $f((x,y) + \theta(dx,dy))$ from above.

It is generally impossible, however, to get the exact minimizer θ^*. Let $0 \leq \tau < 1$, and

$$\Theta(\tau) = \sup\{\theta \geq 0 : \theta dx \geq -\tau x, \quad \theta dy \geq -\tau y\}.$$

Obviously, every $\theta \in [0, \Theta(\tau)]$ satisfies the constraint

$$(x,y) + \theta(dx,dy) \in S_{++}.$$

In Section 4.4, we will show quadratic functions $G^{\tau}_{cen}(\theta)$ and $G^{\tau}(\theta)$ such that

$$\begin{aligned}
&f_{cen}((x,y) + \theta(dx,dy)) \leq f_{cen}(x,y) - G^{\tau}_{cen}(\theta) \quad \text{for every } \theta \in [0, \Theta(\tau)],\\
&G^{\tau}_{cen}(0) = 0, \quad \frac{dG^{\tau}_{cen}(0)}{d\theta} > 0,\\
&f((x,y) + \theta(dx,dy)) \leq f(x,y) - G^{\tau}(\theta) \quad \text{for every } \theta \in [0, \Theta(\tau)],\\
&G^{\tau}(0) = 0, \quad \frac{dG^{\tau}(0)}{d\theta} > 0.
\end{aligned}$$

See Figure 8.

Thus, taking the step size parameter $\hat{\theta}$ which minimizes $f(x,y) - G^{\tau}(\theta)$ subject to

$$f_{cen}(x,y) - G^{\tau}_{cen}(\theta) \leq \alpha_{bd} \quad \text{and} \quad \theta \in [0, \Theta(\tau)],$$

we obtain a new point $(\bar{x}, \bar{y}) = (x, y) + \hat{\theta}(dx, dy)$ such that

$$(\bar{x}, \bar{y}) \in N_{cen}(\alpha_{bd}),$$
$$f((x, y) + \theta^*(dx, dy)) \leq f(\bar{x}, \bar{y}) \leq f(x, y) - G^{\tau}(\hat{\theta}) < f(x, y).$$

Theoretically, the step size parameter $\hat{\theta}$ ensures either the global or the polynomial-time convergence with suitable choices of the parameter β. Practically, it gives an initial value for an inexact line search to get a better approximation of the exact minimizer θ^*.

We now summarize main convergence results with regard to the potential reduction algorithm mentioned so far. Let $\nu > 0$, and let α_{cen}, α_1, α_{bd}, β_{cen} and β_{bd} satisfy (2.12). Let $(x^1, y^1) \in N_{cen}(\alpha_{bd})$. In addition, we assume that at each iteration the direction parameter β is chosen such that the inequalities (2.13) hold, and that the step size parameter $\theta \geq 0$ is taken so that

$$(x, y) + \theta(dx, dy) \in N_{cen}(\alpha_{bd}),$$
$$f((x, y) + \theta(dx, dy)) \leq f((x, y) + \hat{\theta}(dx, dy)).$$

We will specify the values of β_{cen} and β_{bd} below to ensure the global convergence, in polynomial-time in some cases.

The first result is a quite general global convergence one. Suppose that the LCP (1.1) satisfies Condition 2.1. Then the sequence $\{(x^k, y^k)\}$ generated by the potential reduction algorithm is bounded and satisfies $\lim_{k \to \infty} {x^k}^T y^k = 0$ (Corollary 6.4). There are three important cases covered by this global convergence result:

(a) $0 < \alpha_{cen} \leq \alpha_1 < \alpha_{bd} < +\infty$. See Figure 9.
(b) $0 < \alpha_{cen} \leq \alpha_1 < \alpha_{bd} = +\infty$. See Figure 10.
(c) $0 < \alpha_{cen} \leq \alpha_1 = \alpha_{bd} = +\infty$. See Figure 11.

The second result is an extension of the polynomial-time convergence result given by Kojima, Mizuno and Yoshise [36] for the positive semi-definite case. Suppose that the LCP satisfies Condition 2.3. Let $\nu = \sqrt{n}$, $\alpha_1 < +\infty$ and $\beta_{cen} = \beta_{bd} = n/(n + \nu)$. Then the potential reduction algorithm solves the LCP in $O(\sqrt{n}(1 + \kappa)L)$ iterations. We may take either a finite $\alpha_{bd} > \alpha_1$ as in the case (a) (Figure 9) or $\alpha_{bd} = +\infty$ as in the case (b) (Figure 10). See Corollary 6.7.

The last result we state here is a special case of the case (c) of the first convergence result above. Suppose that the LCP satisfies Condition 2.3. Let $\nu = \sqrt{n}$. Choose the parameters $\alpha_{cen} = \alpha_1 = \alpha_{bd} = +\infty$ and $\beta_{cen} = 0$. This choice of the parameters implies $\beta_k = 0$ throughout the iterations of the potential reduction algorithm. In this case the algorithm solves the LCP in $O(\exp\{\sqrt{n}(1 + \kappa)L\})$ iterations (Corollary 6.9). This potential reduction algorithm with the choice of the parameter $\beta_k = 0$ $(k = 1, 2, \ldots)$ turns out to be a direct application of the (damped) Newton method to the system of equations

$$y = Mx + q, \quad x_i y_i = 0 \ (i \in N)$$

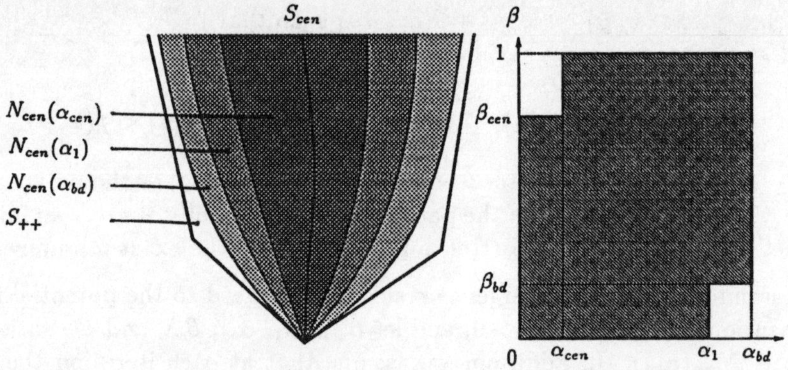

Figure 9: Case (a) $0 < \alpha_{cen} \leq \alpha_1 < \alpha_{bd} < +\infty$.

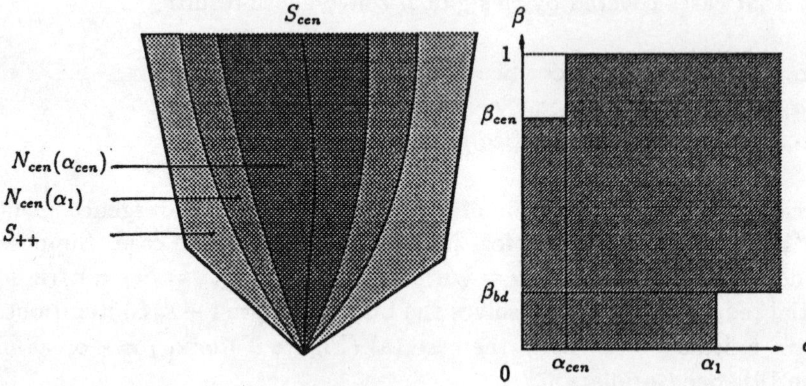

Figure 10: Case (b) $0 < \alpha_{cen} \leq \alpha_1 < \alpha_{bd} = +\infty$.

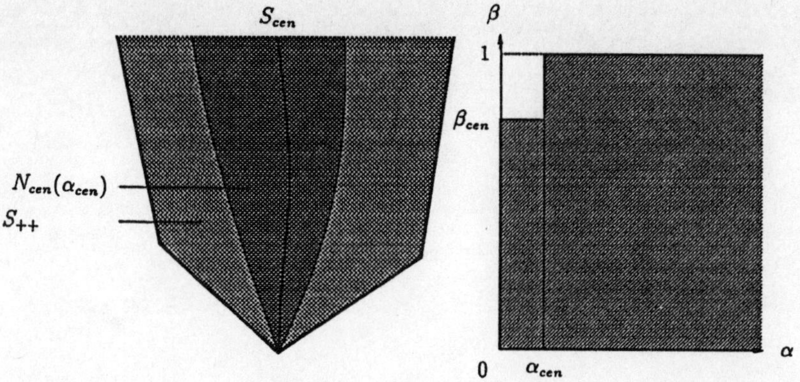

Figure 11: Case (c) $0 < \alpha_{cen} \leq \alpha_1 = \alpha_{bd} = +\infty$.

associated with the LCP. The algorithm may be also regarded as an affine scaling interior point algorithm for the LCP (Lustig [37]) because the search direction at each iteration involves no centering force as in the affine scaling interior point algorithms for linear programs (Barnes [3], Dikin [11], Vanderbei, Meketon and Freedman [76], etc.). It should be noted that the global convergence of the algorithm presented here does not need any nondegeneracy assumption on the LCP, while the global convergence of the affine scaling algorithms for linear programs has been established under nondegeneracy assumptions (Dikin [12], Tsuchiya [73], Vanderbei and Lagarias [75], etc.).

More general global convergence theorems will be established in Section 6.2, from which we can directly derive the results above.

3. The Class of Linear Complementarity Problems with P_0-Matrices

In this section we investigate linear complementarity problems with P_0-matrices. In Section 3.1, we introduce some characteristic numbers related to P_0-matrices. Some subclasses of the P_0-matrices are defined in Section 3.2, and their invariance property under column and row scaling is discussed in Section 3.3. Section 3.4 gives an example of NP-complete linear complementarity problems with P_0-matrices.

3.1. Some Characteristic Numbers Related to P_0-Matrices

An $n \times n$ matrix M is called a P_0-matrix when all the principal minors of M are nonnegative and a P-matrix when they are positive. We also say that M belongs to the classes P_0 or P, respectively. Obviously every P-matrix is a P_0-matrix. It is known that an $n \times n$ matrix M is a P_0-matrix if and only if for each nonzero $\boldsymbol{\xi} \in R^n$ there exists an index $i \in N$ such that $\xi_i \neq 0$ and $\xi_i[M\boldsymbol{\xi}]_i \geq 0$ (Fiedler and Pták [16]), and a P-matrix if and only if for each nonzero $\boldsymbol{\xi} \in R^n$ there is an index $i \in N$ such that $\xi_i[M\boldsymbol{\xi}]_i > 0$ (Fiedler and Pták [15]). Here $N = \{1, 2, \ldots, n\}$ and $[M\boldsymbol{\xi}]_i$ denotes the i-th component of the vector $M\boldsymbol{\xi}$.

For every $n \times n$ matrix M, define

$$\lambda_{min}(M) = \min_{\|\boldsymbol{\xi}\|=1} \boldsymbol{\xi}^T M \boldsymbol{\xi}, \tag{3.1}$$

$$\gamma(M) = \min_{\|\boldsymbol{\xi}\|=1} \max_{i \in N} \xi_i[M\boldsymbol{\xi}]_i \, . \tag{3.2}$$

Then M belongs to the class PSD of positive semi-definite matrices, i.e., $\boldsymbol{\xi}^T M \boldsymbol{\xi} \geq 0$ for every $\boldsymbol{\xi} \in R^n$, if and only if $\lambda_{min}(M) \geq 0$, and to the class P if and only if $\gamma(M) > 0$. The quantity $\lambda_{min}(M)$ turns out to be the minimum eigenvalue of the symmetric matrix $(M + M^T)/2$. We also see that every P-matrix M is nonsingular and that M is a P-matrix if and only if M^{-1} is. Hence $\gamma(M^{-1})$ is well-defined for every P-matrix M, and we denote

$$\bar{\gamma}(M) = \sqrt{\gamma(M)\gamma(M^{-1})} \, . \tag{3.3}$$

Furthermore, the inequality $0 < \bar{\gamma}(M) \leq 1/\sqrt{n}$ holds for every P-matrix M (Theorem 8.13 of [29]).

Remark 3.1. The number $\bar{\gamma}(M)$ was introduced in Kojima, Megiddo and Noma [29] where a path-following algorithm was presented which solved an LCP with a P-matrix M in $O\left(\dfrac{L}{\bar{\gamma}(M)}\right)$ iterations. On the other hand, Ye [78] showed that the potential reduction algorithm given by Kojima, Megiddo and Ye [31] solves an LCP with a P-matrix in $O\left(n^2 L \max\left\{-\frac{\lambda_{min}(M)}{n\gamma(M^T)}, 1\right\}\right)$ iterations.

3.2. Subclasses of the P_0-Matrices

We will be concerned with some subclasses of the class P_0: SS (the class of skew-symmetric matrices), PSD (the class of positive semi-definite matrices), P, $P_*(\kappa)$, P_* and CS (the class of column sufficient matrices). See Sections 2.1 and 3.1 for their definitions.

Let κ be any nonnegative real number. Recall that the class $P_*(\kappa)$ consists of all the $n \times n$ matrices M satisfying

$$(1+4\kappa) \sum_{i \in I_+(\xi)} \xi_i [M\xi]_i + \sum_{i \in I_-(\xi)} \xi_i [M\xi]_i \geq 0 \quad \text{for every } \xi \in R^n, \tag{3.4}$$

where

$$I_+(\xi) = \{i \in N : \xi_i [M\xi]_i > 0\}, \; I_-(\xi) = \{i \in N : \xi_i [M\xi]_i < 0\}.$$

The index sets $I_+(\xi)$ and $I_-(\xi)$ depend on the matrix M though they do not explicitly represent the dependence. It should be noticed that (3.4) can be rewritten as

$$\xi^T M \xi + 4\kappa \sum_{i \in I_+(\xi)} \xi_i [M\xi]_i \geq 0 \quad \text{for every } \xi \in R^n. \tag{3.5}$$

Obviously, $P_*(0) = PSD$ and $P_*(\kappa_1) \subset P_*(\kappa_2)$ if $0 \leq \kappa_1 \leq \kappa_2$. We call M a P_*-matrix if it belongs to the class $P_* = \bigcup_{\kappa \geq 0} P_*(\kappa)$.

A P-matrix M is characterized by the property that the LCP (1.1) has a unique solution for every $q \in R^n$ (Samelson, Thrall and Wesler [60]). A column sufficient matrix M is characterized by the property that the solution set S_{cp} of the LCP (1.1) is convex (possibly empty) for every $q \in R^n$ (Cottle, Pang and Venkateswaran [9]).

Among the subclasses SS, PSD, P, P_* and CS of P_0, we have the following relations:

$$SS \subset PSD, \quad P \cap SS = \emptyset, \quad (PSD \cup P) \subset P_* \subset CS \subset P_0.$$

See Figure 2 at page 9. The first two relations and the last one, i.e., $CS \subset P_0$ are obvious from their definitions. So we will derive the rest of the relations, $(PSD \cup P) \subset P_* \subset CS$, below (Lemmas 3.2 and 3.3).

Lemma 3.2. *Every P_*-matrix is column sufficient, i.e., $P_* \subset CS$.*

Proof: Let M be an $n \times n$ P_*-matrix and assume that $\xi_i [M\xi]_i \leq 0$ $(i \in N)$ for some $\xi \in R^n$. Then $I_+(\xi) = \emptyset$. From (3.4), we have

$$0 \geq \sum_{i \in N} \xi_i [M\xi]_i = \sum_{i \in I_-(\xi)} \xi_i [M\xi]_i \geq 0;$$

hence

$$\sum_{i \in N} \xi_i [M\xi]_i = \sum_{i \in I_-(\xi)} \xi_i [M\xi]_i = 0.$$

It follows that $\xi_i[M\xi]_i = 0$ $(i \in N)$. Hence M is column sufficient. ∎

The next lemma implies that the class P_* contains two important subclasses, *PSD* and P, which makes it possible to deal with them in a unified way.

Lemma 3.3.

(i) *$PSD = P_*(0) \subset P_*$.*

(ii) *Let M be a P-matrix. Define nonnegative numbers κ^* and κ^{**} by*

$$\kappa^* = \max\left\{ \frac{-\lambda_{min}(M)}{4\gamma(M)},\ 0 \right\}, \tag{3.6}$$

$$\kappa^{**} = \frac{1}{4\bar{\gamma}(M)}. \tag{3.7}$$

Then M belongs to $P_*(\kappa^*) \cap P_*(\kappa^{**}) = P_*(\min\{\kappa^*,\ \kappa^{**}\})$. See (3.1), (3.2) and (3.3) for the definitions of $\lambda_{min}(M)$, $\gamma(M)$ and $\bar{\gamma}(M)$.

Proof: The assertion (i) is straightforward from the definitions of the classes *PSD*, $P_*(\kappa)$ and P_*. We will show (ii). Suppose that M is an $n \times n$ P-matrix. By the definitions (3.1) of $\lambda_{min}(M)$ and (3.2) of $\gamma(M)$, we have

$$\xi^T M \xi \geq \lambda_{min}(M)\|\xi\|^2, \tag{3.8}$$

$$\max_{i \in N} \xi_i[M\xi]_i \geq \gamma(M)\|\xi\|^2 \tag{3.9}$$

for every $\xi \in R^n$. Note that $\gamma(M) > 0$ because M is a P-matrix. Hence

$$\begin{aligned}
\xi^T M\xi + 4\kappa^* \sum_{i \in I_+(\xi)} \xi_i[M\xi]_i &\geq \xi^T M\xi + 4\kappa^* \max_{i \in N} \xi_i[M\xi]_i \\
&\geq \lambda_{min}(M)\|\xi\|^2 + 4\kappa^*\gamma(M)\|\xi\|^2 \quad \text{(by (3.8) and (3.9))} \\
&\geq \lambda_{min}(M)\|\xi\|^2 - \frac{\lambda_{min}(M)}{\gamma(M)}\gamma(M)\|\xi\|^2 \quad \text{(by (3.6))} \\
&= 0
\end{aligned}$$

for every $\xi \in R^n$. Thus we have shown $M \in P_*(\kappa^*)$. Since M^{-1} is a P-matrix, we also have

$$\max_{i \in N} \xi_i[M^{-1}\xi]_i \geq \gamma(M^{-1})\|\xi\|^2.$$

Hence, replacing ξ by $M\xi$, we have

$$\max_{i \in N} \xi_i[M\xi]_i \geq \gamma(M^{-1})\|M\xi\|^2 \tag{3.10}$$

for every $\xi \in R^n$. It follows from the inequalities (3.9), (3.10) and the definition (3.3) of $\bar{\gamma}(M)$ that

$$\max_{i\in N} \xi_i[M\xi]_i \geq \bar{\gamma}(M)\|\xi\|\|M\xi\| \geq -\bar{\gamma}(M)\xi^T M\xi. \tag{3.11}$$

Therefore, for every $\xi \in R^n$, we obtain

$$\begin{aligned} \xi^T M\xi + 4\kappa^{**} \sum_{i\in I_+(\xi)} \xi_i[M\xi]_i &\geq \xi^T M\xi + 4\kappa^{**} \max_{i\in N} \xi_i[M\xi]_i \\ &\geq \xi^T M\xi - 4\kappa^{**}\bar{\gamma}(M)\xi^T M\xi \quad \text{(by (3.11))} \\ &= 0 \quad \text{(by (3.7))}, \end{aligned}$$

which implies $M \in P_*(\kappa^{**})$. This completes the proof. ∎

In the lemma above, we cannot say in general that either κ^* or κ^{**} is less than the other. To see this, let $a \in R$ and consider the P-matrices

$$M = \begin{pmatrix} 1 & 2a \\ 0 & 1 \end{pmatrix} \quad \text{and} \quad M^{-1} = \begin{pmatrix} 1 & -2a \\ 0 & 1 \end{pmatrix}.$$

By a simple calculation, we have

$$\begin{aligned} &\lambda_{min}(M) = 1 - |a|, \\ &\gamma(M) = \gamma(M^{-1}) = \bar{\gamma}(M) = \frac{1}{2}\left(1 - \frac{|a|}{\sqrt{a^2+1}}\right); \end{aligned}$$

hence

$$\kappa^* = \max\{|a| - 1, 0\}\,\kappa^{**}.$$

Thus $\kappa^* < \kappa^{**}$ if $|a| < 2$, and $\kappa^* > \kappa^{**}$ if $|a| > 2$.

The lemma below presents another characterization of the class $P_*(\kappa)$ $(\kappa \geq 0)$, which will be utilized in the succeeding discussions to evaluate the reduction of the potential function in each iteration of the UIP method.

Lemma 3.4. *Let $\kappa \geq 0$. The following two statements are equivalent:*

(i) *An $n \times n$ matrix M belongs to the class $P_*(\kappa)$.*
(ii) *For every $n \times n$ positive diagonal matrix D and every $\xi, \eta, h \in R^n$, the relations*

$$\begin{aligned} D^{-1}\xi + D\eta &= h, \\ -M\xi + \eta &= 0 \end{aligned}$$

always imply

$$\xi^T \eta \geq -\kappa\|h\|^2.$$

Proof: Eliminating h in (ii), we obtain an equivalent statement: For every $\xi, \eta \in R^n$, the relation

$$\eta = M\xi$$

always implies

$$\xi^T \eta \geq -\kappa \inf_D \left\| D^{-1}\xi + D\eta \right\|^2 .$$

Here the infimum is taken over all the $n \times n$ diagonal matrices D with positive entries. It will be shown below that

$$\inf_D \left\| D^{-1}\xi + D\eta \right\|^2 = 4 \sum_{i \in I_+(\xi,\eta)} \xi_i \eta_i, \tag{3.12}$$

where

$$I_+(\xi, \eta) = \{i \in N : \xi_i \eta_i > 0\}.$$

Hence we know that (ii) is equivalent to the inequality

$$\xi^T M \xi + 4\kappa \sum_{i \in I_+(\xi)} \xi_i [M\xi]_i \geq 0 \quad \text{for every } \xi \in R^n,$$

which characterizes the class $P_*(\kappa)$ of matrices. Here

$$I_+(\xi) = \{i \in N : \xi_i [M\xi]_i > 0\}.$$

What we have left is to show the equality (3.12). Let

$$D = \text{diag } d = \text{diag } (d_1, d_2, \ldots, d_n).$$

Then

$$\inf_D \left\| D^{-1}\xi + D\eta \right\|^2 = \inf_{d>0} \sum_{i=1}^n \left(\frac{\xi_i}{d_i} + d_i \eta_i \right)^2 = \sum_{i=1}^n \inf_{d_i>0} \left(\frac{\xi_i}{d_i} + d_i \eta_i \right)^2 .$$

Now we will evaluate each term. Denote

$$\alpha(\xi_i, \eta_i) = \inf_{d_i>0} \left(\frac{\xi_i}{d_i} + d_i \eta_i \right)^2 .$$

If $\xi_i \eta_i < 0$, we know $\alpha(\xi_i, \eta_i) = 0$ by taking $d_i = \sqrt{-\xi_i/\eta_i}$. If $\xi_i \eta_i = 0$, i.e., $\xi_i = 0$ or $\eta_i = 0$, we also see $\alpha(\xi_i, \eta_i) = 0$ by taking $d_i \to 0$ or $d_i \to \infty$. In the case that $\xi_i \eta_i > 0$, we have the inequality

$$\left(\frac{\xi_i}{d_i} + d_i \eta_i \right)^2 = 4\xi_i \eta_i + \left(\frac{\xi_i}{d_i} - d_i \eta_i \right)^2 \geq 4\xi_i \eta_i .$$

Since the last inequality above becomes the equality when $d_i = \sqrt{\xi_i/\eta_i}$, we have $\alpha(\xi_i, \eta_i) = 4\xi_i \eta_i$. Summarizing all the cases above, we obtain (3.12). ∎

We now give a geometric characterization to the subclasses of P_0 under consideration in terms of the Hadamard product $(\xi_1[M\xi]_1, \xi_2[M\xi]_2, \ldots, \xi_n[M\xi]_n)^T$, which we will denote by $\zeta_M(\xi)$, of $\xi \in R^n$ and $M\xi$. This is motivated by the paper Cottle, Pang and Venkateswaran [9] where a column sufficient matrix was introduced as a matrix M satisfying

$$\zeta_M(\xi) = 0 \text{ whenever } \zeta_M(\xi) \leq 0.$$

Let

$$\begin{aligned} R^n_- &= \{\zeta \in R^n : \zeta \leq 0\}, \\ Z(\kappa) &= \{\zeta \in R^n : (1+4\kappa) \sum_{i \in I_+(\zeta)} \zeta_i + \sum_{i \in I_-(\zeta)} \zeta_i < 0\} \quad \text{for every } \kappa \geq 0, \\ H_0 &= \{\zeta \in R^n : e^T\zeta = 0\}, \\ H_{--} &= \{\zeta \in R^n : e^T\zeta < 0\}, \end{aligned}$$

where

$$I_+(\zeta) = \{i \in N : \zeta_i > 0\}, \quad I_-(\zeta) = \{i \in N : \zeta_i < 0\}.$$

Then

$$\begin{array}{lll} M \in CS & \text{if and only if} & \zeta_M(R^n \setminus \{0\}) \cap (R^n_- \setminus \{0\}) = \emptyset, \\ M \in P_*(\kappa) & \text{if and only if} & \zeta_M(R^n \setminus \{0\}) \cap Z(\kappa) = \emptyset, \\ M \in PSD & \text{if and only if} & \zeta_M(R^n \setminus \{0\}) \cap H_{--} = \emptyset, \\ M \in P & \text{if and only if} & \zeta_M(R^n \setminus \{0\}) \cap R^n_- = \emptyset, \\ M \in SS & \text{if and only if} & \zeta_M(R^n \setminus \{0\}) \subset H_0. \end{array}$$

Obviously, $H_{--} = Z(0) \supset Z(\kappa_1) \supset Z(\kappa_2) \supset (R^n_- \setminus \{0\})$ if $0 \leq \kappa_1 \leq \kappa_2$. We further observe

$$Z(\kappa) = \{\zeta \in R^n : (1+4\kappa)\sum_{i \in I} \zeta_i + \sum_{i \notin I} \zeta_i < 0 \quad \text{for every } I \subset N\}$$

from the definitions of the index sets $I_+(\zeta)$ and $I_-(\zeta)$. Hence $Z(\kappa)$ turns out the interior of the polyhedral cone

$$\{\zeta \in R^n : (1+4\kappa)\sum_{i \in I} \zeta_i + \sum_{i \notin I} \zeta_i \leq 0 \quad \text{for every } I \subset N\}$$

that contains the nonpositive orthant R^n_-. See Figure 12. It should be noted that the class P_*, which is the union of $P_*(\kappa)$ $(\kappa \geq 0)$, remains a proper subclass of CS although the intersection of $Z(\kappa)$ $(\kappa \geq 0)$ becomes $R^n_- \setminus \{0\}$.

Finally in this section, we remark that all the classes mentioned so far, P_0, CS, P_*, $P_*(\kappa)$, PSD, P and SS, enjoy a nice property that if a matrix M belongs to one of these classes then every principal submatrix of M also belongs to the class. One can easily verify this property.

3.3. Invariance under Column and Row Scalings

We now consider column and row scalings of the LCP (1.1). Let $U = \text{diag}(u_1, u_2, \ldots, u_n)$ and $V = \text{diag}(v_1, v_2, \ldots, v_n)$ be positive diagonal matrices. Introducing new variable

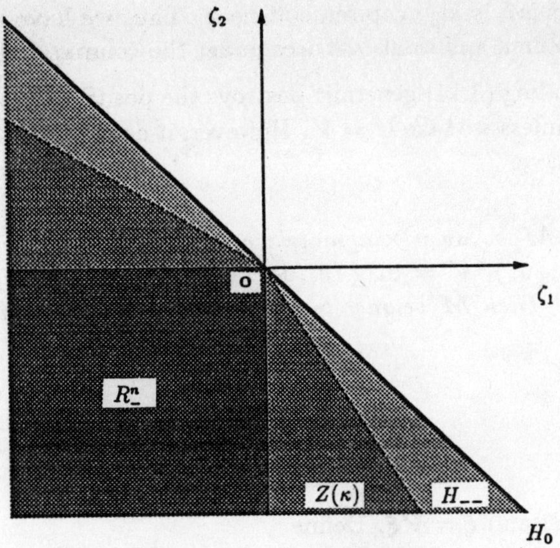

Figure 12: The relations among the sets R^n_-, $Z(\kappa)$, H_0 and H_{--}.

vectors $\hat{\boldsymbol{x}} = \boldsymbol{V}^{-1}\boldsymbol{x} \in R^n$ and $\hat{\boldsymbol{y}} = \boldsymbol{U}\boldsymbol{y}$ into the LCP (1.1), we obtain the $\widehat{\text{LCP}}$: Find an $(\hat{\boldsymbol{x}}, \hat{\boldsymbol{y}}) \in R^{2n}$ such that

$$\hat{\boldsymbol{y}} = \hat{\boldsymbol{M}}\hat{\boldsymbol{x}} + \hat{\boldsymbol{q}}, \ (\hat{\boldsymbol{x}}, \hat{\boldsymbol{y}}) \geq \mathbf{0} \text{ and } \hat{x}_i\hat{y}_i = 0 \ (i \in N). \tag{3.13}$$

Here $\hat{\boldsymbol{q}} = \boldsymbol{U}\boldsymbol{q}$ and

$$\hat{\boldsymbol{M}} = \boldsymbol{U}\boldsymbol{M}\boldsymbol{V}. \tag{3.14}$$

Obviously, the LCP (1.1) and the $\widehat{\text{LCP}}$ (3.13) are equivalent in the sense that $(\boldsymbol{x}, \boldsymbol{y})$ is a solution of the former if and only if $(\hat{\boldsymbol{x}}, \hat{\boldsymbol{y}}) = (\boldsymbol{V}^{-1}\boldsymbol{x}, \boldsymbol{U}\boldsymbol{y})$ is a solution of the latter.

Now, let us investigate how a two-sided scaling of the form (3.14) affects those properties of a P_0-matrix $\boldsymbol{M}$ that have been stated in the previous section. By definition, the classes P_0 and P are invariant under scalings of the form (3.14). That is, $\hat{\boldsymbol{M}}$ is a P_0-matrix (or a P-matrix) if $\boldsymbol{M}$ is. The scaling (3.14) also preserves column sufficiency. To see this, let $\boldsymbol{M}$ be a column sufficient matrix and define $\hat{\boldsymbol{M}}$ by (3.14). Let $\hat{\boldsymbol{\xi}} \in R^n$ and $\boldsymbol{\xi} = \boldsymbol{V}\hat{\boldsymbol{\xi}}$. Then, for every $i \in N$, we obtain

$$\hat{\xi}_i[\hat{\boldsymbol{M}}\hat{\boldsymbol{\xi}}]_i = \hat{\xi}_i[\boldsymbol{U}\boldsymbol{M}\boldsymbol{V}\hat{\boldsymbol{\xi}}]_i = \frac{u_i}{v_i}[\boldsymbol{V}\hat{\boldsymbol{\xi}}]_i[\boldsymbol{M}(\boldsymbol{V}\hat{\boldsymbol{\xi}})]_i = \frac{u_i}{v_i}\xi_i[\boldsymbol{M}\boldsymbol{\xi}]_i \,. \tag{3.15}$$

Hence, by the above equality and the column sufficiency of $\boldsymbol{M}$, we see that

$$\hat{\xi}_i[\hat{\boldsymbol{M}}\hat{\boldsymbol{\xi}}]_i \leq 0 \ \ (i \in N) \ \ \text{ implies } \ \ \hat{\xi}_i[\hat{\boldsymbol{M}}\hat{\boldsymbol{\xi}}]_i = 0 \ \ (i \in N).$$

Therefore the matrix $\hat{M}$ is also column sufficient. Thus we have shown the invariance of the class CS of column sufficient matrices under the column and row scaling (3.14).

The two-sided scaling (3.14) generally destroys the positive semi-definiteness and the skew-symmetricity unless we take $U = V$. However, it does not destroy the P_*-property. More precisely, we have:

Theorem 3.5. *Let M be an $n \times n$ matrix of the class $P_*(\kappa)$ for some $\kappa \geq 0$. Let $U = \text{diag}\,(u_1, u_2, \ldots, u_n)$, $V = \text{diag}\,(v_1, v_2, \ldots, v_n)$ be positive diagonal matrices and define $\hat{M}$ by (3.14). Then $\hat{M}$ belongs to $P_*(\hat{\kappa})$, where $\hat{\kappa}$ is a nonnegative number such that*

$$\frac{1+4\hat{\kappa}}{1+4\kappa} = \frac{\max_{i \in N} \frac{u_i}{v_i}}{\min_{i \in N} \frac{u_i}{v_i}}.$$

Proof: Let $\hat{\xi} \in R^n$ and $\xi = V\hat{\xi}$. Define

$$I_+(\xi) = \{i \in N : \xi_i[M\xi]_i > 0\}, \qquad I_-(\xi) = \{i \in N : \xi_i[M\xi]_i < 0\},$$
$$\hat{I}_+(\hat{\xi}) = \{i \in N : \hat{\xi}_i[\hat{M}\hat{\xi}]_i > 0\}, \qquad \hat{I}_-(\hat{\xi}) = \{i \in N : \hat{\xi}_i[\hat{M}\hat{\xi}]_i < 0\}.$$

Then we observe from (3.15) that

$$\hat{I}_+(\hat{\xi}) = I_+(\xi), \quad \hat{I}_-(\hat{\xi}) = I_-(\xi).$$

Hence, for every $\hat{\xi} \in R^n$, we have

$$\begin{aligned}
&(1+4\hat{\kappa}) \sum_{i \in \hat{I}_+(\hat{\xi})} \hat{\xi}_i[\hat{M}\hat{\xi}]_i + \sum_{i \in \hat{I}_-(\hat{\xi})} \hat{\xi}_i[\hat{M}\hat{\xi}]_i \\
= \ & (1+4\hat{\kappa}) \sum_{i \in I_+(\xi)} \frac{u_i}{v_i}\xi_i[M\xi]_i + \sum_{i \in I_-(\xi)} \frac{u_i}{v_i}\xi_i[M\xi]_i \quad \text{(by (3.15))} \\
\geq \ & (1+4\hat{\kappa}) \left(\min_{i \in N} \frac{u_i}{v_i}\right) \sum_{i \in I_+(\xi)} \xi_i[M\xi]_i + \left(\max_{i \in N} \frac{u_i}{v_i}\right) \sum_{i \in I_-(\xi)} \xi_i[M\xi]_i \\
= \ & (1+4\kappa) \left(\max_{i \in N} \frac{u_i}{v_i}\right) \sum_{i \in I_+(\xi)} \xi_i[M\xi]_i + \left(\max_{i \in N} \frac{u_i}{v_i}\right) \sum_{i \in I_-(\xi)} \xi_i[M\xi]_i \\
= \ & \left(\max_{i \in N} \frac{u_i}{v_i}\right) \left\{ (1+4\kappa) \sum_{i \in I_+(\xi)} \xi_i[M\xi]_i + \sum_{i \in I_-(\xi)} \xi_i[M\xi]_i \right\} \\
\geq \ & 0 \quad (\text{since } M \in P_*(\kappa)).
\end{aligned}$$

Thus we have shown that $\hat{M}$ belongs to $P_*(\hat{\kappa})$. ∎

The theorem above shows, in particular, that every column and row scaled matrix $\hat{M}$ of a positive semi-definite matrix M is a P_*-matrix.

3.4. An NP-Complete Linear Complementarity Problem with a P_0-Matrix

In this section we show that the class of all the linear complementarity problems with P_0-matrices is NP-complete. For this purpose we consider the knapsack problem: Given an integer vector $\boldsymbol{a} = (a_1, a_2, \ldots, a_m)^T$ and an integer b, find a solution $\boldsymbol{u} = (u_1, u_2, \ldots, u_m)^T \in R^m$ of

$$\boldsymbol{a}^T\boldsymbol{u} = b \quad \text{and} \quad u_i \in \{0,1\} \ (i = 1,2,\ldots,m). \tag{3.16}$$

The knapsack problem is known to be NP-complete (see, for example, Schrijver [61]). We will reduce it to a linear complementarity problem with a P_0-matrix.

Let $\bar{\boldsymbol{a}} = (\bar{a}_1, \bar{a}_2, \ldots, \bar{a}_{4m+2})^T \in R^{4m+2}$ be such that

$$\bar{a}_i = \begin{cases} a_j & \text{if } i = 4j-3 \ (j = 1,2,\ldots,m), \\ 0 & \text{otherwise.} \end{cases}$$

Obviously, (3.16) can be rewritten as

$$\bar{\boldsymbol{a}}^T\boldsymbol{x} = b \quad \text{and} \quad x_i \in \{0,1\} \ (i = 1,5,\ldots,4m-3). \tag{3.17}$$

Here, $\boldsymbol{x} \in R^{4m+2}$ is a variable vector. Define

$$\boldsymbol{B} = \begin{pmatrix} 0 & 0 & 0 & 0 \\ 1 & 0 & 0 & 0 \\ 1 & 1 & 0 & 0 \\ -1 & 0 & 0 & 0 \end{pmatrix} \quad \text{and} \quad \boldsymbol{p} = \begin{pmatrix} 0 \\ 0 \\ -1 \\ 1 \end{pmatrix}.$$

Now consider the linear complementarity problem: Find a $(\boldsymbol{v}, \boldsymbol{w}) \in R^8$, if it exists, such that

$$\boldsymbol{w} = \boldsymbol{B}\boldsymbol{v} + \boldsymbol{p}, \ (\boldsymbol{v}, \boldsymbol{w}) \geq \boldsymbol{0} \ \text{and} \ \boldsymbol{v}^T\boldsymbol{w} = 0 \tag{3.18}$$

or equivalently

$$\begin{aligned} &w_1 = 0, \ v_1 \geq 0, \ v_1 w_1 = 0, \\ &w_2 = v_1, \ v_2 \geq 0, \ v_2 w_2 = 0, \\ &w_3 = v_1 + v_2 - 1 \geq 0, \ v_3 \geq 0, \ v_3 w_3 = 0, \\ &w_4 = -v_1 + 1 \geq 0, \ v_4 \geq 0, \ v_4 w_4 = 0. \end{aligned}$$

We can easily verify that the solution set of the LCP above is the union of the three disjoint sets:

$$\begin{aligned} &\{(\boldsymbol{v}, \boldsymbol{w}) : v_1 = 0, \ v_2 = 1, \ v_3 \geq 0, \ v_4 = 0, \ w_1 = w_2 = w_3 = 0, \ w_4 = 1\}, \\ &\{(\boldsymbol{v}, \boldsymbol{w}) : v_1 = 0, \ v_2 > 1, \ v_3 = 0, \ v_4 = 0, \ w_1 = w_2 = 0, \ w_3 = v_2 - 1, \ w_4 = 1\}, \\ &\{(\boldsymbol{v}, \boldsymbol{w}) : v_1 = 1, \ v_2 = 0, \ v_3 \geq 0, \ v_4 \geq 0, \ w_1 = 0, \ w_2 = 1, \ w_3 = w_4 = 0\}. \end{aligned}$$

It follows that $v_1 \in \{0,1\}$ if and only if $(\boldsymbol{v}, \boldsymbol{w})$ is a solution of the LCP (3.18) for some $v_2, v_3, v_4 \in R$ and $\boldsymbol{w} \in R^4$. Hence we can utilize m copies of the LCP (3.18) to represent the condition $x_i \in \{0,1\}$ $(i = 1, 5, \ldots, 4m-3)$ in (3.17) :

$$\boldsymbol{w}^i = B\boldsymbol{v}^i + \boldsymbol{p}, \ (\boldsymbol{v}^i, \boldsymbol{w}^i) \geq 0 \ \text{and} \ \boldsymbol{v}^{iT}\boldsymbol{w}^i = 0 \ (i = 1, 2, \ldots, m), \tag{3.19}$$

where

$$\boldsymbol{x} = (\boldsymbol{v}^1, \boldsymbol{v}^2, \ldots, \boldsymbol{v}^m, x_{4m+1}, x_{4m+2}).$$

Thus we obtain a linear complementarity problem which is equivalent to (3.17): Find an $(\boldsymbol{x}, \boldsymbol{y}) = (\boldsymbol{v}^1, \boldsymbol{v}^2, \ldots, \boldsymbol{v}^m, x_{4m+1}, x_{4m+2}, \boldsymbol{w}^1, \boldsymbol{w}^2, \ldots, \boldsymbol{w}^m, y_{4m+1}, y_{4m+2})$ satisfying (3.19),

$$\begin{aligned} y_{4m+1} &= \bar{\boldsymbol{a}}^T\boldsymbol{x} - b \geq 0, \ x_{4m+1} \geq 0, \ x_{4m+1}y_{4m+1} = 0, \\ y_{4m+2} &= -\bar{\boldsymbol{a}}^T\boldsymbol{x} + b \geq 0, \ x_{4m+2} \geq 0, \ x_{4m+2}y_{4m+2} = 0. \end{aligned}$$

Finally we observe that the coefficient matrix

$$M = \begin{pmatrix} B & O & \cdots & O & 0 & 0 \\ O & B & \ddots & \vdots & 0 & 0 \\ \vdots & \ddots & \ddots & O & \vdots & \vdots \\ O & \cdots & O & B & 0 & 0 \\ & & \bar{\boldsymbol{a}}^T & & & \\ & & -\bar{\boldsymbol{a}}^T & & & \end{pmatrix}$$

associated with the LCP above is a $(4m+2) \times (4m+2)$ lower triangular matrix with zero diagonal entries so it is a P_0-matrix.

4. Basic Analysis of the UIP Method

This section is devoted to basic analysis of the UIP method. In Section 4.1, we establish some fundamental lemmas and theorems under Conditions 2.1 and 2.3. Section 4.2 introduces some neighborhoods of the path of centers and then shows relationships among them. Section 4.3 investigates a smooth version of the UIP method. Finally in Section 4.4, we evaluate the change of the potential function at a new point $(\boldsymbol{x},\boldsymbol{y})+\theta(d\boldsymbol{x},d\boldsymbol{y})$ generated in Step 4 of the UIP method, in terms of quadratic functions in the step size parameter θ.

4.1. Some Lemmas and Theorems

The lemma below makes it possible to determine the search direction $(d\boldsymbol{x},d\boldsymbol{y}) \in R^{2n}$ consistently and uniquely from the system (2.8) of equations in Step 3 of the UIP method whenever M is a P_0-matrix.

Lemma 4.1. *The matrix*

$$\bar{M} = \begin{pmatrix} Y & X \\ -M & I \end{pmatrix} \tag{4.1}$$

is nonsingular for any positive diagonal matrices X and Y if and only if M is a P_0-matrix. Here I denotes the identity matrix.

Proof: Suppose that M is an $n \times n$ P_0-matrix. Let $X = \text{diag}\,(x_1, x_2, \ldots, x_n)$ and $Y = \text{diag}\,(y_1, y_2, \ldots, y_n)$ be arbitrary positive diagonal matrices. Assume that the matrix $\bar{M}$ defined by (4.1) is singular. Then $\bar{M}\boldsymbol{\zeta} = \mathbf{0}$ for some nonzero $\boldsymbol{\zeta} = (\boldsymbol{\xi}, \boldsymbol{\eta}) \in R^{2n}$, i.e., $y_i\xi_i + x_i\eta_i = 0$ $(i \in N)$, and $\boldsymbol{\eta} = M\boldsymbol{\xi}$. It follows that $\boldsymbol{\xi} \neq \mathbf{0}$ and hence we can find an index $i \in N$ such that $\xi_i \neq 0$ and $\xi_i\eta_i \geq 0$ since M is a P_0-matrix. On the other hand, $\xi_i\eta_i = -y_i(\xi_i)^2/x_i < 0$, which is a contradiction. Thus we have shown the nonsingularity of $\bar{M}$. We suppose, in turn, that M is not a P_0-matrix. Then there exists a nonzero $\boldsymbol{\xi} \in R^n$ such that $\xi_i = 0$ or $\xi_i\eta_i < 0$ for every $i \in N$. Here $\boldsymbol{\eta} = M\boldsymbol{\xi}$. Perturbing the vector $\boldsymbol{\xi}$ if necessary, we may assume that $(\xi_i, \eta_i) = (0,0)$ or $\xi_i\eta_i < 0$ for every $i \in N$. Now define $(x_i, y_i) = (1,1)$ in the former case and $(x_i, y_i) = (|\xi_i|, |\eta_i|)$ in the latter case. Let $X = \text{diag}\,(x_1, x_2, \ldots, x_n)$, $Y = \text{diag}\,(y_1, y_2, \ldots, y_n)$ and define $\bar{M}$ by (4.1). We then see that $\bar{M}\boldsymbol{\zeta} = \mathbf{0}$ for $\boldsymbol{\zeta} = (\boldsymbol{\xi}, \boldsymbol{\eta}) \neq \mathbf{0}$. Hence the matrix $\bar{M}$ is singular. ∎

We define a mapping $\boldsymbol{u} : R^{2n}_{+} \to R^n_{+}$ by

$$\boldsymbol{u}(\boldsymbol{x},\boldsymbol{y}) = X\boldsymbol{y} = (x_1y_1, x_2y_2, \ldots, x_ny_n)^T \quad \text{for every } (\boldsymbol{x},\boldsymbol{y}) \in R^{2n}_{+}.$$

It should be noted that the LCP (1.1) can be rewritten as

$$u(x, y) = 0 \quad \text{and} \quad (x, y) \in S_+,$$

and the path of centers S_{cen} as

$$S_{cen} = \{(x, y) \in S_{++} : u(x, y) = te \quad \text{for some } t > 0\} \tag{4.2}$$

(see (2.6)). Assuming Condition 2.1, we will show that the mapping u maps S_{++} onto R^n_{++} diffeomorphically and that the path of centers S_{cen} is a one-dimensional smooth curve leading to a solution of the LCP (1.1).

Lemma 4.2. *The mapping u is one-to-one on $S_{++} = \{(x, y) \in R^{2n}_{++} : y = Mx + q\}$ whenever M is a P_0-matrix.*

Proof: Assume on the contrary that $u(x^1, y^1) = u(x^2, y^2)$ for some distinct $(x^1, y^1), (x^2, y^2) \in S_{++}$. Then

$$M(x^1 - x^2) = y^1 - y^2 \text{ and } x^1_i y^1_i = x^2_i y^2_i > 0 \ (i \in N).$$

Since the matrix M is a P_0-matrix, we can find an index j such that

$$x^1_j \neq x^2_j \text{ and } 0 \leq (x^1_j - x^2_j)[M(x^1 - x^2)]_j = (x^1_j - x^2_j)(y^1_j - y^2_j).$$

We may assume without loss of generality that $x^1_j > x^2_j$. Then the inequality above implies that $y^1_j \geq y^2_j$. This contradicts the equality $x^1_j y^1_j = x^2_j y^2_j > 0$. ∎

Lemma 4.3. *Suppose that Condition 2.1 holds. Then the system*

$$u(x, y) = a \quad \text{and} \quad (x, y) \in S_{++}$$

has a solution for every $a \in R^n_{++}$.

Proof: Let $a \in R^n_{++}$. Define $a^1 = (x^1_1 y^1_1, x^1_2 y^1_2, \ldots, x^1_n y^1_n)^T \in R^n_{++}$, where $(x^1, y^1) \in S_{++}$ is a point given in Condition 2.1. Now we consider the family of systems of equations with a parameter $t \in [0, 1]$:

$$u(x, y) = (1 - t)a^1 + ta \text{ and } (x, y) \in S_{++}. \tag{4.3}$$

Let $\bar{t} \leq 1$ be the supremum of $\hat{t}$'s such that the system (4.3) has a solution for every $t \in [0, \hat{t}]$. Then there exists a sequence $\{(x^k, y^k, t^k)\}$ of solutions of the system (4.3) such that $\lim_{k \to \infty} t^k = \bar{t}$. Since ${x^k}^T y^k = e^T u(x^k, y^k) = (1 - t^k)e^T a^1 + t^k e^T a \leq e^T a^1 + e^T a$, (iii) of Condition 2.1 ensures that the sequence $\{(x^k, y^k)\}$ is bounded. Hence we may assume that it converges to some $(\bar{x}, \bar{y}) \in S_+$. By the continuity of the mapping u, we have

$$u(\bar{x}, \bar{y}) = (1 - \bar{t})a^1 + \bar{t}a.$$

The right-hand side $(1-\bar{t})a^1 + \bar{t}a$ of the system of equations above is a positive vector, so we see $(\bar{x}, \bar{y}) \in R^{2n}_{++}$ by the definition of the mapping u. It follows that the point $(\bar{x}, \bar{y}, \bar{t})$ satisfies the system (4.3). Hence if $\bar{t} = 1$ then the desired result follows. Assume on the contrary that $\bar{t} < 1$. In view of Lemma 4.2, the restriction of the mapping u to S_{++} is a local homeomorphism at $(\bar{x}, \bar{y}) \in S_{++}$. (See the domain invariance theorem in Schwartz [62].) Hence the system (4.3) has a solution for every t sufficiently close to $\bar{t}$. This contradicts the definition of $\bar{t}$. ∎

Theorem 4.4. *Suppose that Condition 2.1 holds. Then*

(i) *The mapping u is a diffeomorphism from S_{++} onto R^n_{++}.*
(ii) *The path of centers S_{cen} defined by (2.6) or (4.2) is a one-dimensional smooth curve.*
(iii) *A point $u^{-1}(te)$ on the path of centers S_{cen} converges to a solution of the LCP (1.1) as t (> 0) tends to 0. In particular, the LCP has a solution.*

Proof: We see $u(S_{++}) \subset R^n_{++}$ by the definition of u, and $R^n_{++} \subset u(S_{++})$ by Lemma 4.3. Hence u maps S_{++} onto R^n_{++}. Furthermore, the mapping u is one-to-one on S_{++} by Lemma 4.2. The Jacobian matrix of the restriction of u to S_{++} with respect to x is $Y + XM$, where $X = \text{diag } x$ and $Y = \text{diag } y$. By Lemma 4.1, the Jacobian matrix is nonsingular under Condition 2.1 because the singularity of the Jacobian matrix coincides with that of the matrix $\bar{M}$ defined by (4.1). Hence the mapping u is a diffeomorphism between S_{++} and R^n_{++}. Thus we have shown (i). The assertion (ii) follows from (i) and the expression (4.2) of the path of centers S_{cen}. We will show (iii). Let $\bar{t} > 0$. By (iii) of Condition 2.1, the subset $\{u^{-1}(te) : 0 < t \leq \bar{t}\}$ of the path of centers S_{cen} is bounded. Hence there is at least one accumulation point of $u^{-1}(te)$ as $t \to 0$. By the continuity, every accumulation point is a solution of the LCP (1.1). Now we utilize some result on real algebraic varieties. We call a subset V of R^m a real algebraic variety if there exist a finite number of polynomials g_i $(i = 1, 2, \ldots, l)$ such that

$$V = \{x \in R^m : g_i(x) = 0 \ (i = 1, 2, \ldots, l)\}.$$

We know that a real algebraic variety has a triangulation (see, for example, Hironaka [25]). That is, it is homeomorphic to a locally finite simplicial complex. Let

$$V = \{(x, y, t) \in R^{2n+1} : y = Mx + q, \ x_i y_i = t \ (i \in N)\}.$$

Obviously, the set V is a real algebraic variety, so it has a triangulation. Let $(\bar{x}, \bar{y})$ be an accumulating point of $u^{-1}(te)$ as $t \to 0$. Then the point $v = (\bar{x}, \bar{y}, 0)$ lies in V. Since the triangulation of V is locally finite, we can find a sequence $\{t^p > 0\}$ and a subset σ of V which is homeomorphic to a one-dimensional simplex such that

$$\lim_{p \to \infty} t^p = 0, \ \ \lim_{p \to \infty} u^{-1}(t^p e) = (\bar{x}, \bar{y}) \ \text{ and } \ (u^{-1}(t^p e), t^p) \in \sigma \ (p = 1, 2, \ldots).$$

On the other hand, we know that $V \cap R^{2n+1}_{++}$ coincides with the one-dimensional curve $\{(u^{-1}(te), t) : t > 0\}$. Thus, the subset $\{(u^{-1}(te), t) : t^{p+1} \leq t \leq t^p\}$ of the curve must be contained in the set σ for every p, since otherwise σ is not arcwise connected. This ensures that $u^{-1}(te)$ converges to $(\bar{x}, \bar{y})$ as $t \to 0$. ∎

The next lemma shows that Condition 2.3, which will be assumed while discussing the computational complexity of the UIP method, is stronger than Condition 2.1. Hence, by Theorem 4.4, there exists a solution of the LCP (1.1) under Condition 2.3 as well as under Condition 2.1.

Lemma 4.5. *Suppose that M is a P_*-matrix and that a point $(x^1, y^1) \in S_{++}$ is known. Then Condition 2.1 holds.*

Proof: It suffices to show (iii) of Condition 2.1. Assume $M \in P_*(\kappa)$ for some $\kappa \geq 0$. Let $t^1 = {x^1}^T y^1$ and $t \geq 0$. Choose an arbitrary $(x, y) \in S_+^t = \{(x, y) \in S_+ : x^T y \leq t\}$. Since $y - y^1 = M(x - x^1)$, we know that

$$\begin{aligned}(x - x^1)^T(y - y^1) &\geq -4\kappa \sum_{i \in I_+}(x_i - x_i^1)(y_i - y_i^1) \quad \text{(by (3.5))}\\ &\geq -4\kappa \sum_{i \in I_+}(x_i y_i + x_i^1 y_i^1) \quad (\text{since } (x, y),\ (x^1, y^1) \geq 0)\\ &\geq -4\kappa(x^T y + {x^1}^T y^1) \quad (\text{since } (x, y),\ (x^1, y^1) \geq 0)\\ &\geq -4\kappa(t + t^1).\end{aligned}$$

Here

$$I_+ = \{i \in N : (x_i - x_i^1)(y_i - y_i^1) > 0\}.$$

Hence we obtain

$$\begin{aligned}{y^1}^T x + {x^1}^T y &= x^T y + {x^1}^T y^1 - (x - x^1)^T(y - y^1)\\ &\leq t + t^1 + 4\kappa(t + t^1)\\ &= (1 + 4\kappa)(t + t^1).\end{aligned}$$

Therefore the set S_+^t is included in the bounded set

$$\{(x, y) \geq 0 : {y^1}^T x + {x^1}^T y \leq (1 + 4\kappa)(t + t^1)\}.$$

Thus we have shown (iii) of Condition 2.1. ∎

From Lemma 4.5 and Theorem 4.4, we can see that, for the existence of a solution of the LCP (1.1), it is sufficient to assume that M is a P_*-matrix and that the interior S_{++} of the feasible region S_+ of the LCP is nonempty. It should be noted that we cannot replace "a P_*-matrix" by "a column sufficient matrix"; the choice

$$M = \begin{pmatrix} 1 & 0 \\ 1 & 0 \end{pmatrix}, \quad q = \begin{pmatrix} 0 \\ -1 \end{pmatrix}$$

gives a counterexample. On the other hand, we may weaken the assumption $S_{++} \neq \emptyset$ into $S_+ \neq \emptyset$:

Theorem 4.6. *Suppose that M is a P_*-matrix and that the LCP (1.1) is feasible, i.e., $S_+ \neq \emptyset$. Then the LCP has a solution, i.e., $S_{cp} \neq \emptyset$.*

Proof: Consider the perturbed linear complementarity problem, LCP($\bar{q}$): Find an $(\boldsymbol{x}, \boldsymbol{y}) \in R^{2n}$ such that

$$\boldsymbol{y} = M\boldsymbol{x} + \bar{\boldsymbol{q}}, \ (\boldsymbol{x}, \boldsymbol{y}) \geq \boldsymbol{0} \text{ and } x_i y_i = 0 \ (i \in N),$$

where $\bar{\boldsymbol{q}} \in R^n$. Then the set Q_{cp} of all the vectors $\bar{\boldsymbol{q}}$ for which the LCP($\bar{\boldsymbol{q}}$) has a solution is a closed subset of R^n because it is the union of all the complementary cones

$$\{\bar{\boldsymbol{q}} \in R^n : \bar{\boldsymbol{q}} = \boldsymbol{y} - M\boldsymbol{x} \ \text{ for some } (\boldsymbol{x}, \boldsymbol{y}) \geq \boldsymbol{0} \ \text{ with } x_i = 0 \ (i \in I), \ y_i = 0 \ (i \notin I)\}$$

$(I \subset N)$. On the other hand, we know from the assumption that the interior

$$S_{++}(\boldsymbol{q} + \epsilon \boldsymbol{e}) = \{(\boldsymbol{x}, \boldsymbol{y}) > \boldsymbol{0} : \boldsymbol{y} = M\boldsymbol{x} + \boldsymbol{q} + \epsilon \boldsymbol{e}\}$$

is nonempty for every $\epsilon > 0$ and that the LCP($\boldsymbol{q} + \epsilon\boldsymbol{e}$) has a solution, i.e., $\boldsymbol{q} + \epsilon\boldsymbol{e} \in Q_{cp}$ for every $\epsilon > 0$, where $\boldsymbol{e}$ denotes the n-dimensional vector of ones. Thus the desired result follows by taking the limit $\epsilon \to 0$. ∎

The theorem above can be restated as $P_* \subset Q_0$, where Q_0 is known as the class of matrices M such that a linear complementarity problem with M has a solution whenever it is feasible (see, for example, Aganagić and Cottle [2]).

4.2. The Path of Centers and Its Neighborhoods

The path of centers (or the central trajectory) S_{cen} for the LCP (1.1), which was defined by (2.6), can be rewritten as

$$S_{cen} = \{(\boldsymbol{x}, \boldsymbol{y}) \in S_{++} : \boldsymbol{u}(\boldsymbol{x}, \boldsymbol{y}) = t\boldsymbol{e} \quad \text{for some } t > 0\}, \tag{4.4}$$

where $\boldsymbol{u} : R^{2n}_+ \to R^n_+$ is the mapping defined by

$$\boldsymbol{u}(\boldsymbol{x}, \boldsymbol{y}) = X\boldsymbol{y} = (x_1 y_1, x_2 y_2, \ldots, x_n y_n)^T \quad \text{for every } (\boldsymbol{x}, \boldsymbol{y}) \in R^{2n}_+. \tag{4.5}$$

Besides the definition (2.6) or (4.4), there are several representations of the path of centers S_{cen}. We have already seen in Section 2.2 the representation

$$S_{cen} = \{(\boldsymbol{x}, \boldsymbol{y}) \in S_{++} : f_{cen}(\boldsymbol{x}, \boldsymbol{y}) = 0\} \tag{4.6}$$

in terms of the function f_{cen}.

For every $(\boldsymbol{x}, \boldsymbol{y}) \in R^{2n}_{++}$, define

$$\begin{aligned} \mu(\boldsymbol{x}, \boldsymbol{y}) &= \frac{\boldsymbol{x}^T \boldsymbol{y}}{n}, \\ \chi(\boldsymbol{x}, \boldsymbol{y}) &= \left\| \frac{\boldsymbol{u}(\boldsymbol{x}, \boldsymbol{y})}{\mu(\boldsymbol{x}, \boldsymbol{y})} - \boldsymbol{e} \right\|. \end{aligned}$$

Let $(x, y) \in S_{++}$. Then it is easily seen that

$$u(x, y) = te \quad \text{for some } t > 0$$

if and only if

$$\chi(x, y) = 0.$$

Thus we obtain

$$S_{cen} = \{(x, y) \in S_{++} : \chi(x, y) = 0\}. \tag{4.7}$$

To derive some other representations of S_{cen}, we further define, for every $(x, y) \in R^{2n}_{++}$,

$$\left.\begin{aligned}
v(x, y) &= (\sqrt{x_1y_1}, \sqrt{x_2y_2}, \ldots, \sqrt{x_ny_n}\,)^T, \\
V(x, y) &= \text{diag } v(x, y), \\
v_{min}(x, y) &= \min_{i \in N} \sqrt{x_iy_i} = \min_{i \in N} v_i(x, y), \\
\omega(x, y) &= v_{min}(x, y) \left\| \frac{v(x, y)}{\mu(x, y)} - V(x, y)^{-1}e \right\|, \\
\pi(x, y) &= \frac{v_{min}(x, y)^2}{\mu(x, y)}.
\end{aligned}\right\} \tag{4.8}$$

Remark 4.7. When the vector $(x, y) \in R^{2n}_{++}$ is fixed or the dependence on the vector (x, y) is clear from the context, we often omit it from the functions $u(x, y)$, $v(x, y)$, $v_{min}(x, y)$, $f_{cen}(x, y)$, $\mu(x, y)$, $\chi(x, y)$, $\omega(x, y)$, $\pi(x, y)$, etc.; for example, we use v to denote $v(x, y)$.

It is easily verified that

$$\begin{aligned}
\omega(x, y) &= 0 \quad \text{if and only if} \quad (x, y) \in S_{cen}, \\
1 - \pi(x, y) &= 0 \quad \text{if and only if} \quad (x, y) \in S_{cen}.
\end{aligned}$$

Hence we have

$$S_{cen} = \{(x, y) \in S_{++} : \omega(x, y) = 0\}, \tag{4.9}$$

$$S_{cen} = \{(x, y) \in S_{++} : 1 - \pi(x, y) = 0\}. \tag{4.10}$$

Remark 4.8. In the papers Kojima, Mizuno and Yoshise [35] and Kojima, Mizuno and Noma [33, 32], the path of centers S_{cen} was characterized in terms of the minimization of the logarithmic barrier function

$$x^Ty - t\sum_{i=1}^{n} \log x_iy_i$$

subject to the constraint $(x, y) \in S_{++}$; we can prove under Condition 2.1 that $(x, y) \in S_{++}$ belongs to S_{cen} if and only if it is a minimizer of the logarithmic barrier function over S_{++} for some $t > 0$.

The real valued functions f_{cen}, χ, ω and $1-\pi$ in the representations (4.6), (4.7), (4.9), (4.10) of S_{cen} give us certain quantities to measure the deviation from the path of centers S_{cen}. All the functions take nonnegative values at every $(\boldsymbol{x}, \boldsymbol{y}) \in S_{++}$, and zero if and only if $(\boldsymbol{x}, \boldsymbol{y}) \in S_{cen}$. In the succeeding discussions, the reduction of the potential function f will be evaluated in terms of ω and π. Using these functions, we define neighborhoods of the path of centers S_{cen} as follows:

$$\begin{aligned} N_{cen}(\alpha) &= \{(\boldsymbol{x}, \boldsymbol{y}) \in S_{++} : f_{cen}(\boldsymbol{x}, \boldsymbol{y}) \leq \alpha\}, \\ N_{\chi}(\alpha) &= \{(\boldsymbol{x}, \boldsymbol{y}) \in S_{++} : \chi(\boldsymbol{x}, \boldsymbol{y}) \leq \alpha\}, \\ N_{\omega}(\alpha) &= \{(\boldsymbol{x}, \boldsymbol{y}) \in S_{++} : \omega(\boldsymbol{x}, \boldsymbol{y}) \leq \alpha\}, \\ N_{\pi}(\alpha) &= \{(\boldsymbol{x}, \boldsymbol{y}) \in S_{++} : 1-\pi(\boldsymbol{x}, \boldsymbol{y}) \leq \alpha\}, \end{aligned}$$

where $\alpha \geq 0$. We also define $N_{cen}(+\infty) = S_{++}$. Obviously, $N_{cen}(0) = N_{\chi}(0) = N_{\omega}(0) = N_{\pi}(0) = S_{cen}$. The neighborhood $N_{cen}(\alpha)$ was introduced in Tanabe [67, 68, 69], $N_{\chi}(\alpha)$ in Kojima, Mizuno and Yoshise [35], and $N_{\pi}(\alpha)$ in Kojima, Mizuno and Yoshise [34], respectively. Among these neighborhoods we have relations as stated in the following theorem:

Theorem 4.9.

(i) $N_{cen}\left(\frac{\alpha^2}{6}\right) \subset N_{\chi}(\alpha) \subset N_{cen}\left(\frac{\alpha^2}{2(1-\alpha)}\right)$ *for each* $\alpha \in [0,1)$, *i.e.*, $\frac{\chi^2}{6} \leq f_{cen}$ *if* $f_{cen} \in \left[0, \frac{1}{6}\right)$ *and* $f_{cen} \leq \frac{\chi^2}{2(1-\chi)}$ *if* $\chi \in [0,1)$.

(ii) (a) $N_{\chi}(\alpha) \subset N_{\omega}(\alpha)$ *for each* $\alpha \in [0,\infty)$, *i.e.*, $\omega \leq \chi$.

(b) $N_{\omega}(\alpha) \subset N_{\chi}\left(\frac{\alpha}{1-\alpha}\right)$ *for each* $\alpha \in [0,1)$, *i.e.*, $\chi \leq \frac{\omega}{1-\omega}$ *if* $\omega \in [0,1)$.

(iii) $N_{\chi}(\alpha) \subset N_{\pi}(\alpha) \subset N_{\chi}(n\alpha)$ *for each* $\alpha \in [0,\infty)$, *i.e.*, $1-\pi \leq \chi \leq n(1-\pi)$.

(iv) $N_{\omega}(\alpha) \subset N_{\pi}(\alpha) \subset N_{\omega}(\sqrt{n\alpha})$ *for each* $\alpha \in [0,\infty)$, *i.e.*, $1-\pi \leq \omega \leq \sqrt{n(1-\pi)}$.

(v) *Let* $n \geq 2$. $N_{\pi}\left(1-\exp\left(-\frac{\alpha}{n-1}\right)\right) \subset N_{cen}(\alpha) \subset N_{\pi}(1-\exp(-\alpha-1))$ *for each* $\alpha \in [0,\infty)$, *i.e.*, $\exp\left(-\frac{f_{cen}}{n-1}\right) \geq \pi \geq \exp(-f_{cen}-1)$.

(vi) (a) $N_{\omega}(\bar{\omega}(\alpha)) \subset N_{cen}(\alpha)$ *for each* $\alpha \in [0,\infty)$, *i.e.*, $\bar{\omega}(f_{cen}) \leq \omega$.

Here $\bar{\omega}(\alpha) = \dfrac{\sqrt{\alpha^2+2\alpha}-\alpha}{\sqrt{\alpha^2+2\alpha}-\alpha+1}$.

(b) $N_{cen}(\alpha) \subset N_{\omega}(\sqrt{6\alpha})$ *for each* $\alpha \in \left[0, \frac{1}{6}\right)$, *i.e.*, $\omega \leq \sqrt{6 f_{cen}}$ *if* $f_{cen} \in \left[0, \frac{1}{6}\right)$.

The remainder of Section 4.2 is devoted to proving the above theorem. We prepare the following three lemmas before going into the proof. The first lemma includes the inequalities that have been used repeatedly in many papers on interior point algorithms. See, for example, Freund [18], Karmarkar [28], Todd and Ye [72], Ye [77], etc.

Lemma 4.10.

(i) *If* $1+\xi>0$ *then* $\log(1+\xi)\le\xi$.
(ii) *Let* $\tau\in[0,1)$. *If* $\boldsymbol{\xi}\in R^n$ *satisfies* $\mathbf{e}+\boldsymbol{\xi}\ge(1-\tau)\mathbf{e}$ *then*

$$\sum_{i=1}^n \log(1+\xi_i)\ge \mathbf{e}^T\boldsymbol{\xi}-\frac{\|\boldsymbol{\xi}\|^2}{2(1-\tau)}.$$

(iii) *If* $\boldsymbol{\xi}\in R^n$ *satisfies* $\mathbf{e}+\boldsymbol{\xi}>\mathbf{0}$ *then*

$$\sum_{i=1}^n \log(1+\xi_i)\le \mathbf{e}^T\boldsymbol{\xi}-\frac{\|\boldsymbol{\xi}\|^2}{2}+\frac{\|\boldsymbol{\xi}\|^3}{3}.$$

Here $\|\boldsymbol{\xi}\|$ *denotes the Euclidean norm of the vector* $\boldsymbol{\xi}$.

Proof: One can easily see the following inequalities:

$$\log(1+\xi) \le \xi \quad \text{if } 1+\xi>0, \tag{4.11}$$

$$\log(1+\xi) \ge \xi-\frac{\xi^2}{2} \quad \text{if } \xi\ge 0, \tag{4.12}$$

$$\log(1+\xi) \le \xi-\frac{\xi^2}{2}+\frac{\xi^3}{3} \quad \text{if } 1+\xi>0. \tag{4.13}$$

The assertion (i) is the inequality (4.11) itself. To see (ii), it is sufficient to show

$$\log(1+\xi)\ge\xi-\frac{\xi^2}{2(1-\tau)}$$

if $\xi\ge-\tau$ for some $\tau\in[0,1)$. In the case $\xi\ge 0$, the inequality above immediately follows from (4.12). Furthermore, if $|\xi|\le\tau$, we observe that

$$\begin{aligned}\log(1+\xi) &= \xi-\frac{\xi^2}{2}+\frac{\xi^3}{3}-\cdots\\ &\ge \xi-\frac{\xi^2}{2}(1+|\xi|+|\xi|^2+\cdots)\\ &= \xi-\frac{\xi^2}{2(1-|\xi|)}\\ &\ge \xi-\frac{\xi^2}{2(1-\tau)}.\end{aligned}$$

Thus we have shown (ii). Finally the assertion (iii) follows from (4.13) and

$$\sum_{i=1}^n(\xi_i)^3\le\sum_{i=1}^n|\xi_i|^3\le\|\boldsymbol{\xi}\|^3.$$

∎

Lemma 4.11. *Let $(\boldsymbol{x}, \boldsymbol{y}) \in S_{++}$. Assume that $\omega = \omega(\boldsymbol{x}, \boldsymbol{y}) < 1$. Then we have:*

(i) $v_{min} \geq \sqrt{(1-\omega)\mu}$.

(ii) $v_{max} \leq \sqrt{\dfrac{\mu}{1-\omega}}$.

Here $v_{min} = v_{min}(\boldsymbol{x}, \boldsymbol{y}) = \min_{i \in N} v_i(\boldsymbol{x}, \boldsymbol{y})$ and $v_{max} = v_{max}(\boldsymbol{x}, \boldsymbol{y}) = \max_{i \in N} v_i(\boldsymbol{x}, \boldsymbol{y})$.

Proof: By the definition (4.8) of ω, we see that

$$\omega = v_{min} \left\| \frac{\boldsymbol{v}}{\mu} - \boldsymbol{V}^{-1}\boldsymbol{e} \right\| \geq v_{min} \left| \frac{v_{min}}{\mu} - \frac{1}{v_{min}} \right| = \frac{\mu - v_{min}^2}{\mu} .$$

Hence the assertion (i) follows. To prove the assertion (ii), we observe that

$$\begin{aligned} \omega &= v_{min} \left\| \frac{\boldsymbol{v}}{\mu} - \boldsymbol{V}^{-1}\boldsymbol{e} \right\| \\ &\geq v_{min} \left| \frac{v_{max}}{\mu} - \frac{1}{v_{max}} \right| \\ &= v_{min} \left(\frac{v_{max}^2 - \mu}{\mu v_{max}} \right) \\ &\geq \sqrt{(1-\omega)\mu} \left(\frac{v_{max}^2 - \mu}{\mu v_{max}} \right) \quad \text{(by (i))} \end{aligned}$$

or equivalently

$$\sqrt{1-\omega}\; v_{max}^2 - \omega\sqrt{\mu}\; v_{max} - \sqrt{1-\omega}\; \mu \leq 0.$$

This inequality implies the assertion (ii). ∎

Lemma 4.12. *Let $n \geq 2$, $\boldsymbol{s} \in R^n_{++}$ and $\tilde{\pi} \in (0,1]$. Assume $\boldsymbol{e}^T\boldsymbol{s} = n$ and $\min_{i \in N} s_i = \tilde{\pi}$. Then we have:*

(i) $\sqrt{\dfrac{n}{n-1}}(1-\tilde{\pi}) \leq \|\boldsymbol{s} - \boldsymbol{e}\| \leq \sqrt{n(n-1)}(1-\tilde{\pi})$.

(ii) $-\log \tilde{\pi} - (n-1)\log \dfrac{n-\tilde{\pi}}{n-1} \leq -\sum_{i=1}^{n} \log s_i \leq -(n-1)\log \tilde{\pi} - \log\{n-(n-1)\tilde{\pi}\}$.

Proof: Let

$$S = \{\boldsymbol{s} \in R^n : \boldsymbol{e}^T\boldsymbol{s} = n \text{ and } \min_{i \in N} s_i = \tilde{\pi}\},$$

$$\tilde{\chi}(\boldsymbol{s}) = \|\boldsymbol{s} - \boldsymbol{e}\| = \sqrt{\sum_{i=1}^{n}(s_i - 1)^2} \quad \text{for every } \boldsymbol{s} \in R^n_{++}.$$

The function $\tilde{\chi}(\boldsymbol{s})$ has both its maximum and minimum over the compact set S. We will evaluate the maximum and minimum values of the function $\tilde{\chi}(\boldsymbol{s})$ to derive the inequality (i). Let $\boldsymbol{s}^* \in R^n$ and $\boldsymbol{s}_* \in R^n$ be such that

$$\begin{aligned} \boldsymbol{s}^* &= (n-(n-1)\tilde{\pi},\ \tilde{\pi},\ \tilde{\pi},\ \ldots,\ \tilde{\pi})^T, \\ \boldsymbol{s}_* &= \left(\frac{n-\tilde{\pi}}{n-1},\ \frac{n-\tilde{\pi}}{n-1},\ \ldots,\ \frac{n-\tilde{\pi}}{n-1},\ \tilde{\pi}\right)^T. \end{aligned}$$

We will show below that $\boldsymbol{s}^*$ is a maximizer of $\tilde{\chi}(\boldsymbol{s})$ over S and that $\boldsymbol{s}_*$ is a minimizer of $\tilde{\chi}(\boldsymbol{s})$ over S. To see this, we utilize the inequality

$$(a-1)^2+(b-1)^2 < (a-\epsilon-1)^2+(b+\epsilon-1)^2 \tag{4.14}$$

which holds for every a, b and ϵ with $0 < a-\epsilon < a \le b$. Assume that

$$\bar{\boldsymbol{s}} = (\bar{s}_1, \bar{s}_2, \ldots, \bar{s}_n)^T \in S,\quad \bar{s}_1 \ge \bar{s}_2 \ge \ldots \ge \bar{s}_n,\quad \bar{\boldsymbol{s}} \ne \boldsymbol{s}^*, \tag{4.15}$$

$$\hat{\boldsymbol{s}} = (\hat{s}_1, \hat{s}_2, \ldots, \hat{s}_n)^T \in S,\quad \hat{s}_1 \ge \hat{s}_2 \ge \ldots \ge \hat{s}_n,\quad \hat{\boldsymbol{s}} \ne \boldsymbol{s}_*. \tag{4.16}$$

It should be noted that these assumptions imply $n \ge 3$. We then observe that

$$\begin{aligned} n-(n-1)\tilde{\pi} > \bar{s}_1 \ge \bar{s}_2 > \tilde{\pi}, \\ \hat{s}_1 > \frac{n-\tilde{\pi}}{n-1} > \hat{s}_{n-1}. \end{aligned}$$

Defining $\bar{\boldsymbol{s}}' = (\bar{s}'_1, \bar{s}'_2, \ldots, \bar{s}'_n)^T$ and $\hat{\boldsymbol{s}}' = (\hat{s}'_1, \hat{s}'_2, \ldots, \hat{s}'_n)^T$ by

$$\begin{aligned} &\bar{s}'_1 = \bar{s}_1 + \epsilon,\quad \bar{s}'_2 = \bar{s}_2 - \epsilon,\quad \bar{s}'_i = \bar{s}_i \quad (i \ne 1, 2) \quad \text{and} \\ &\hat{s}'_1 = \hat{s}_1 - \epsilon,\quad \hat{s}'_{n-1} = \hat{s}_{n-1} + \epsilon,\quad \hat{s}'_i = \hat{s}_i \quad (i \ne 1, n-1), \end{aligned}$$

we have

$$\bar{\boldsymbol{s}}' \in S,\quad \tilde{\chi}(\bar{\boldsymbol{s}}') > \tilde{\chi}(\bar{\boldsymbol{s}}) \quad \text{and} \quad \hat{\boldsymbol{s}}' \in S,\quad \tilde{\chi}(\hat{\boldsymbol{s}}') < \tilde{\chi}(\hat{\boldsymbol{s}})$$

for every sufficiently small $\epsilon > 0$ in view of the inequality (4.14). Hence we have shown that $\bar{\boldsymbol{s}}$ is not a maximizer of the function $\tilde{\chi}(\boldsymbol{s})$ whenever $\bar{\boldsymbol{s}}$ satisfies (4.15) and that $\hat{\boldsymbol{s}}$ is not a minimizer of $\tilde{\chi}(\boldsymbol{s})$ whenever $\hat{\boldsymbol{s}}$ satisfies (4.16). On the other hand, we can see that there exist a maximizer and a minimizer of $\tilde{\chi}(\boldsymbol{s})$ over S in the set

$$\{\boldsymbol{s} \in S : s_1 \ge s_2 \ge \ldots \ge s_n\}.$$

Thus we conclude that the function $\tilde{\chi}(\boldsymbol{s})$ attains its maximum at $\boldsymbol{s} = \boldsymbol{s}^*$ and its minimum at $\boldsymbol{s} = \boldsymbol{s}_*$. Therefore we have the inequality (i) because

$$\begin{aligned} \tilde{\chi}(\boldsymbol{s}^*) &= \sqrt{\{n-(n-1)\tilde{\pi}-1\}^2+(n-1)(\tilde{\pi}-1)^2} = \sqrt{n(n-1)}(1-\tilde{\pi}), \\ \tilde{\chi}(\boldsymbol{s}_*) &= \sqrt{(n-1)\left(\frac{n-\tilde{\pi}}{n-1}-1\right)^2+(\tilde{\pi}-1)^2} = \sqrt{\frac{n}{n-1}}(1-\tilde{\pi}). \end{aligned}$$

Noting that the inequality

$$-\log a - \log b < -\log(a-\epsilon) - \log(b+\epsilon)$$

holds for every a, b and ϵ with $0 < a - \epsilon < a \leq b$, we can show the inequality (ii) in a similar way. ∎

We are now ready to prove Theorem 4.9.

Proof of Theorem 4.9.

Proof of (i).

Let $(\boldsymbol{x}, \boldsymbol{y}) \in S_{++}$, $\boldsymbol{r} = \boldsymbol{r}(\boldsymbol{x}, \boldsymbol{y}) = \dfrac{X\boldsymbol{y}}{\mu} - \boldsymbol{e} \in R^n$ and $\hat{f}_{cen}(\boldsymbol{r}) = -\sum_{i=1}^{n} \log(1 + r_i)$. Since $\chi(\boldsymbol{x}, \boldsymbol{y}) = \|\boldsymbol{r}\|$ and $f_{cen}(\boldsymbol{x}, \boldsymbol{y}) = \hat{f}_{cen}(\boldsymbol{r})$, it suffices to show that

$$\frac{\|\boldsymbol{r}\|^2}{6} \leq \hat{f}_{cen}(\boldsymbol{r}) \text{ if } \hat{f}_{cen}(\boldsymbol{r}) < \frac{1}{6},$$

$$\hat{f}_{cen}(\boldsymbol{r}) \leq \frac{\|\boldsymbol{r}\|^2}{2(1 - \|\boldsymbol{r}\|)} \text{ if } \|\boldsymbol{r}\| < 1.$$

The second relation above follows from (ii) of Lemma 4.10 since $\boldsymbol{e}^T\boldsymbol{r} = 0$. To prove the first relation above, we assume $\hat{f}_{cen}(\boldsymbol{r}) < 1/6$ and $\boldsymbol{r} \neq \boldsymbol{0}$. Define

$$\hat{g}(\theta) = \hat{f}_{cen}(\theta\boldsymbol{r}) = -\sum_{i=1}^{n} \log(1 + \theta r_i) \quad \text{for every } \theta \in \hat{\Theta},$$

where $\hat{\Theta} = \{\theta \geq 0 : \boldsymbol{e} + \theta\boldsymbol{r} > \boldsymbol{0}\}$. By the definition of $\boldsymbol{r}$, we have $1 \in \hat{\Theta}$. Furthermore, it follows from $\boldsymbol{e}^T\boldsymbol{r} = 0$ and $\boldsymbol{r} \neq \boldsymbol{0}$ that $\dfrac{1}{\|\boldsymbol{r}\|} \in \hat{\Theta}$. In fact, $1 + \dfrac{r_i}{\|\boldsymbol{r}\|} \leq 0$ for some $i \in N$ would imply $r_i < 0$ and $r_j = 0$ $(j \in N \setminus \{i\})$, which contradicts $\boldsymbol{e}^T\boldsymbol{r} = 0$. By (iii) of Lemma 4.10 and $\boldsymbol{e}^T\boldsymbol{r} = 0$, we have

$$\hat{g}(\theta) \geq \frac{\|\theta\boldsymbol{r}\|^2}{2} - \frac{\|\theta\boldsymbol{r}\|^3}{3} \quad \text{for every } \theta \in \hat{\Theta}. \tag{4.17}$$

Furthermore, the function $\hat{g}$ is monotone nondecreasing in $\theta \in \hat{\Theta}$ since

$$\frac{d\hat{g}(\theta)}{d\theta} = -\sum_{i=1}^{n} \frac{r_i}{1 + \theta r_i} \geq -\sum_{i=1}^{n} r_i = 0.$$

Hence, if $\|\boldsymbol{r}\| \geq 1$ then

$$\hat{f}_{cen}(\boldsymbol{r}) = \hat{g}(1) \geq \hat{g}\left(\frac{1}{\|\boldsymbol{r}\|}\right) \geq \frac{1}{2} - \frac{1}{3} = \frac{1}{6} \quad \text{(by (4.17))}.$$

Therefore, we have $\|\boldsymbol{r}\| < 1$ because $\hat{f}_{cen}(\boldsymbol{r}) < 1/6$. Finally, by (4.17) again, we obtain

$$\hat{f}_{cen}(\boldsymbol{r}) = \hat{g}(1) \geq \frac{\|\boldsymbol{r}\|^2}{2} - \frac{\|\boldsymbol{r}\|^3}{3} \geq \frac{\|\boldsymbol{r}\|^2}{6}.$$

Thus we have shown the assertion (i).

Proof of (ii).
The assertion (a) follows from

$$\omega = v_{min}\left\|\frac{v}{\mu} - V^{-1}e\right\| \leq \left\|V\left(\frac{v}{\mu} - V^{-1}e\right)\right\| = \left\|\frac{V^2e}{\mu} - e\right\| = \chi.$$

To show the assertion (b), assume $\omega < 1$. Then we have

$$\begin{aligned}
\chi &= \left\|\frac{V^2e}{\mu} - e\right\| \\
&= \left\|V\left(\frac{v}{\mu} - V^{-1}e\right)\right\| \\
&\leq v_{max}\left\|\frac{v}{\mu} - V^{-1}e\right\| \\
&\leq \frac{\sqrt{\mu}}{\sqrt{1-\omega}}\left\|\frac{v}{\mu} - V^{-1}e\right\| \quad \text{(by (ii) of Lemma 4.11)} \\
&\leq \frac{v_{min}}{1-\omega}\left\|\frac{v}{\mu} - V^{-1}e\right\| \quad \text{(by (i) of Lemma 4.11)} \\
&= \frac{\omega}{1-\omega}.
\end{aligned}$$

Proof of (iii).
The case $n = 1$ is trivial because $\chi = 1 - \pi = 0$ for every $(x, y) \in S_{++}$. Let $n \geq 2$, $(x, y) \in S_{++}$ and $s = s(x, y) = \dfrac{Xy}{\mu}$. Then $e^T s = n$, $\pi(x, y) = \min_{i \in N} s_i$ and $\chi(x, y) = \|s - e\|$. By (i) of Lemma 4.12, we have

$$\sqrt{\frac{n}{n-1}}(1 - \pi) \leq \chi \leq \sqrt{n(n-1)}(1 - \pi);$$

hence

$$1 - \pi \leq \chi \leq n(1 - \pi).$$

This completes the proof of (iii).

Proof of (iv).
The first relation follows from

$$\omega = v_{min}\left\|\frac{v}{\mu} - V^{-1}e\right\| \geq v_{min}\left|\frac{v_{min}}{\mu} - \frac{1}{v_{min}}\right| = \left|\frac{v_{min}^2}{\mu} - 1\right| = 1 - \pi$$

and the second from

$$\omega^2 = v_{min}^2\left\|\frac{nv}{\|v\|^2} - V^{-1}e\right\|^2$$

$$
\begin{aligned}
&= v_{min}^2\left(e^TV^{-2}e - \frac{n^2}{\|v\|^2}\right)\\
&= \sum_{i=1}^{n}\frac{v_{min}^2}{v_i^2} - \frac{n^2v_{min}^2}{\|v\|^2}\\
&\leq n - n\pi\\
&= n(1-\pi).
\end{aligned}
$$

Proof of (v).

Let $n \geq 2$, $(x,y) \in S_{++}$ and $s = s(x,y) = \dfrac{Xy}{\mu}$. Then $e^Ts = n$, $\pi(x,y) = \min_{i\in N} s_i$ and $f_{cen}(x,y) = -\sum_{i=1}^{n}\log s_i$. Hence we see by (ii) of Lemma 4.12 that

$$
-\log\pi - (n-1)\log\frac{n-\pi}{n-1} \leq f_{cen} \leq -(n-1)\log\pi - \log\{n-(n-1)\pi\}.
$$

It follows that

$$
-\log\pi - 1 \leq f_{cen} \leq -(n-1)\log\pi
$$

or equivalently

$$
\exp(-f_{cen}-1) \leq \pi \leq \exp\left(-\frac{f_{cen}}{n-1}\right).
$$

This completes the proof of (v).

Proof of (vi).

The assertion (vi) follows from the assertions (i) and (ii) of this theorem. From (i) and (ii)-(b), we have

$$
\begin{aligned}
\chi &\geq \sqrt{f_{cen}^2 + 2f_{cen}} - f_{cen},\\
\omega &\geq \frac{\chi}{1+\chi};
\end{aligned}
$$

hence

$$
\omega \geq \frac{\sqrt{f_{cen}^2 + 2f_{cen}} - f_{cen}}{\sqrt{f_{cen}^2 + 2f_{cen}} - f_{cen} + 1}.
$$

Thus we have shown the assertion (a). The assertion (b) also follows immediately from (i) and (ii)-(a).

4.3. A Smooth Version of the UIP Method

In each iteration of the UIP method presented in Section 2.2, we first compute the search direction (dx, dy) at the current point $(x, y) \in S_{++}$ by solving the system (2.8) of equations and then proceed in the direction (dx, dy) to generate a new point $(x, y) + \theta(dx, dy)$, where $\theta \geq 0$ is a step size parameter. We now deal with a simple situation in which the parameter $\beta \in [0, 1]$ to determine the direction (dx, dy) is fixed throughout the iterations. Then the UIP method can be considered a sort of numerical integration of the vector field $\{(dx, dy)\}$ over S_{++} consisting of the solutions of the system (2.8) with the fixed β. If we employ a smaller step size parameter θ and update the direction (dx, dy) more often, we can perform the integration more precisely. If we take the step size parameter θ to be infinitesimal in the UIP method as a limit, the sequence $\{(x^k, y^k)\}$ generated by the method comes to a smooth trajectory such that the search direction (dx, dy) is tangent to the trajectory at each point (x, y) on it.

In this section, we will analyze the smooth version of the UIP method stated above, which could be given as the system of differential equations:

$$\begin{pmatrix} Y & X \\ -M & I \end{pmatrix} \begin{pmatrix} \dot{x} \\ \dot{y} \end{pmatrix} = \begin{pmatrix} \beta \dfrac{x^T y}{n} e - Xy \\ 0 \end{pmatrix}, \tag{4.18}$$

where $\dot{x} = \dfrac{dx}{ds}$, $\dot{y} = \dfrac{dy}{ds}$ and $s \geq 0$. Given an initial point $(x(0), y(0)) = (x^0, y^0) \in S_{++}$, we have a trajectory, a solution curve, $\{(x(s), y(s)) : s \geq 0\}$ integrating the system (4.18). The tangent direction of the solution curve coincides with the search direction of the UIP method, i.e.,

$$\left(\frac{dx(s)}{ds}, \frac{dy(s)}{ds} \right) = (dx, dy). \tag{4.19}$$

Recall that the mapping $u : S_{++} \to R^n_{++}$ defined by (4.5) is diffeomorphic (Theorem 4.4). With this mapping u we will transform the system (4.18) of differential equations into the one in $u = u(x, y)$. Let

$$\dot{u} = \frac{du}{ds} \quad \text{and} \quad u(s) = u(x(s), y(s)) \quad \text{for every } s \geq 0.$$

Then

$$\dot{u} = Y\dot{x} + X\dot{y}$$

and we obtain, from (4.18), the system of differential equations

$$\dot{u} = \beta \frac{e^T u}{n} e - u. \tag{4.20}$$

The trajectory $\{u(s) : s \geq 0\}$ is a solution curve of this system.

The system (4.20) is easier to analyze than the system (4.18). First we observe that the system (4.20) can be rewritten as

$$\dot{u} = -(I - \beta P)u. \tag{4.21}$$

Here I denotes the $n \times n$ identity matrix, and P the orthogonal projection matrix from R^n_{++} onto $u(S_{cen}) = \{te : t > 0\}$, i.e., $P = ee^T/n$.

Let $\beta \in (0,1)$. We will see that each trajectory leads to the origin $\mathbf{0}$ at which it is tangent to the ray $u(S_{cen}) = \{te : t > 0\}$. Let $Q = I - P$, i.e., Q be the orthogonal projection matrix from R^n onto the subspace $\{u \in R^n : e^T u = 0\}$. Then $P^2 = P$ and $QP = O$, where O denotes the $n \times n$ zero matrix. Hence the system (4.21) of differential equations can be further rewritten as

$$\begin{aligned} P\dot{u} &= -(1-\beta)Pu, \\ Q\dot{u} &= -Qu. \end{aligned}$$

Solving this system with the initial condition $u(0) = u^0 \in R^n_{++}$, we obtain

$$\begin{aligned} Pu(s) &= \exp\{-(1-\beta)s\}Pu^0, \\ Qu(s) &= \exp(-s)Qu^0. \end{aligned}$$

It follows that

$$\begin{aligned} u(s) &= Pu(s) + Qu(s) \\ &= \exp\{-(1-\beta)s\}Pu^0 + \exp(-s)Qu^0, \\ Qu(s) &= \left(\frac{\|Pu(s)\|}{\|Pu^0\|}\right)^{\frac{1}{1-\beta}} Qu^0. \end{aligned}$$

From these equalities, we see that $u(s) \in R^n_{++}$ for every $s \geq 0$ and that, if $\beta \in (0,1)$, $u(s)$ tends to the origin $\mathbf{0}$ while it asymptotically approaches the ray $u(S_{cen}) = \{te : t > 0\}$ as $s \to \infty$. The two extreme cases are $\beta = 0$ and $\beta = 1$. When $\beta = 0$, the solution curve $\{u(s) : s \geq 0\}$ equals the line segment $\{tu^0 : 0 < t \leq 1\}$ connecting the initial point u^0 and the origin $\mathbf{0}$. When $\beta = 1$, the solution curve equals the line segment $\{Pu^0 + tQu^0 : 0 < t \leq 1\}$ connecting u^0 and Pu^0. See Figure 13.

Remark 4.13. The properties of the system of differential equations (4.21) above are quite similar to the ones that were given by Tanabe [68]. Similar studies were also done in Bayer and Lagarias [5, 6] and Megiddo and Shub [43].

We now proceed to study the relationships between the system (4.18) of differential equations and its solution curves and the potential function f defined by (2.2). We begin by showing that the search direction (dx, dy) determined by the system (2.8) is a descent direction of the potential function f. Recall that the search direction (dx, dy) depends on the parameter $\beta \in [0,1]$ and can be regarded as a convex combination of the centering direction (dx^c, dy^c) and the affine scaling direction (dx^a, dy^a), which correspond to the cases $\beta = 1$ and $\beta = 0$, respectively. See the equality (2.10).

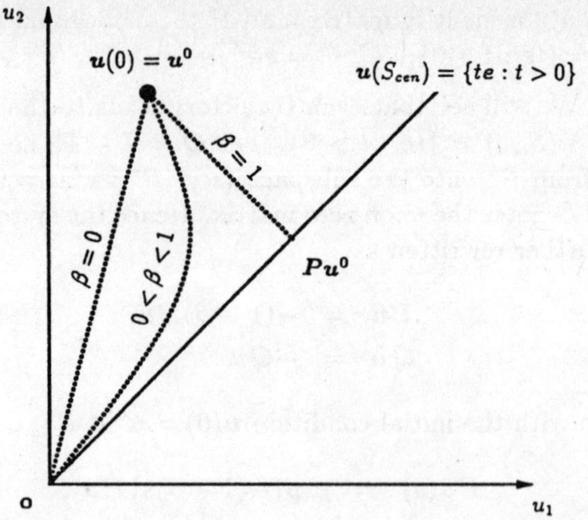

Figure 13: Solution curves of the system (4.20).

Lemma 4.14. *Let ∇ denote, as usual the gradient operator. Then,*

$$\nabla f_{cp}(x,y)^T \begin{pmatrix} dx^c \\ dy^c \end{pmatrix} = 0, \quad \nabla f_{cp}(x,y)^T \begin{pmatrix} dx^a \\ dy^a \end{pmatrix} = -1,$$

$$\nabla f_{cp}(x,y)^T \begin{pmatrix} dx \\ dy \end{pmatrix} = -(1-\beta), \tag{4.22}$$

$$\nabla f_{cen}(x,y)^T \begin{pmatrix} dx^c \\ dy^c \end{pmatrix} = -\frac{\omega^2}{\pi}, \quad \nabla f_{cen}(x,y)^T \begin{pmatrix} dx^a \\ dy^a \end{pmatrix} = 0,$$

$$\nabla f_{cen}(x,y)^T \begin{pmatrix} dx \\ dy \end{pmatrix} = -\frac{\beta\omega^2}{\pi}, \tag{4.23}$$

$$\nabla f(x,y)^T \begin{pmatrix} dx^c \\ dy^c \end{pmatrix} = -\frac{\omega^2}{\pi}, \quad \nabla f(x,y)^T \begin{pmatrix} dx^a \\ dy^a \end{pmatrix} = -\nu,$$

$$\nabla f(x,y)^T \begin{pmatrix} dx \\ dy \end{pmatrix} = -\left\{\nu(1-\beta) + \frac{\beta\omega^2}{\pi}\right\}$$

for every $(x,y) \in S_{++}$.

Proof: We need only to show the equalities (4.22) and (4.23) because the others follow directly from the relations (2.3) and (2.10).

We now observe that

$$\nabla f_{cp}(x,y)^T \begin{pmatrix} dx \\ dy \end{pmatrix} = \frac{1}{x^T y} \begin{pmatrix} y \\ x \end{pmatrix}^T \begin{pmatrix} dx \\ dy \end{pmatrix}$$

$$
\begin{aligned}
&= \frac{1}{x^T y} e^T (Y dx + X dy) \\
&= \frac{1}{x^T y} e^T \left(\beta \frac{x^T y}{n} e - X y \right) \quad \text{(by (2.8))} \\
&= -(1-\beta), \\
\nabla f_{cen}(x,y)^T \begin{pmatrix} dx \\ dy \end{pmatrix} &= \left\{ \frac{n}{x^T y} \begin{pmatrix} y \\ x \end{pmatrix} - \begin{pmatrix} X^{-1} e \\ Y^{-1} e \end{pmatrix} \right\}^T \begin{pmatrix} dx \\ dy \end{pmatrix} \\
&= \left(\frac{n}{x^T y} e - X^{-1} Y^{-1} e \right)^T (Y dx + X dy) \\
&= \left(\frac{n}{x^T y} e - X^{-1} Y^{-1} e \right)^T \left(\beta \frac{x^T y}{n} e - X y \right) \quad \text{(by (2.8))} \\
&= \left(\frac{e}{\mu} - V^{-2} e \right)^T (\beta \mu e - V^2 e) \quad \text{(by } V^2 = XY) \\
&= \left(\frac{v}{\mu} - V^{-1} e \right)^T (\beta \mu V^{-1} e - v) \\
&= \beta \left(\frac{v}{\mu} - V^{-1} e \right)^T (\mu V^{-1} e - v) \\
&\qquad \left(\text{since } \left(\frac{v}{\mu} - V^{-1} e \right)^T v = 0 \right) \\
&= -\beta \mu \left\| \frac{v}{\mu} - V^{-1} e \right\|^2 \\
&= -\frac{\beta \omega^2}{\pi} \quad \text{(by (4.8)).}
\end{aligned}
$$

This completes the proof. ∎

It is remarkable that the vectors (dx^c, dy^c) and (dx^a, dy^a) at the point $(x, y) \in S_{++}$ are normal to the gradient vectors $\nabla f_{cp}(x, y)$ and $\nabla f_{cen}(x, y)$, respectively. Moreover, we can see that the term ω^2/π in the lemma above vanishes if and only if $(x, y) \in S_{++}$ lies on the path of centers S_{cen}, while it grows larger as (x, y) goes farther from S_{cen}.

The potential function f can be regarded as a function of $v = v(x, y) = (\sqrt{x_1 y_1}, \sqrt{x_2 y_2}, \ldots, \sqrt{x_n y_n}\,)^T$, which we denote by p, i.e.,

$$
p(v) = (n + \nu) \log \|v\|^2 - \sum_{i=1}^{n} \log(v_i)^2 - n \log n \quad \text{for every } v \in R^n_{++}.
$$

We shall show that the continuous steepest descent method for minimizing the potential function $p(v)$ induces the same trajectories as the system (4.20) of equations. Let $\nabla p(v)$ denote the gradient vector of p at $v \in R^n_{++}$, and consider the system of differential equations

$$
\dot{v} = -\nabla p(v) = -2 \left\{ \frac{(n + \nu) v}{\|v\|^2} - V^{-1} e \right\}. \tag{4.24}
$$

The continuous steepest descent method traces a trajectory, a solution curve of the system of differential equations above, from a given initial point $\boldsymbol{v}(0) = \boldsymbol{v}^0 \in R^n_{++}$. By the relation $\boldsymbol{u} = \boldsymbol{V}^2\boldsymbol{e}$, we have $\dot{\boldsymbol{u}} = 2\boldsymbol{V}\dot{\boldsymbol{v}}$. Hence the system (4.24) of differential equations in the space of $\boldsymbol{v}$ can be rewritten as the system of differential equations in the space of $\boldsymbol{u}$:

$$\dot{\boldsymbol{u}} = -4\left\{\frac{(n+\nu)\boldsymbol{u}}{\boldsymbol{e}^T\boldsymbol{u}} - \boldsymbol{e}\right\}. \tag{4.25}$$

Choose the parameters $\beta \in (0,1)$ and $\nu > 0$ such that $\beta = n/(n+\nu)$. Then we can easily verify that the right-hand side of the system (4.25) differs from that of the system (4.20) only by a scalar multiple $\dfrac{4n}{\beta\boldsymbol{e}^T\boldsymbol{u}}$. Therefore the system (4.25) induces the same trajectories as the system (4.20). We will see in Lemma 6.5 that the choice of the parameters β and ν above gives rise to a large reduction in the potential function f.

Now we evaluate the reduction of the potential function f along the trajectories. The theorem below follows immediately from Lemma 4.14 and the relation (4.19):

Theorem 4.15. *Let $(\boldsymbol{x}(s), \boldsymbol{y}(s))$ $(s \geq 0)$ be a solution of the system (4.18). Then*

$$\begin{aligned}
\frac{df_{cp}(\boldsymbol{x}(s),\boldsymbol{y}(s))}{ds} &= -(1-\beta), \\
\frac{df_{cen}(\boldsymbol{x}(s),\boldsymbol{y}(s))}{ds} &= -\frac{\beta\omega(\boldsymbol{x}(s),\boldsymbol{y}(s))^2}{\pi(\boldsymbol{x}(s),\boldsymbol{y}(s))}, \\
\frac{df(\boldsymbol{x}(s),\boldsymbol{y}(s))}{ds} &= -\left\{\nu(1-\beta) + \frac{\beta\omega(\boldsymbol{x}(s),\boldsymbol{y}(s))^2}{\pi(\boldsymbol{x}(s),\boldsymbol{y}(s))}\right\}
\end{aligned}$$

for every $s \geq 0$.

Recall that the potential function f is the sum of νf_{cp} and f_{cen}. In view of the theorem above, we see that f_{cp} decreases constantly at the speed of $(1-\beta)$ along each trajectory $\{(\boldsymbol{x}(s),\boldsymbol{y}(s)) : s \geq 0\}$, while the decreasing speed of f_{cen} depends on the location of the point $(\boldsymbol{x}(s),\boldsymbol{y}(s))$. If the point $(\boldsymbol{x}(s),\boldsymbol{y}(s))$ lies on the path of centers S_{cen} for some $s \geq 0$, the value $f_{cen}(\boldsymbol{x}(s),\boldsymbol{y}(s))$ and the speed $\dfrac{df_{cen}(\boldsymbol{x}(s),\boldsymbol{y}(s))}{ds}$ are both zero so that the trajectory runs exactly on S_{cen}. When the trajectory starts from a point $(\boldsymbol{x}(0),\boldsymbol{y}(0)) \notin S_{cen}$, the nearer the point $(\boldsymbol{x}(s),\boldsymbol{y}(s))$ approaches the path of centers S_{cen}, the smaller the decreasing speed $-\dfrac{df_{cen}(\boldsymbol{x}(s),\boldsymbol{y}(s))}{ds} = \dfrac{\beta\omega(\boldsymbol{x}(s),\boldsymbol{y}(s))^2}{\pi(\boldsymbol{x}(s),\boldsymbol{y}(s))}$ becomes. It should be noted that the decreasing speed of the functions f_{cp}, f_{cen} and f along the trajectory $\{(\boldsymbol{x}(s),\boldsymbol{y}(s)) : s \geq 0\}$ depends on the parametrization. Recall that the trajectory has been represented as a solution of the system (4.18) of differential equations. A discrete version of Theorem 4.15 will be given in Section 4.4. See Theorem 4.17.

4.4. Quadratic Approximations of the Potential Function

Let $(\boldsymbol{x},\boldsymbol{y}) \in S_{++}$, and let $(d\boldsymbol{x},d\boldsymbol{y}) \in R^{2n}$ be the direction computed in Step 3 of the UIP method by solving the the Newton equation (2.8). This section establishes two theorems, Theorems 4.17 and 4.18, to evaluate a reduction in the potential function at a new point $(\boldsymbol{x},\boldsymbol{y}) + \theta(d\boldsymbol{x},d\boldsymbol{y})$ in terms of quadratic functions in the step size parameter θ. Theorem 4.17 will provide us with an initial value for approximating the minimizer of the potential function along the line $\{(\boldsymbol{x},\boldsymbol{y}) + \theta(d\boldsymbol{x},d\boldsymbol{y}) : \theta \geq 0\}$ in Step 4 of the UIP method, while Theorem 4.18, which will be derived from Theorem 4.17, plays a key role in Section 6 where we will establish the global and/or polynomial-time convergence of potential reduction algorithms that are special cases of the UIP method.

In addition to the symbols $\boldsymbol{v} = \boldsymbol{v}(\boldsymbol{x},\boldsymbol{y})$, $\boldsymbol{V} = \boldsymbol{V}(\boldsymbol{x},\boldsymbol{y})$, $v_{min} = v_{min}(\boldsymbol{x},\boldsymbol{y})$, $\omega = \omega(\boldsymbol{x},\boldsymbol{y})$ and $\pi = \pi(\boldsymbol{x},\boldsymbol{y})$ defined by (4.8), we often use the following symbols.

$$\left.\begin{aligned} \boldsymbol{h}_{cp} &= \boldsymbol{h}_{cp}(\boldsymbol{x},\boldsymbol{y}) = \frac{\boldsymbol{v}}{\|\boldsymbol{v}\|^2}, \\ \boldsymbol{h}_{cen} &= \boldsymbol{h}_{cen}(\boldsymbol{x},\boldsymbol{y}) = \frac{\boldsymbol{v}}{\mu} - \boldsymbol{V}^{-1}\boldsymbol{e}, \\ \boldsymbol{h}(\beta) &= \boldsymbol{h}(\beta,\boldsymbol{x},\boldsymbol{y}) = \boldsymbol{V}^{-1}(\beta\mu\boldsymbol{e} - \boldsymbol{X}\boldsymbol{y}) \text{ for every } \beta \in [0,1]. \end{aligned}\right\} \tag{4.26}$$

Among these symbols we have the following relations. Their proofs are straightforward and omitted here.

Lemma 4.16.

$$\begin{aligned} &\|\boldsymbol{h}_{cen}\| = \frac{\omega}{v_{min}}, \\ &\|\boldsymbol{h}_{cp}\| = \frac{1}{\|\boldsymbol{v}\|} = \frac{1}{\sqrt{n\mu}}, \\ &\boldsymbol{h}_{cp}^T\boldsymbol{h}_{cen} = 0, \\ &\boldsymbol{h}(\beta) = -\mu\{(1-\beta)n\boldsymbol{h}_{cp} + \beta\boldsymbol{h}_{cen}\} \quad \textit{for every } \beta \in [0,1], \\ &\boldsymbol{h}_{cp}^T\boldsymbol{h}(\beta) = -(1-\beta) \quad \textit{for every } \beta \in [0,1], \\ &\boldsymbol{h}_{cen}^T\boldsymbol{h}(\beta) = -\frac{\beta\omega^2}{\pi} \quad \textit{for every } \beta \in [0,1], \\ &\|\boldsymbol{h}(\beta)\| = \frac{v_{min}}{\pi}\sqrt{(1-\beta)^2 n\pi + \beta^2\omega^2} \quad \textit{for every } \beta \in [0,1]. \end{aligned}$$

It will be convenient to transform the system (2.8) of Newton equations into the equivalent system of equations

$$\boldsymbol{V}^{-1}(\boldsymbol{Y}d\boldsymbol{x} + \boldsymbol{X}d\boldsymbol{y}) = \boldsymbol{h}(\beta), \quad -\boldsymbol{M}d\boldsymbol{x} + d\boldsymbol{y} = \boldsymbol{0}, \tag{4.27}$$

which we obtain by multiplying (2.8) by the diagonal matrix

$$\boldsymbol{V}^{-1} = \text{diag}\left(\frac{1}{v_1},\frac{1}{v_2},\ldots,\frac{1}{v_n}\right) = \text{diag}\left(\frac{1}{\sqrt{x_1y_1}},\frac{1}{\sqrt{x_2y_2}},\ldots,\frac{1}{\sqrt{x_ny_n}}\right).$$

Theorem 4.17. *Let* $\nu > 0$, $\tau \in [0,1)$, $(\boldsymbol{x},\boldsymbol{y}) \in S_{++}$, $\beta \in [0,1]$ *and* $\beta \neq 1$ *if* $(\boldsymbol{x},\boldsymbol{y}) \in S_{cen}$. *Define*

$$\Theta(\tau) = \sup\{\theta \geq 0 : \theta d\boldsymbol{x} \geq -\tau\boldsymbol{x}, \theta d\boldsymbol{y} \geq -\tau\boldsymbol{y}\},$$

and the quadratic functions G_{cp}, G^{τ}_{cen} *and* $G^{\tau} : R \to R$ *by*

$$\left.\begin{aligned} G_{cp}(\theta) &= (1-\beta)\theta - \frac{d\boldsymbol{x}^T d\boldsymbol{y}}{\boldsymbol{x}^T\boldsymbol{y}}\theta^2, \\ G^{\tau}_{cen}(\theta) &= \frac{\beta\omega^2}{\pi}\theta - \left\{ n\frac{d\boldsymbol{x}^T d\boldsymbol{y}}{\boldsymbol{x}^T\boldsymbol{y}} + \frac{\|\boldsymbol{X}^{-1}d\boldsymbol{x}\|^2 + \|\boldsymbol{Y}^{-1}d\boldsymbol{y}\|^2}{2(1-\tau)} \right\}\theta^2, \\ G^{\tau}(\theta) &= \nu G_{cp}(\theta) + G^{\tau}_{cen}(\theta). \end{aligned}\right\} \tag{4.28}$$

Assume that $\theta \in [0, \Theta(\tau)]$ *and* $(\bar{\boldsymbol{x}}, \bar{\boldsymbol{y}}) = (\boldsymbol{x},\boldsymbol{y}) + \theta(d\boldsymbol{x}, d\boldsymbol{y})$. *Then we have:*

$$\Theta(\tau) < +\infty, \tag{4.29}$$

$$(\bar{\boldsymbol{x}}, \bar{\boldsymbol{y}}) \in S_{++}, \tag{4.30}$$

$$\left.\begin{aligned} f_{cp}(\bar{\boldsymbol{x}}, \bar{\boldsymbol{y}}) - f_{cp}(\boldsymbol{x},\boldsymbol{y}) &\leq -G_{cp}(\theta), \\ f_{cen}(\bar{\boldsymbol{x}}, \bar{\boldsymbol{y}}) - f_{cen}(\boldsymbol{x},\boldsymbol{y}) &\leq -G^{\tau}_{cen}(\theta), \\ f(\bar{\boldsymbol{x}}, \bar{\boldsymbol{y}}) - f(\boldsymbol{x},\boldsymbol{y}) &\leq -G^{\tau}(\theta). \end{aligned}\right\} \tag{4.31}$$

Theorem 4.18. *Let* $\nu > 0$, $(\boldsymbol{x},\boldsymbol{y}) \in S_{++}$, $\beta \in [0,1]$ *and* $\beta \neq 1$ *if* $(\boldsymbol{x},\boldsymbol{y}) \in S_{cen}$. *Define*

$$\Delta(\beta) = \max\left\{0, -\frac{d\boldsymbol{x}^T d\boldsymbol{y}}{\|\boldsymbol{h}(\beta)\|^2}\right\}, \tag{4.32}$$

$$\left.\begin{aligned} g_{cp}(\beta) = g_{cp}(\beta,\boldsymbol{x},\boldsymbol{y}) &= \frac{(1-\beta)\pi}{\sqrt{(1+2\Delta(\beta))\{(1-\beta)^2 n\pi + \beta^2\omega^2\}}}, \\ g_{cen}(\beta) = g_{cen}(\beta,\boldsymbol{x},\boldsymbol{y}) &= \frac{\beta\omega^2}{\sqrt{(1+2\Delta(\beta))\{(1-\beta)^2 n\pi + \beta^2\omega^2\}}}, \\ g(\nu,\beta) = g(\nu,\beta,\boldsymbol{x},\boldsymbol{y}) &= \frac{\nu(1-\beta)\pi + \beta\omega^2}{\sqrt{(1+2\Delta(\beta))\{(1-\beta)^2 n\pi + \beta^2\omega^2\}}}. \end{aligned}\right\} \tag{4.33}$$

If

$$\theta = \frac{v_{min}\tau}{\sqrt{1+2\Delta(\beta)}\|\boldsymbol{h}(\beta)\|} \tag{4.34}$$

for some $\tau \in [0,1)$, *then the new point* $(\bar{\boldsymbol{x}}, \bar{\boldsymbol{y}}) = (\boldsymbol{x},\boldsymbol{y}) + \theta(d\boldsymbol{x}, d\boldsymbol{y})$ *satisfies*

$$(\bar{\boldsymbol{x}}, \bar{\boldsymbol{y}}) \in S_{++}, \tag{4.35}$$

$$\left.\begin{aligned} f_{cp}(\bar{\boldsymbol{x}}, \bar{\boldsymbol{y}}) - f_{cp}(\boldsymbol{x},\boldsymbol{y}) &\leq -G_{cp}(\theta) \leq -g_{cp}(\beta)\tau + \frac{\tau^2}{4n}, \\ f_{cen}(\bar{\boldsymbol{x}}, \bar{\boldsymbol{y}}) - f_{cen}(\boldsymbol{x},\boldsymbol{y}) &\leq -G^{\tau}_{cen}(\theta) \leq -g_{cen}(\beta)\tau + \left\{\frac{1}{4} + \frac{1}{2(1-\tau)}\right\}\tau^2, \\ f(\bar{\boldsymbol{x}}, \bar{\boldsymbol{y}}) - f(\boldsymbol{x},\boldsymbol{y}) &\leq -G^{\tau}(\theta) \leq -g(\nu,\beta)\tau + \left\{\frac{\nu}{4n} + \frac{1}{4} + \frac{1}{2(1-\tau)}\right\}\tau^2. \end{aligned}\right\} \tag{4.36}$$

Before proceeding to proofs of the theorems, we give some remark on the quantities $\Delta(\beta)$, $g_{cp}(\beta)$, $g_{cen}(\beta)$ and $g(\nu,\beta)$ that appeared in Theorem 4.18. By Lemma 4.16, we see

$$\|h(\beta)\| = \frac{v_{min}}{\pi}\sqrt{(1-\beta)^2 n\pi + \beta^2\omega^2}.$$

The term $\sqrt{(1-\beta)^2 n\pi + \beta^2\omega^2}$ on the right-hand side, which appeared also in the definition (4.33) of $g_{cp}(\beta)$, $g_{cen}(\beta)$ and $g(\nu,\beta)$, is zero if and only if $\beta = 1$ and $(x,y) \in S_{cen}$ hold simultaneously. Hence all the $\Delta(\beta)$, $g_{cp}(\beta)$, $g_{cen}(\beta)$ and $g(\nu,\beta)$ are well-defined under the assumptions of Theorem 4.18. The quantity $\Delta(\beta)$ generally depends on not only the point (x,y) but also the direction parameter β because the direction (dx,dy) is a solution of the system (2.8) of equations with the parameter β. It may diverge to infinity as (x,y) approaches the boundary of S_{++}. However, in the case where the matrix M belongs to the class P_* we can derive an upper bound for $\Delta(\beta)$ over all $(x,y) \in S_{++}$ and $\beta \in [0,1]$ except the case that $(x,y) \in S_{cen}$ and $\beta = 1$. In fact, if we denote $V^{-1}X$ by D, we can rewrite the system (4.27) as

$$D^{-1}dx + D dy = h(\beta), \quad -M dx + dy = 0.$$

Hence, by Lemma 3.4 with $\xi = dx$ and $\eta = dy$, we obtain:

Lemma 4.19. *Let $\beta \in [0,1]$ and $\beta \neq 1$ if $(x,y) \in S_{cen}$. Assume that the matrix M belongs to the class $P_*(\kappa)$ for some $\kappa \geq 0$. Then $\Delta(\beta) \leq \kappa$.*

Now we will prove the two theorems, Theorems 4.17 and 4.18.

Proof of Theorem 4.17.

First we prove the relation (4.29). Assume, on the contrary, that $\Theta(\tau) = +\infty$, which implies $(dx,dy) \geq 0$. We then observe by (2.8) that

$$0 \leq y^T dx + x^T dy = e^T(Y dx + X dy) = e^T(\beta\mu e - Xy) = -(1-\beta)x^T y \leq 0.$$

It follows that $(dx,dy) = 0$ and $\beta = 1$. On the other hand, by the equation (2.8) again, $(dx,dy) = 0$ implies $(x,y) \in S_{cen}$. This contradicts the assumption that $\beta \neq 1$ if $(x,y) \in S_{cen}$. Thus we have shown (4.29).

We next show the relation (4.30). Since (dx,dy) is a solution of the Newton equation (2.8) and $(x,y) \in S_{++}$, the new point $(\bar{x},\bar{y}) = (x,y) + \theta(dx,dy)$ satisfies the system of linear equations $\bar{y} = M\bar{x} + q$. We further see that

$$(\bar{x},\bar{y}) = (x,y) + \theta(dx,dy) \geq (1-\tau)(x,y) > 0 \tag{4.37}$$

because $\theta \in [0,\Theta(\tau)]$ and $\tau \in [0,1)$. Thus we have the relation (4.30).

We now evaluate the left-hand side of the second inequality in (4.31):

$$
\begin{aligned}
& f_{cen}(\bar{x},\bar{y}) - f_{cen}(x,y) \\
= \;& f_{cen}(x+\theta dx, y+\theta dy) - f_{cen}(x,y) \\
= \;& n\log\left\{x^Ty + \theta(y^Tdx + x^Tdy) + \theta^2 dx^Tdy\right\} - \sum_{i=1}^{n}(\log(x_i+\theta dx_i) + \log(y_i+\theta dy_i)) \\
& - n\log x^Ty + \sum_{i=1}^{n}(\log x_i + \log y_i) \\
= \;& n\log\left\{1 + \frac{\theta(y^Tdx + x^Tdy)}{x^Ty} + \frac{\theta^2 dx^Tdy}{x^Ty}\right\} \\
& - \sum_{i=1}^{n}\left\{\log\left(1+\frac{\theta dx_i}{x_i}\right) + \log\left(1+\frac{\theta dy_i}{y_i}\right)\right\}.
\end{aligned}
$$

In the equality above, we note by (4.37) that

$$
1 + \frac{\theta(y^Tdx + x^Tdy)}{x^Ty} + \frac{\theta^2 dx^Tdy}{x^Ty} = \frac{(x+\theta dx)^T(y+\theta dy)}{x^Ty} > 0,
$$

$$
e + \theta X^{-1}dx \geq (1-\tau)e, \quad e + \theta Y^{-1}dy \geq (1-\tau)e.
$$

Hence we see

$$
\begin{aligned}
& f_{cen}(\bar{x},\bar{y}) - f_{cen}(x,y) \\
\leq \;& n\left\{\frac{\theta(y^Tdx + x^Tdy)}{x^Ty} + \frac{\theta^2 dx^Tdy}{x^Ty}\right\} \\
& - \theta e^T(X^{-1}dx + Y^{-1}dy) + \frac{\|\theta X^{-1}dx\|^2 + \|\theta Y^{-1}dy\|^2}{2(1-\tau)} \qquad \text{(by Lemma 4.10)} \\
= \;& \theta\left\{\frac{ne^T(Ydx + Xdy)}{\|v\|^2} - e^TV^{-2}(Ydx + Xdy)\right\} \\
& + \theta^2\left\{\frac{ndx^Tdy}{x^Ty} + \frac{\|X^{-1}dx\|^2 + \|Y^{-1}dy\|^2}{2(1-\tau)}\right\} \\
= \;& \theta\left\{\left(\frac{v}{\mu} - V^{-1}e\right)^T V^{-1}(Ydx + Xdy)\right\} \\
& + \theta^2\left\{\frac{ndx^Tdy}{x^Ty} + \frac{\|X^{-1}dx\|^2 + \|Y^{-1}dy\|^2}{2(1-\tau)}\right\} \\
= \;& \theta h_{cen}^T h(\beta) + \theta^2\left\{\frac{ndx^Tdy}{x^Ty} + \frac{\|X^{-1}dx\|^2 + \|Y^{-1}dy\|^2}{2(1-\tau)}\right\} \qquad \text{(by (4.26) and (4.27))} \\
= \;& -G_{cen}^{\tau}(\theta) \quad \text{(by Lemma 4.16 and the definition (4.28) of } G_{cen}^{\tau}(\theta)).
\end{aligned}
$$

Thus we have shown the second inequality of (4.31).

The first inequality of (4.31) on the function f_{cp} could be derived similarly to the second inequality on the function f_{cen}, and the proof is omitted here. The last inequality of (4.31) on the potential function f follows directly from the first two inequalities because of the relations (2.3) and (4.28). This completes the proof of Theorem 4.17.

For Theorem 4.18 we need the following lemma:

Lemma 4.20.

(i) $dx^T dy \leq \|h(\beta)\|^2/4$.
(ii) $\|X^{-1}dx\|^2 + \|Y^{-1}dy\|^2 \leq (1+2\Delta(\beta))\|h(\beta)\|^2/v_{min}^2$.

Proof: We see from the first equation of (4.27) that

$$\begin{aligned} 4dx^T dy &= 4(V^{-1}Y dx)^T(V^{-1}X dy) \\ &= \|V^{-1}Y dx + V^{-1}X dy\|^2 - \|V^{-1}Y dx - V^{-1}X dy\|^2 \\ &\leq \|h(\beta)\|^2. \end{aligned}$$

We also see that

$$\begin{aligned} \|X^{-1}dx\|^2 + \|Y^{-1}dy\|^2 &= \|V^{-1}(V^{-1}Y dx)\|^2 + \|V^{-1}(V^{-1}X dy)\|^2 \\ &\leq (\|V^{-1}Y dx\|^2 + \|V^{-1}X dy\|^2)/v_{min}^2 \\ &= (\|V^{-1}Y dx + V^{-1}X dy\|^2 - 2dx^T dy)/v_{min}^2 \\ &= (\|h(\beta)\|^2 - 2dx^T dy)/v_{min}^2 \quad \text{(by (4.27))} \\ &\leq (1+2\Delta(\beta))\|h(\beta)\|^2/v_{min}^2 \quad \text{(by (4.32)).} \end{aligned}$$

∎

Proof of Theorem 4.18.

By the definition (4.34) of θ and (ii) of Lemma 4.20, we see that

$$\begin{aligned} \theta^2(\|X^{-1}dx\|^2 + \|Y^{-1}dy\|^2) &\leq \left\{\frac{v_{min}^2\tau^2}{(1+2\Delta(\beta))\|h(\beta)\|^2}\right\}\left\{\frac{(1+2\Delta(\beta))\|h(\beta)\|^2}{v_{min}^2}\right\} \\ &= \tau^2. \end{aligned} \tag{4.38}$$

The inequality above guarantees $\theta \leq \Theta(\tau)$ and permits us to apply Theorem 4.17. Therefore the relation (4.35) and the left inequalities in (4.36) immediately follow from Theorem 4.17.

What we have left is to prove the right-hand side inequalities in (4.36). From (4.34) and Lemma 4.16, we obtain

$$\begin{aligned} \theta &= \left(\frac{v_{min}\tau}{\sqrt{1+2\Delta(\beta)}}\right)\left(\frac{\pi}{v_{min}\sqrt{(1-\beta)^2 n\pi + \beta^2\omega^2}}\right) \\ &= \frac{\tau\pi}{\sqrt{(1+2\Delta(\beta))\{(1-\beta)^2 n\pi + \beta^2\omega^2\}}}. \end{aligned}$$

Using this expression of θ, we can easily see that the linear terms in θ of $G_{cp}(\theta)$, $G^{\tau}_{cen}(\theta)$ and $G^{\tau}(\theta)$ become $g_{cp}(\beta)\tau$, $g_{cen}(\beta)\tau$ and $g(\nu,\beta)\tau$, respectively (see (4.28) and (4.33)). We also obtain the following inequalities with regard to the quadratic terms:

$$\begin{aligned}
\frac{dx^T dy}{x^T y}\theta^2 &\leq \frac{\|h(\beta)\|^2}{4x^T y}\theta^2 \text{ (by (i) of Lemma 4.20)} \\
&= \left(\frac{\|h(\beta)\|^2}{4\|v\|^2}\right)\left\{\frac{v_{min}^2\tau^2}{(1+2\Delta(\beta))\|h(\beta)\|^2}\right\} \quad \text{(by (4.34))} \\
&= \frac{v_{min}^2\tau^2}{4(1+2\Delta(\beta))\|v\|^2} \\
&\leq \frac{\tau^2}{4n} \quad \text{(since } nv_{min}^2 \leq \|v\|^2 \text{ and } \Delta(\beta) \geq 0 \text{),} \\
\frac{\|X^{-1}dx\|^2 + \|Y^{-1}dy\|^2}{2(1-\tau)}\theta^2 &\leq \frac{\tau^2}{2(1-\tau)} \quad \text{(by (4.38)).}
\end{aligned}$$

Thus we have completed the proof of Theorem 4.18.

5. Initial Points and Stopping Criteria

The UIP method for the LCP (1.1) presented in Section 2.2 starts from an $(\boldsymbol{x}^1, \boldsymbol{y}^1)$ which lies in the interior S_{++} of the feasible region of the LCP, and generates a sequence $\{(\boldsymbol{x}^k, \boldsymbol{y}^k)\} \subset S_{++}$ which generally never attains an exact solution of the LCP. Here we have two important problems: how to prepare an initial point $(\boldsymbol{x}^1, \boldsymbol{y}^1) \in S_{++}$ and how to compute an exact solution of the LCP in a finite number of operations. The former is dealt with in Section 5.1, and the latter in Section 5.2. These two problems, as well as some inequalities given in Section 5.3, are essential for evaluating the theoretical computational complexity of the UIP method.

5.1. Initial Points

In general, we may not have an available initial point $(\boldsymbol{x}^1, \boldsymbol{y}^1) \in S_{++}$ for the UIP method to solve the LCP (1.1). In order to overcome the difficulty, we reduce the LCP to an artificial linear complementarity problem with an apparent interior feasible point from which we can start the UIP method. We denote the artificial problem by LCP′: Find an $(\boldsymbol{x}', \boldsymbol{y}') \in R^{2n'}$ such that

$$\boldsymbol{y}' = M'\boldsymbol{x}' + \boldsymbol{q}', \ (\boldsymbol{x}', \boldsymbol{y}') \geq \boldsymbol{0} \ \text{and} \ x_i' y_i' = 0 \ (i \in N'), \tag{5.1}$$

where M' is an $n' \times n'$ matrix, $\boldsymbol{q}' \in R^{n'}$ and $N' = \{1, 2, \ldots, n'\}$. We also use the symbols S'_+ and S'_{++} for the set of all the feasible solutions and all the interior feasible solutions to the LCP′, respectively:

$$\begin{aligned} S'_+ &= \{(\boldsymbol{x}', \boldsymbol{y}') \geq \boldsymbol{0} : \boldsymbol{y}' = M'\boldsymbol{x}' + \boldsymbol{q}'\}, \\ S'_{++} &= \{(\boldsymbol{x}', \boldsymbol{y}') > \boldsymbol{0} : \boldsymbol{y}' = M'\boldsymbol{x}' + \boldsymbol{q}'\}. \end{aligned}$$

The artificial problem LCP′ must have a readily available initial point $(\boldsymbol{x}'^1, \boldsymbol{y}'^1) \in S'_{++}$ for the UIP method. We need, in addition, to know about the solution of the original LCP (1.1) from a solution of the artificial LCP′ (5.1) which would be obtained by applying the UIP method to the LCP′. More precisely, it is necessary that a solution to the LCP′ (5.1) informs us either of a solution to the LCP (1.1) or of the fact that the LCP (1.1) has no solution.

We now give a method of constructing the artificial problem LCP′ (5.1). This method is due to Pang [56]. Let

$$n' = 2n, \ \boldsymbol{x}' = \begin{pmatrix} \boldsymbol{x} \\ \tilde{\boldsymbol{x}} \end{pmatrix}, \ \boldsymbol{y}' = \begin{pmatrix} \boldsymbol{y} \\ \tilde{\boldsymbol{y}} \end{pmatrix}, \ M' = \begin{pmatrix} M & I \\ -I & O \end{pmatrix}, \ \boldsymbol{q}' = \begin{pmatrix} \boldsymbol{q} \\ \tilde{\boldsymbol{q}} \end{pmatrix}. \tag{5.2}$$

Here $\tilde{x}$, $\tilde{y} \in R^n$ are artificial variable vectors and $\tilde{q} \in R^n$ is a positive constant vector. In order to ensure the reducibility of the LCP to the LCP′, we choose a vector $\tilde{q}$ such that $\tilde{q} > x$ for every basic feasible solution (x, y) of the system

$$y = Mx + q, \quad (x, y) \geq 0. \tag{5.3}$$

Since each basic component of a basic feasible solution to the system above is represented as a ratio Δ_1/Δ_2, where Δ_1 denotes a minor of order n of the $n \times (2n+1)$ matrix $(-M \;\; I \;\; q)$ and Δ_2 a nonzero minor of order n of the $n \times 2n$ matrix $(-M \;\; I)$, it suffices to choose a $\tilde{q}$ such that

$$\tilde{q} > \rho_{max} e, \tag{5.4}$$

where ρ_{max} denotes the maximum value of the ratios Δ_1/Δ_2 for all minors Δ_1 of order n of the matrix $(-M \;\; I \;\; q)$ and all nonzero minors Δ_2 of order n of the matrix $(-M \;\; I)$, and hence $\rho_{max}(\geq 1)$ gives an upper bound of all the basic components of basic feasible solutions of the system (5.3). See Lemma 5.4 for a reason of the choice (5.4) of $\tilde{q}$.

We assume that all the entries of M and q are integral. Define $\bar{L}$ and L by

$$\bar{L} = \sum_{i=1}^{n}\sum_{j=1}^{n} \log_2(|m_{ij}|+1) + \sum_{i=1}^{n} \log_2(|q_i|+1) + 2\log_2 n, \tag{5.5}$$

$$L = \sum_{i=1}^{n}\sum_{j=1}^{n} \lceil \log_2(|m_{ij}|+1) \rceil + \sum_{i=1}^{n} \lceil \log_2(|q_i|+1) \rceil + 2\lceil \log_2(n+1) \rceil + n(n+1). \tag{5.6}$$

Here $\lceil z \rceil$ denotes the smallest integer not less than $z \in R$. We have defined L as a size of the LCP (1.1) in Section 2.3. Obviously $L \geq \bar{L}$. By the definition (5.5) of $\bar{L}$, we have

$$\frac{2^{\bar{L}}}{n^2} = \left\{ \prod_{i=1}^{n}\prod_{j=1}^{n}(|m_{ij}|+1) \right\} \left\{ \prod_{i=1}^{n}(|q_i|+1) \right\}. \tag{5.7}$$

Every minor of the matrix $(-M \;\; I \;\; q)$ is integral and its absolute value is less than $2^L/n^2$ because of the equality (5.7); hence $\rho_{max} < 2^L/n^2$. Let

$$\tilde{q} = \frac{2^{L+1}}{n^2} e. \tag{5.8}$$

Then all the entries of M' and q' are integral (see (5.7)) and $\tilde{q}$ satisfies the inequality (5.4).

If we choose an $x^1 \in R^n$ and an $\tilde{x}^1 \in R^n$ such that

$$0 < x^1 < \tilde{q}, \quad \tilde{x}^1 > 0 \quad \text{and} \quad \tilde{x}^1 > -Mx^1 - q, \tag{5.9}$$

the point $(x'^1, y'^1) = (x^1, \tilde{x}^1, y^1, \tilde{y}^1)$ with

$$y^1 = Mx^1 + \tilde{x}^1 + q, \quad \tilde{y}^1 = -x^1 + \tilde{q} \tag{5.10}$$

lies in the interior S'_{++} of the feasible region of the LCP′ and serves as an initial point of the UIP method applied to the LCP′. In order to obtain a better computational complexity, however, it is necessary to find an initial point with a smaller value of the potential function f' defined similarly to (2.3), i.e.,

$$\left.\begin{aligned} &f'(x', y') = \nu' f'_{cp}(x', y') + f'_{cen}(x', y'), \\ &f'_{cp}(x', y') = \log x'^T y', \\ &f'_{cen}(x', y') = n' \log x'^T y' - \sum_{i=1}^{n'} \log x'_i y'_i - n' \log n' = \sum_{i=1}^{n'} \log \frac{x'^T y'/n'}{x'_i y'_i}. \end{aligned}\right\} \quad (5.11)$$

The lemma below gives us a way of finding such a point $(x'^1, y'^1) \in S'_{++}$.

Lemma 5.1. *Let $n \geq 2$. Suppose all the entries of M and q are integral. Construct the artificial problem LCP′ (5.1) by using (5.2) and (5.8). Let $\alpha \in (0, 5]$. Then the point $(x'^1, y'^1) = (x^1, \tilde{x}^1, y^1, \tilde{y}^1)$ defined by*

$$x^1 = \frac{2^L}{n^2} e, \quad \tilde{x}^1 = \left(\frac{5}{\alpha}\right) \frac{2^{2L}}{n^3} e,$$
$$y^1 = Mx^1 + \tilde{x}^1 + q = \frac{2^L}{n^2} Me + \left(\frac{5}{\alpha}\right) \frac{2^{2L}}{n^3} e + q, \quad \tilde{y}^1 = -x^1 + \frac{2^{L+1}}{n^2} e = \frac{2^L}{n^2} e$$

satisfies

$$(x'^1, y'^1) \in S'_{++}, \quad (5.12)$$
$$f'_{cp}(x'^1, y'^1) \leq \left(3 + \frac{5}{\alpha}\right) L, \quad (5.13)$$
$$f'_{cen}(x'^1, y'^1) \leq \alpha. \quad (5.14)$$

Proof: To see (5.12), we only have to show $y^1 > 0$. It follows from (5.7) that

$$-\frac{2^L}{n^2} e \leq Me + \frac{n^2}{2^L} q \leq \frac{2^L}{n^2} e.$$

Hence we have

$$\left(\frac{5}{\alpha} - \frac{1}{n}\right) \frac{2^{2L}}{n^3} e \leq y^1 \leq \left(\frac{5}{\alpha} + \frac{1}{n}\right) \frac{2^{2L}}{n^3} e. \quad (5.15)$$

Thus $y^1 > 0$ because $n \geq 2$ and $\alpha \in (0, 5]$, and hence we have shown (5.12). Next we will evaluate $f'_{cp}(x'^1, y'^1)$ and $f'_{cen}(x'^1, y'^1)$. From the definition of (x'^1, y'^1) and (5.15), we have

$$\left(\frac{5}{\alpha} - \frac{1}{n}\right) \frac{2^{3L}}{n^5} \leq x_i^1 y_i^1 \leq \left(\frac{5}{\alpha} + \frac{1}{n}\right) \frac{2^{3L}}{n^5} \quad (i \in N),$$
$$\tilde{x}_i^1 \tilde{y}_i^1 = \left(\frac{5}{\alpha}\right) \frac{2^{3L}}{n^5} \quad (i \in N),$$
$$x'^{1T} y'^1 \leq \left(\frac{10}{\alpha} + \frac{1}{n}\right) \frac{2^{3L}}{n^4},$$
$$\frac{x'^{1T} y'^1}{n'} \leq \left(\frac{5}{\alpha} + \frac{1}{2n}\right) \frac{2^{3L}}{n^5}.$$

Hence it follows that

$$\begin{aligned}
f'_{cp}(x'^1, y'^1) &= \log x'^{1T} y'^1 \\
&\leq 3\bar{L}\log 2 + \log\left(1 + \frac{10}{\alpha}\right) \\
&\leq 3\bar{L} + \frac{10}{\alpha} \quad \text{(by (i) of Lemma 4.10)} \\
&\leq \left(3 + \frac{5}{\alpha}\right) L \quad (\text{since } L \geq \bar{L} \geq 2\log_2 n \geq 2), \\
f'_{cen}(x'^1, y'^1) &= \sum_{i=1}^{n'} \log \frac{x'^{1T} y'^1 / n'}{x_i'^1 y_i'^1} \\
&= \sum_{i=1}^{n} \left(\log \frac{x'^{1T} y'^1/n'}{x_i^1 y_i^1} + \log \frac{x'^{1T} y'^1/n'}{\tilde{x}_i^1 \tilde{y}_i^1} \right) \\
&\leq \sum_{i=1}^{n} \left(\log \frac{5/\alpha + 1/(2n)}{5/\alpha - 1/n} + \log \frac{5/\alpha + 1/(2n)}{5/\alpha} \right) \\
&= n \log \frac{\{1 + \alpha/(10n)\}^2}{1 - \alpha/(5n)} \\
&\leq n \log\left(1 + \frac{\alpha}{n}\right) \quad (\text{since } n \geq 2 \text{ and } \alpha \in (0, 5]) \\
&\leq \alpha \quad \text{(by (i) of Lemma 4.10).}
\end{aligned}$$

Thus we have shown (5.13) and (5.14). ∎

The artificial problem LCP′ (5.1) determined by (5.2) enjoys further nice properties:

Lemma 5.2. *Construct the artificial problem LCP′ (5.1) by using (5.2). Then the set* $S'^t_+ = \{(x', y') \in S'_+ : x'^T y' \leq t\}$ *is bounded for every* $t \geq 0$.

Proof: Let $(x', y') = (x, \tilde{x}, y, \tilde{y}) \in S'^t_+$, i.e.,

$$(x, \tilde{x}, y, \tilde{y}) \geq 0, \tag{5.16}$$
$$y = Mx + \tilde{x} + q, \tag{5.17}$$
$$\tilde{y} = -x + \tilde{q}, \tag{5.18}$$
$$x'^T y' = x^T M x + q^T x + \tilde{q}^T \tilde{x} \leq t. \tag{5.19}$$

First we observe $0 \leq x \leq \tilde{q}$, $0 \leq \tilde{y} \leq \tilde{q}$ from (5.16) and (5.18). Hence, by (5.19), $\tilde{q}^T \tilde{x}$ is bounded from above, which implies the boundedness of $\tilde{x}$ because $\tilde{q} > 0$ and $\tilde{x} \geq 0$. Finally, by (5.17), we see that y is also bounded. Thus the set S'^t_+ is bounded. ∎

Lemma 5.3. *Let C be one of the classes P_0, CS, P_*, $P_*(\kappa)$, PSD and SS. Then the matrix* $M' = \begin{pmatrix} M & I \\ -I & O \end{pmatrix}$ *belongs to the class C if and only if M belongs to C.*

Proof: Since the "only if" part follows directly from the final remark of Section 3.2 that every principal submatrix inherits those properties of its mother matrix, we will just show the "if" part. The case that $C = PSD$ or SS is obvious. We first consider the case $C = P_0$. Every principal submatrix $\bar{M}'$ of M' is of the form

$$\bar{M}' = \begin{pmatrix} \bar{M} & \bar{I} \\ -\bar{I}^T & O \end{pmatrix}.$$

Here $\bar{M}$ is a principal submatrix of M and $\bar{I}$ is a submatrix of the identity matrix I. Hence all entries of each column in $\bar{I}$ are 0 but at most one 1. One can see that the determinant of $\bar{M}'$, unless it vanishes, coincides with a principal minor of $\bar{M}$; hence of M. Therefore M' is a P_0-matrix if M is. Next, we consider the case $C = CS$. Suppose that M is an $n \times n$ column sufficient matrix. Let $N = \{1, 2, \ldots, n\}$ and $N' = \{1, 2, \ldots, 2n\}$. Assume that

$$\xi'_i[M'\xi']_i \le 0 \quad (i \in N')$$

for some $\xi' = (\xi, \tilde{\xi}) \in R^{2n}$, i.e.,

$$\xi_i([M\xi]_i + \tilde{\xi}_i) \le 0, \quad \tilde{\xi}_i(-\xi_i) \le 0 \quad (i \in N). \tag{5.20}$$

It follows that $\xi_i[M\xi]_i \le 0 \ \ (i \in N)$; and hence $\xi_i[M\xi]_i = 0 \ \ (i \in N)$ because M is column sufficient. From (5.20) we see $\xi_i\tilde{\xi}_i = 0 \ \ (i \in N)$. Thus we have

$$\xi'_i[M'\xi']_i = 0 \quad (i \in N'),$$

which implies that M' is column sufficient. The case $C = P_*$ being an immediate consequence of the case $C = P_*(\kappa)$, we finally deal with the case $C = P_*(\kappa)$. Suppose that an $n \times n$ matrix M belongs to $P_*(\kappa)$ for some $\kappa \ge 0$. Let $\xi \in R^n$, $\tilde{\xi} \in R^n$, $\xi' = (\xi, \tilde{\xi}) \in R^{2n}$, $N = \{1, 2, \ldots, n\}$ and $N' = \{1, 2, \ldots, 2n\}$. Define

$$\begin{aligned} I_+ &= \{i \in N : \xi_i[M\xi]_i > 0\}, \\ I'_+ &= \{i \in N' : \zeta'_i[M'\zeta']_i > 0\}, \\ \bar{I}_+ &= \{i \in N : \xi'_i[M'\xi']_i > 0\} \ = \ \{i \in N : \xi_i([M\xi]_i + \tilde{\xi}_i) > 0\}, \\ \tilde{I}_+ &= \{i \in N : \xi'_{n+i}[M'\xi']_{n+i} > 0\} \ = \ \{i \in N : -\xi_i\tilde{\xi}_i > 0\}. \end{aligned}$$

Then

$$\begin{aligned} & \xi'^T M'\xi' + 4\kappa \sum_{i \in I'_+} \xi'_i[M'\xi']_i \\ = \ & \xi^T(M\xi + \tilde{\xi}) + \tilde{\xi}^T(-\xi) + 4\kappa \left(\sum_{i \in \bar{I}_+} \xi_i([M\xi]_i + \tilde{\xi}_i) + \sum_{i \in \tilde{I}_+} (-\xi_i\tilde{\xi}_i) \right) \\ \ge \ & \xi^T M\xi + 4\kappa \left(\sum_{i \in I_+} \xi_i([M\xi]_i + \tilde{\xi}_i) + \sum_{i \in I_+} (-\xi_i\tilde{\xi}_i) \right) \\ = \ & \xi^T M\xi + 4\kappa \sum_{i \in I_+} \xi_i[M\xi]_i \\ \ge \ & 0 \quad (\text{since } M \subset P_*(\kappa)\ ). \end{aligned}$$

Here the first inequality above follows from the definitions of the index sets $\bar{I}_+$ and $\tilde{I}_+$. Thus we have shown $M' \subset P_*(\kappa)$. This completes the proof. ∎

As we have already pointed out, we wish to know about the solution of the LCP (1.1) from a solution of the LCP′ (5.1). We have the following lemma, which was in essence obtained by Pang [56].

Lemma 5.4. *Construct the artificial problem LCP′ (5.1) by using (5.2) and (5.4). Let* $(\boldsymbol{x}', \boldsymbol{y}') = (\boldsymbol{x}, \tilde{\boldsymbol{x}}, \boldsymbol{y}, \tilde{\boldsymbol{y}})$ *be a solution of the LCP′ (5.1). Then*

(i) *If* $\tilde{\boldsymbol{x}} = \mathbf{0}$, $(\boldsymbol{x}, \boldsymbol{y})$ *is a solution of the LCP (1.1).*
(ii) *If* M *is column sufficient and* $\tilde{\boldsymbol{x}} \neq \mathbf{0}$, *the LCP (1.1) has no solution.*

Proof: The assertion (i) is clear. In a way similar to the proof of Proposition 2 in Pang [56], we can show that the assertion (ii) is true if $\tilde{\boldsymbol{q}} > \boldsymbol{x}$ for every basic feasible solution $(\boldsymbol{x}, \boldsymbol{y})$ of the system (5.3). As we have already seen, the choice (5.4) satisfies this requirement. ∎

It is interesting to consider how the assumption, the column sufficiency of M, can be weaken in the assertion (ii) of the lemma above. We now give a negative answer; let

$$M = \begin{pmatrix} 0 & 1 \\ 0 & 0 \end{pmatrix}, \quad \boldsymbol{q} = \begin{pmatrix} -1 \\ 0 \end{pmatrix}.$$

Then M is a P_0-matrix, though not column sufficient, and the LCP (1.1) has a solution, for example, $(\boldsymbol{x}, \boldsymbol{y}) = (0, 1, 0, 0)$. However, the artificial problem LCP′ (5.1) determined by (5.2) and (5.4) has a solution $(\boldsymbol{x}', \boldsymbol{y}') = (\boldsymbol{x}, \tilde{\boldsymbol{x}}, \boldsymbol{y}, \tilde{\boldsymbol{y}})$ with $\tilde{\boldsymbol{x}} \neq \mathbf{0}$. Indeed,

$$M' = \begin{pmatrix} 0 & 1 & 1 & 0 \\ 0 & 0 & 0 & 1 \\ -1 & 0 & 0 & 0 \\ 0 & -1 & 0 & 0 \end{pmatrix}, \quad \boldsymbol{q}' = \begin{pmatrix} -1 \\ 0 \\ \tilde{q}_1 \\ \tilde{q}_2 \end{pmatrix}, \quad \begin{pmatrix} \tilde{q}_1 \\ \tilde{q}_2 \end{pmatrix} > \begin{pmatrix} 1 \\ 1 \end{pmatrix},$$

and $(\boldsymbol{x}, \tilde{\boldsymbol{x}}, \boldsymbol{y}, \tilde{\boldsymbol{y}}) = (\tilde{q}_1, 0, 1, 0, 0, 0, 0, \tilde{q}_2)$ is a solution to the LCP′.

Now we present two conditions associated with the LCP (1.1), neither of which involves an interior feasible point of the LCP:

Condition 5.5. M is a column sufficient matrix.

Condition 5.6.

(i) All the entries of M and $\boldsymbol{q}$ are integral.
(ii) The matrix M belongs to the class P_*, i.e., to the class $P_*(\kappa)$ for some nonnegative number κ.

It should be noted that Condition 5.6 coincides with (i) and (ii) of Condition 2.3. In view of Lemmas 5.1, 5.2 and 5.3, we have:

Lemma 5.7.

(i) *If the LCP (1.1) satisfies Condition 5.5 then the artificial problem LCP′ (5.1) determined by (5.2) and (5.4) satisfies Condition 2.1.*
(ii) *Let $n \geq 2$. If the LCP (1.1) satisfies Condition 5.6 then the artificial problem LCP′ (5.1) determined by (5.2) and (5.8) satisfies Condition 2.3.*

In both cases, it is assumed that the quantities $\boldsymbol{M}$, $\boldsymbol{q}$, S_{++}, f_{cp}, f_{cen}, etc. for the LCP (1.1) in Conditions 2.1 and 2.3 are replaced adequately by the correspondents $\boldsymbol{M}'$, $\boldsymbol{q}'$, S'_{++}, f'_{cp}, f'_{cen}, etc. for the LCP′ (5.1).

We presented in Section 2.4 a class of potential reduction algorithms, which will be described again in detail in Section 6.1, as special cases of the UIP method. It will be shown in Section 6.2 ((i) of Corollary 6.4) that a potential reduction algorithm in the class solves the LCP (1.1) under Condition 2.1. Hence the lemma above ensures that the algorithm can also solve the LCP′ (5.1) constructed by using (5.2) and (5.4) from the LCP (1.1) satisfying Condition 5.5. From the solution of the LCP′ (5.1) obtained as a result of applying the algorithm to the LCP′, we either have a solution to the LCP (1.1) or know that the LCP (1.1) has no solution because of Lemma 5.4. See (ii) of Corollary 6.4. To be brief, we can solve the LCP by solving the LCP′. Under Condition 2.3 we will further have two convergence results of the algorithm (Corollaries 6.7 and 6.9), both of which will also be extended to the ones under Condition 5.6 (Corollary 6.10) on account of Lemmas 5.4 and 5.7.

In the case that $\boldsymbol{M}$ is a positive semi-definite matrix, we might as well construct the artificial problem LCP′ (5.1) in a simpler way: Assume that all the entries of $\boldsymbol{M}$ and $\boldsymbol{q}$ are integral, and let

$$n' = n+1,\ \boldsymbol{x}' = \begin{pmatrix} \boldsymbol{x} \\ \tilde{x} \end{pmatrix},\ \boldsymbol{y}' = \begin{pmatrix} \boldsymbol{y} \\ \tilde{y} \end{pmatrix},\ \boldsymbol{M}' = \begin{pmatrix} \boldsymbol{M} & \boldsymbol{e} \\ -\boldsymbol{e}^T & 0 \end{pmatrix},\ \boldsymbol{q}' = \begin{pmatrix} \boldsymbol{q} \\ \tilde{q} \end{pmatrix} \tag{5.21}$$

and

$$\tilde{q} = \frac{(n+1)2^L}{n^2}, \tag{5.22}$$

where $\tilde{x} \in R$ and $\tilde{y} \in R$ are artificial variables. Obviously the matrix $\boldsymbol{M}'$ remains positive semi-definite. This type of artificial problem was proposed originally in the paper Kojima, Mizuno and Yoshise [35], where some theorems similar to Lemmas 5.1 and 5.4 of this paper were established so that the LCP(1.1) could be reduced to the artificial problem LCP′ of this type. See Section 6 of the paper [35] for details.

It should be noted that the matrix $\boldsymbol{M}' = \begin{pmatrix} \boldsymbol{M} & \boldsymbol{e} \\ -\boldsymbol{e}^T & 0 \end{pmatrix}$ may not be a P_*-matrix even if $\boldsymbol{M}$ is. Indeed the matrix $\boldsymbol{M}'$ corresponding to the P_*-matrix $\boldsymbol{M} = \begin{pmatrix} 0 & 3 \\ -1 & 1 \end{pmatrix}$ is not even a P_0-matrix. Therefore, it does not seem proper to construct the artificial problem LCP′ (5.1) by using (5.21) and (5.22) when M is a P_*-matrix but not a positive semi-definite matrix.

The previous ways, (5.2) with (5.8) and (5.21) with (5.22), of constructing the artificial problem LCP′ (5.1) involve such a large number as 2^L, which could not be practical for implementing the UIP method on computers. Their significance is only for evaluating the theoretical computational complexity. Now we present a way of constructing the artificial problem LCP′ (5.1) without such a large number. We assume that the matrix M is a P_*-matrix and that the interior S_{++} of the feasible region of the LCP (1.1) is not empty though we do not know an interior feasible point from which the UIP method can start. In this case there is always a solution of the LCP (Theorem 4.6). Define

$$n' = n+1,\ \boldsymbol{x}' = \begin{pmatrix} \boldsymbol{x} \\ \tilde{x} \end{pmatrix},\ \boldsymbol{y}' = \begin{pmatrix} \boldsymbol{y} \\ \tilde{y} \end{pmatrix},\ M' = \begin{pmatrix} M & \boldsymbol{d} \\ \boldsymbol{0}^T & c \end{pmatrix},\ \boldsymbol{q}' = \begin{pmatrix} \boldsymbol{q} \\ \tilde{q} \end{pmatrix}, \tag{5.23}$$

where $\tilde{x}$ and $\tilde{y}$ are 1-dimensional artificial variables, $\boldsymbol{d} \in R^n$ is a positive constant vector, $c \geq 0$ and $\tilde{q} > 0$ are scalar constants.

Lemma 5.8. *Suppose that the matrix M is a P_*-matrix and that the interior S_{++} of the feasible region of the LCP is nonempty. Construct the artificial problem LCP′ (5.1) by using (5.23). Then the LCP′ satisfies Condition 2.1 where the symbols for the LCP are replaced by the correspondents for the LCP′.*

Proof: By construction, M' is a P_0-matrix because M is. Taking $\tilde{x}$ sufficiently large, we can find an interior feasible point of the LCP′. Therefore, we only have to show that the LCP′ satisfies (iii) of Condition 2.1. Let $t \geq 0$ and consider

$$\begin{aligned} S_+^{\prime t} &= \{(\boldsymbol{x}', \boldsymbol{y}') \geq 0 : \boldsymbol{y}' = M'\boldsymbol{x}' + \boldsymbol{q}' \text{ and } \boldsymbol{x}'^T\boldsymbol{y}' \leq t\} \\ &= \{(\boldsymbol{x}, \tilde{x}, \boldsymbol{y}, \tilde{y}) \geq \boldsymbol{0} : \boldsymbol{y} = M\boldsymbol{x} + \boldsymbol{d}\tilde{x} + \boldsymbol{q},\ \tilde{y} = c\tilde{x} + \tilde{q} \text{ and } \boldsymbol{x}^T\boldsymbol{y} + \tilde{x}\tilde{y} \leq t\}. \end{aligned}$$

Choose an arbitrary $(\boldsymbol{x}, \tilde{x}, \boldsymbol{y}, \tilde{y}) \in S_+^{\prime t}$. Then we have

$$t \geq \boldsymbol{x}^T\boldsymbol{y} + \tilde{x}\tilde{y} \geq \tilde{x}\tilde{y} = \tilde{x}(c\tilde{x} + \tilde{q}) \geq \tilde{q}\tilde{x};$$

hence

$$0 \leq \tilde{x} \leq \frac{t}{\tilde{q}}. \tag{5.24}$$

It follows that

$$\tilde{q} \leq \tilde{y} \leq \tilde{q} + \frac{ct}{\tilde{q}}.$$

What we have left to show is that $(\boldsymbol{x}, \boldsymbol{y})$ lies in a bounded subset of R^{2n}. Let $(\hat{\boldsymbol{x}}, \hat{\boldsymbol{y}}) \in S_{++}$. Define

$$\bar{\boldsymbol{y}} = \hat{\boldsymbol{y}} + \boldsymbol{d}\tilde{x} = M\hat{\boldsymbol{x}} + \boldsymbol{d}\tilde{x} + \boldsymbol{q}.$$

Note that $\bar{y} \geq \hat{y} > 0$ because $d > 0$ and $\tilde{x} \geq 0$. Since M is a P_*-matrix and $y - \bar{y} = (Mx + d\tilde{x} + q) - (M\hat{x} + d\tilde{x} + q) = M(x - \hat{x})$, there is a $\kappa \geq 0$ such that

$$\begin{aligned}(x-\hat{x})^T(y-\bar{y}) &\geq -4\kappa \sum_{i\in I_+}(x_i-\hat{x}_i)(y_i-\bar{y}_i)\\ &\geq -4\kappa \sum_{i\in I_+}(x_iy_i+\hat{x}_i\bar{y}_i) \quad (\text{since } (x,y)\geq 0,\ \hat{x}>0 \text{ and } \bar{y}>0)\\ &\geq -4\kappa(x^Ty+\hat{x}^T\bar{y}) \quad (\text{since } (x,y)\geq 0,\ \hat{x}>0 \text{ and } \bar{y}>0),\end{aligned}$$

where $I_+ = \{i \in N : (x_i - \hat{x}_i)(y_i - \bar{y}_i) > 0\}$. Therefore, we see

$$\begin{aligned}\hat{y}^Tx + \hat{x}^Ty &= (\bar{y} - d\tilde{x})^Tx + \hat{x}^Ty\\ &\leq \bar{y}^Tx + \hat{x}^Ty \quad (\text{since } d>0,\ \tilde{x}\geq 0 \text{ and } x \geq 0)\\ &= x^Ty + \hat{x}^T\bar{y} - (x-\hat{x})^T(y-\bar{y})\\ &\leq (1+4\kappa)(x^Ty+\hat{x}^T\bar{y})\\ &= (1+4\kappa)\{x^Ty + \hat{x}^T(\hat{y}+d\tilde{x})\}\\ &\leq (1+4\kappa)\left(t+\hat{x}^T\hat{y}+\frac{t}{\tilde{q}}d^T\hat{x}\right) \quad (\text{since } x^Ty \leq x'^Ty' \leq t \text{ and (5.24) }).\end{aligned}$$

Thus the point (x, y) lies in the bounded set

$$\left\{(x,y)\geq 0 : \hat{y}^Tx+\hat{x}^Ty \leq (1+4\kappa)\left(t+\hat{x}^T\hat{y}+\frac{t}{\tilde{q}}d^T\hat{x}\right)\right\}.$$

This completes the proof. ∎

Under the assumptions of the lemma above, the potential reduction algorithm which will be described as a special case of the UIP method in Section 6.1 computes a solution $(x^*, \tilde{x}^*, y^*, \tilde{y}^*)$ of the LCP′ (5.1) (Corollary 6.4). Then $\tilde{x}^* = 0$ because $\tilde{y}^* = c\tilde{x}^* + \tilde{q} > 0$. Hence (x^*, y^*) is a solution of the LCP (1.1). It should be noted that Corollary 6.7, which ensures the global linear convergence of the potential reduction algorithm in the case of a P_*-matrix, and if the step size parameter θ and the direction parameter β are properly chosen, does not apply to the artificial problem LCP′ (5.1) since the matrix $M' = \begin{pmatrix} M & d \\ 0^T & c \end{pmatrix}$ is not necessarily a P_*-matrix; for example, take $M = (0)$, $d = (1)$ and $c = 0$.

In addition to the assumptions of Lemma 5.8, suppose that $c = 0$ and $\tilde{q} = 1$. Then the path of centers S'_{cen} of the artificial problem LCP′ is characterized by the system of equations

$$y = Mx + q + d\tilde{x},\ \tilde{y} = 1,\ x_iy_i = t\ \ (i \in N),\ \tilde{x} = t,\ (x, \tilde{x}, y, \tilde{y}) > 0,\ t > 0. \qquad (5.25)$$

The artificial variables $\tilde{x}$ and $\tilde{y}$ are always equal to the parameter t and the constant 1 in the system above. Thus, deleting those artificial variables from (5.25), we have the system

$$y = Mx + q + dt,\ x_iy_i = t\ \ (i \in N),\ (x, y) > 0,\ t > 0, \qquad (5.26)$$

which is equivalent to (5.25). In view of Theorem 4.4, the solution set $S' = \{(\boldsymbol{x}(t), \boldsymbol{y}(t)) : t > 0\}$ of the system (5.26) is a smooth curve converging to a solution of the LCP as $t \to 0$. This fact was shown in the paper Kojima, Mizuno and Noma [32] for the case that M is a P-matrix, and in the paper Kojima, Mizuno and Noma [33] for the case that M is positive semi-definite. A numerical method for tracing S' was proposed in the paper Kojima, Megiddo and Noma [29].

Generally, the curve S' does not lie within the feasible region S_+ of the LCP. Therefore, the application of the UIP method to the artificial problem LCP′ can be interpreted as an "exterior" point method for the LCP (1.1). It is noteworthy that, for any given $\boldsymbol{x}^1 > \boldsymbol{0}$, if we take $\boldsymbol{d}$ and $t > 0$ satisfying

$$\begin{aligned} d_i &= \frac{1}{x_i^1} - \frac{[M\boldsymbol{x}^1]_i + q_i}{t} > 0 \ (i \in N), \\ \boldsymbol{d} &= (d_1, d_2, \ldots, d_n)^T, \end{aligned}$$

then the point $(\boldsymbol{x}^1, \boldsymbol{y}^1)$ with $\boldsymbol{y}^1 = M\boldsymbol{x}^1 + \boldsymbol{q} + \boldsymbol{d}t$ lies on the curve S'. Therefore we can start the exterior point method from any $\boldsymbol{x}^1 > \boldsymbol{0}$ in the $\boldsymbol{x}$-space.

5.2. Stopping Criteria

In Step 2 of the UIP method, we adopted the stopping criterion of the type

$$\boldsymbol{x}^T\boldsymbol{y} \le \epsilon. \tag{5.27}$$

Here ϵ is a positive constant number. If a point $(\boldsymbol{x}, \boldsymbol{y}) \in S_+$ satisfies the inequality above for sufficiently small $\epsilon > 0$, it might be regarded as an approximate solution of the LCP (1.1). More precisely, we have the following results.

Suppose that a point $(\hat{\boldsymbol{x}}, \hat{\boldsymbol{y}}) \in S_+$ satisfies the stopping criterion (5.27), i.e.,

$$\hat{\boldsymbol{x}}^T\hat{\boldsymbol{y}} \le \epsilon. \tag{5.28}$$

Letting

$$I = \{i \in N : \hat{x}_i \le \sqrt{\epsilon}\,\} \quad \text{and} \quad J = \{j \in N : \hat{y}_j \le \sqrt{\epsilon}\,\}, \tag{5.29}$$

we have $I \cup J = N$. Hence, if

$$(\boldsymbol{x}^*, \boldsymbol{y}^*) \in S_+, \ \ x_i^* = 0 \ \text{ for every } i \in I \ \text{ and } \ y_j^* = 0 \ \text{ for every } j \in J, \tag{5.30}$$

the point $(\boldsymbol{x}^*, \boldsymbol{y}^*)$ is a solution of the LCP (1.1).

Lemma 5.9. *Suppose that $(\hat{\boldsymbol{x}}, \hat{\boldsymbol{y}}) \in S_+$ satisfies the inequality (5.28). Define the index sets I and J by (5.29). If*

$$\epsilon < \left(\frac{\rho_{min}}{n+1}\right)^2 \tag{5.31}$$

then there exists a solution $(\boldsymbol{x}^*, \boldsymbol{y}^*)$ of the LCP (1.1) such that the relation (5.30) holds. Here $\rho_{min}(\leq 1)$ is the positive minimum value of the ratios Δ_1/Δ_2 for all minors Δ_1 of order n of the matrix $(-M \quad I \quad q)$ and all nonzero minors Δ_2 of order n of the matrix $(-M \quad I)$. Furthermore, we can compute such a solution $(\boldsymbol{x}^*, \boldsymbol{y}^*)$ in $O(n^3)$ arithmetic operations from $(\hat{\boldsymbol{x}}, \hat{\boldsymbol{y}})$.

The proof of this lemma is quite similar to that of Lemma B in Appendix B of Kojima, Mizuno and Yoshise [35]. We will give an outline of the proof below. Each basic component of a basic feasible solution of the system (5.3), or a vertex of the feasible region S_+ of the LCP(1.1), is represented as a ratio Δ_1/Δ_2, where Δ_1 is a minor of order n of the matrix $(-M \quad I \quad q)$ and Δ_2 a nonzero minor of order n of the matrix $(-M \quad I)$. Therefore each nonzero component of a vertex of S_+ is not less than ρ_{min}. In view of Carathéodory's theorem, we have

$$(\hat{\boldsymbol{x}}, \hat{\boldsymbol{y}}) = \sum_{\ell=1}^{p} c_\ell(\boldsymbol{x}^\ell, \boldsymbol{y}^\ell) + (\boldsymbol{\xi}, \boldsymbol{\eta}),$$

where $p \leq n+1$, $\sum_{\ell=1}^{p} c_\ell = 1$, $c_\ell \geq 0$ $(\ell = 1, \dots, p)$, $(\boldsymbol{x}^\ell, \boldsymbol{y}^\ell)$ is a vertex of S_+ for $\ell = 1, \dots, p$ and $(\boldsymbol{\xi}, \boldsymbol{\eta})$ is an unbounded direction of S_+, i.e., $\boldsymbol{\eta} = M\boldsymbol{\xi}$ and $(\boldsymbol{\xi}, \boldsymbol{\eta}) \geq \mathbf{0}$. Among $(\boldsymbol{x}^\ell, \boldsymbol{y}^\ell)$ $(\ell = 1, \dots, p)$, we can find a vertex $(\boldsymbol{x}^*, \boldsymbol{y}^*)$ of S_+ such that $c_\ell \geq 1/(n+1)$. It follows that

$$(\hat{\boldsymbol{x}}, \hat{\boldsymbol{y}}) \geq \frac{1}{n+1}(\boldsymbol{x}^*, \boldsymbol{y}^*).$$

One can show that $(\boldsymbol{x}^*, \boldsymbol{y}^*)$ satisfies the relation (5.30) and hence it is a solution of the LCP (1.1). Indeed, otherwise it would follow that

$$\hat{x}_i \geq \frac{x_i^*}{n+1} \geq \frac{\rho_{min}}{n+1} > \sqrt{\epsilon} \quad \text{for some } i \in I$$

or

$$\hat{y}_j \geq \frac{y_j^*}{n+1} \geq \frac{\rho_{min}}{n+1} > \sqrt{\epsilon} \quad \text{for some } j \in J.$$

This is a contradiction to the definitions (5.29) of I and J. We can compute such a solution $(\boldsymbol{x}^*, \boldsymbol{y}^*)$ of the LCP in $O(n^3)$ arithmetic operations in the way presented in Appendix B of [35].

This result gives us a theoretical goal of the UIP method. That is, we can employ the inequality

$$\boldsymbol{x}^T\boldsymbol{y} \leq \epsilon \quad \text{for a given constant } \epsilon \text{ with } 0 < \epsilon < \left(\frac{\rho_{min}}{n+1}\right)^2 \tag{5.32}$$

as the stopping criterion of the method. If all the entries of the coefficient matrix M and the constant vector q of the LCP (1.1) are integral, we might take $\epsilon = 2^{-2L}$, where L is the size of the LCP defined by (5.6). That is, we could utilize the inequality

$$\boldsymbol{x}^T\boldsymbol{y} \leq 2^{-2L} \tag{5.33}$$

as the stopping criterion. This was shown in Kojima, Mizuno and Yoshise [35], and is an immediate consequence of Lemma 5.9 as shown below. Here we remark that the size L employed in this paper is greater than the size L given in the paper [35].

Corollary 5.10. *Let $n \geq 2$. Assume that all the entries of M and q are integral. Suppose that $(\hat{x}, \hat{y}) \in S_+$ satisfies $\hat{x}^T \hat{y} \leq 2^{-2L}$. Define the index sets I and J by (5.29) with $\epsilon = 2^{-2L}$. Then there exists a solution (x^*, y^*) of the LCP (1.1) such that the relation (5.30) holds. Furthermore, we can compute such a solution (x^*, y^*) in $O(n^3)$ arithmetic operations from $(\hat{x}, \hat{y})$.*

Proof: In view of the equality (5.7) and the definition of ρ_{min}, we see

$$\rho_{min} > \frac{n^2}{2^L} > \frac{n+1}{2^L} \quad \text{(since } n \geq 2 \text{ and } L \geq \bar{L} \geq 2\log_2 n \geq 2).$$

Thus we have shown

$$2^{-2L} < \left(\frac{\rho_{min}}{n+1}\right)^2$$

and the assertion follows from the previous lemma. ∎

We next consider the situation that the artificial problem LCP′ (5.1) is constructed and that the UIP method is applied to the LCP′. In this case, the stopping criterion (5.32) for the LCP (1.1) will be reformed into

$$x'^T y' \leq \epsilon' \quad \text{for a given constant } \epsilon' \text{ with } 0 < \epsilon' < \left(\frac{\rho'_{min}}{n'+1}\right)^2 \tag{5.34}$$

and (5.33) into

$$x'^T y' \leq 2^{-2L'}. \tag{5.35}$$

Here ρ'_{min} is the positive minimum value of the ratios Δ'_1/Δ'_2 for all minors Δ'_1 of order n' of the matrix $(-M' \;\; I \;\; q')$ and all nonzero minors Δ'_2 of order n' of the matrix $(-M' \;\; I)$, and L' is the input size of the LCP′ (5.1) defined similarly to L. Owing to the structure of the artificial problem LCP′, however, there may exist a better stopping criterion that would reduce the theoretical computational complexity if a good initial point of the UIP method for the LCP′ is available.

Let $n \geq 2$. Assume that all the entries of M and q are integral. Construct the artificial problem LCP′ (5.1) by using (5.2) and (5.8). Then we may employ the inequality

$$x'^T y' \leq 2^{-3L} \tag{5.36}$$

instead of (5.35) as the stopping criterion of the UIP method applied to the LCP′. In fact we can compute an exact solution (x'^*, y'^*) of the LCP′ in $O(n'^3) = O(n^3)$ arithmetic operations from any point $(\hat{x}', \hat{y}') \in S'_+$ satisfying (5.36). To see this, it suffices to show that

$$2^{-3L} < \left(\frac{\rho'_{min}}{n'+1}\right)^2. \tag{5.37}$$

Since each nonzero minor of the matrix

$$(-M' \ \ I) = \begin{pmatrix} -M & -I & I & O \\ I & O & O & I \end{pmatrix}$$

coincides, up to the absolute values, with a nonzero minor of M and hence its absolute value is less than $2^L/n^2$ by (5.7), the positive minimum ratio ρ'_{min} is greater than $n^2/2^L$. Therefore we have

$$\frac{\rho'_{min}}{n'+1} > \frac{n^2}{(2n+1)2^L} \geq \frac{4}{5}2^{-L} > 2^{-\frac{3}{2}L} \quad (\text{since } n \geq 2 \text{ and } L \geq \bar{L} \geq 2\log_2 n \geq 2),$$

which implies (5.37).

The point $(\boldsymbol{x}'^1, \boldsymbol{y}'^1) \in S'_{++}$ given in Lemma 5.1 serves as a good initial point of the UIP method to solve the LCP$'$ (5.1) constructed by using (5.2) and (5.8) since $f'_{cp}(\boldsymbol{x}'^1, \boldsymbol{y}'^1) = O(L)$ which is generally much smaller than $O(L')$. The combination of the initial point $(\boldsymbol{x}'^1, \boldsymbol{y}'^1)$ and the stopping criterion (5.36) will lead to better theoretical computational complexity of potential reduction algorithms that are special cases of the UIP method (Corollary 6.10).

5.3. Inequalities for Evaluating the Computational Complexity of the UIP Method

Suppose that Condition 2.3 holds for the LCP (1.1). In particular, the point $(\boldsymbol{x}^1, \boldsymbol{y}^1) \in S_{++}$ which serves as an initial point of the UIP method satisfies

$$f_{cp}(\boldsymbol{x}^1, \boldsymbol{y}^1) = \log {\boldsymbol{x}^1}^T \boldsymbol{y}^1 = O(L), \quad f_{cen}(\boldsymbol{x}^1, \boldsymbol{y}^1) = O(1) \tag{5.38}$$

and hence

$${\boldsymbol{x}^1}^T \boldsymbol{y}^1 = 2^{O(L)}, \quad f(\boldsymbol{x}^1, \boldsymbol{y}^1) = \nu f_{cp}(\boldsymbol{x}^1, \boldsymbol{y}^1) + f_{cen}(\boldsymbol{x}^1, \boldsymbol{y}^1) = O(\nu L). \tag{5.39}$$

Here we have assumed that $\nu L \geq 1$. If this assumption did not hold, we would have to replace νL by $\max\{\nu L, 1\}$ in the following argument. Applying the UIP method to the LCP, we have a sequence $\{(\boldsymbol{x}^k, \boldsymbol{y}^k)\} \subset S_{++}$ starting from the initial point $(\boldsymbol{x}^1, \boldsymbol{y}^1)$. Each iteration of the method takes $O(n^3)$ arithmetic operations. We shall present some fundamental inequalities on the sequence $\{(\boldsymbol{x}^k, \boldsymbol{y}^k)\}$ which will play an important role in the evaluation of the number of iterations necessary to reach an approximate solution $(\hat{\boldsymbol{x}}, \hat{\boldsymbol{y}}) \in S_+$ of the LCP satisfying the stopping criterion (5.33), i.e., $\hat{\boldsymbol{x}}^T \hat{\boldsymbol{y}} \leq 2^{-2L}$. When we have such an approximate solution $(\hat{\boldsymbol{x}}, \hat{\boldsymbol{y}})$, we can compute an exact solution of the LCP in $O(n^3)$ arithmetic operations (Corollary 5.10).

The inequality

$${\boldsymbol{x}^{k+1}}^T \boldsymbol{y}^{k+1} \leq (1 - \bar{\delta}) {\boldsymbol{x}^k}^T \boldsymbol{y}^k \quad (k = 1, 2, \ldots) \tag{5.40}$$

implies global linear convergence of the inner product $\boldsymbol{x}^T \boldsymbol{y}$ to 0. Here $\bar{\delta} \in (0,1)$ denotes a constant. If this inequality holds, then the sequence $\{(\boldsymbol{x}^k, \boldsymbol{y}^k)\}$ attains an approximate solution $(\boldsymbol{x}, \boldsymbol{y}) = (\boldsymbol{x}^k, \boldsymbol{y}^k) \in S_+$ satisfying (5.33) in $O(L/\delta)$ iterations because of (5.39). Here $\delta = -\log(1-\bar{\delta})$. Inequalities of this kind have been utilized to show the polynomial-time convergence of path-following algorithms in several papers (Gonzaga [22], Kojima, Mizuno and Yoshise [34, 35], Renegar [57], etc.). It should be noted that the inequality (5.40) can be rewritten in terms of the function $f_{cp}(\boldsymbol{x}, \boldsymbol{y}) = \log \boldsymbol{x}^T \boldsymbol{y}$ as

$$f_{cp}(\boldsymbol{x}^{k+1}, \boldsymbol{y}^{k+1}) \leq f_{cp}(\boldsymbol{x}^k, \boldsymbol{y}^k) - \delta \ \ (k = 1, 2, \ldots). \tag{5.41}$$

Here $\delta = -\log(1 - \bar{\delta})$. It follows that

$$f_{cp}(\boldsymbol{x}^k, \boldsymbol{y}^k) \leq f_{cp}(\boldsymbol{x}^1, \boldsymbol{y}^1) - \delta(k-1) \ \ (k = 1, 2, \ldots).$$

Replacing $(k-1)$ by $\log k$ in the inequality above, we have another type of inequalities:

$$f_{cp}(\boldsymbol{x}^k, \boldsymbol{y}^k) \leq f_{cp}(\boldsymbol{x}^1, \boldsymbol{y}^1) - \delta \log k \ \ (k = 1, 2, \ldots). \tag{5.42}$$

This inequality ensures that the stopping criterion (5.33) is satisfied in $O(\exp(L/\delta))$ iterations because of (5.38).

Let δ be a positive constant. The inequality

$$f(\boldsymbol{x}^{k+1}, \boldsymbol{y}^{k+1}) \leq f(\boldsymbol{x}^k, \boldsymbol{y}^k) - \delta \ \ (k = 1, 2, \ldots), \tag{5.43}$$

which means a constant reduction in the potential function f, has been utilized in many potential reduction algorithms since Karmarkar [28]. In view of the relation (2.5), i.e., $f(\boldsymbol{x}, \boldsymbol{y}) \geq \nu \log \boldsymbol{x}^T \boldsymbol{y}$, the inequality

$$f(\boldsymbol{x}, \boldsymbol{y}) \leq -2\nu L$$

implies the stopping criterion (5.33). On the other hand, the relation (5.39) holds for the initial point $(\boldsymbol{x}^1, \boldsymbol{y}^1)$ of the UIP method. Thus, if the inequality (5.43) holds, the method stops within $O(\nu L/\delta)$ iterations.

Summarizing the discussion so far, we have the following theorem. Inequalities of the types (5.42) and (5.43) will appear in Theorems 6.8 and 6.6, respectively.

Theorem 5.11. *Let $n \geq 2$. Suppose that the LCP (1.1) satisfies Condition 2.3. Let $\{(\boldsymbol{x}^k, \boldsymbol{y}^k)\}$ be a sequence generated by the UIP method applied to the LCP, with the initial point $(\boldsymbol{x}^1, \boldsymbol{y}^1) \in S_{++}$ given in Condition 2.3 and the stopping criterion (5.33).*

(i) *If the inequality (5.40) or (5.41) holds, the UIP method stops within $O(L/\delta)$ iterations. Here $\delta = -\log(1-\bar{\delta})$.*
(ii) *If the inequality (5.42) holds, the UIP method stops within $O(\exp(L/\delta))$ iterations.*
(iii) *If the inequality (5.43) holds, the UIP method stops within $O(\nu L/\delta)$ iterations.*

In any case, each iteration takes $O(n^3)$ arithmetic operations and we can compute an exact solution of the LCP in $O(n^3)$ arithmetic operations from the final iterate of the UIP method.

Suppose that the LCP (1.1) satisfies Condition 5.6. Namely, we give up (iii) of Condition 2.3 that requires an initial point $(\boldsymbol{x}^1, \boldsymbol{y}^1) \in S_{++}$ for the UIP method known in advance. Let $n \geq 2$. Construct the artificial problem LCP′ (5.1) by using (5.2) and (5.8), and apply the UIP method to the LCP′ with the initial point $(\boldsymbol{x}'^1, \boldsymbol{y}'^1) \in S'_{++}$ given in Lemma 5.1 and the stopping criterion (5.36). We may say that the UIP method solves the LCP (1.1) if it does the LCP′ (5.1): If an approximate solution $(\boldsymbol{x}', \boldsymbol{y}') \in S'_{+}$ of the LCP′ satisfying the stopping criterion (5.36) is obtained as a final iterate of the UIP method for the LCP′, an exact solution $(\boldsymbol{x}'^*, \boldsymbol{y}'^*)$ of the LCP′ can be computed in $O(n'^3) = O(n^3)$ arithmetic operations (see Section 5.2); according to the artificial components of the solution $(\boldsymbol{x}'^*, \boldsymbol{y}'^*)$ of the LCP′, we either have a solution of the LCP or know the infeasibility of the LCP, i.e., $S_+ = \emptyset$ (Lemma 5.4 and Theorem 4.6). We will discuss the computational complexity when we solve the LCP in this way, providing that the sequence $\{(\boldsymbol{x}'^k, \boldsymbol{y}'^k)\}$ generated by the UIP method for solving the LCP′ satisfies a certain inequality corresponding to (5.41), (5.42) or (5.43). Recall that $f'_{cp}(\boldsymbol{x}'^1, \boldsymbol{y}'^1) = O(L)$ and $f'_{cen}(\boldsymbol{x}'^1, \boldsymbol{y}'^1) = O(1)$ for the point $(\boldsymbol{x}'^1, \boldsymbol{y}'^1) \in S'_{++}$ given in Lemma 5.1. Similar to the preceding theorem, we have:

Theorem 5.12. *Let $n \geq 2$. Suppose that the LCP (1.1) satisfies Condition 5.6. Construct the artificial problem LCP′ (5.1) by using (5.2) and (5.8). Let $\{(\boldsymbol{x}'^k, \boldsymbol{y}'^k)\}$ be a sequence generated by the UIP method applied to the LCP′, with the initial point $(\boldsymbol{x}'^1, \boldsymbol{y}'^1) \in S'_{++}$ given in Lemma 5.1 and the stopping criterion (5.36).*

(i) *If the inequality*

$$f'_{cp}(\boldsymbol{x}'^{k+1}, \boldsymbol{y}'^{k+1}) \leq f'_{cp}(\boldsymbol{x}'^k, \boldsymbol{y}'^k) - \delta' \quad (k = 1, 2, \ldots)$$

holds, the UIP method stops in $O(L/\delta')$ iterations.

(ii) *If the inequality*

$$f'_{cp}(\boldsymbol{x}'^k, \boldsymbol{y}'^k) \leq f'_{cp}(\boldsymbol{x}'^1, \boldsymbol{y}'^1) - \delta' \log k \quad (k = 1, 2, \ldots)$$

holds, the UIP method stops in $O(\exp(L/\delta'))$ iterations.

(iii) *If the inequality*

$$f'(\boldsymbol{x}'^{k+1}, \boldsymbol{y}'^{k+1}) \leq f'(\boldsymbol{x}'^k, \boldsymbol{y}'^k) - \delta' \quad (k = 1, 2, \ldots)$$

holds, the UIP method stops in $O(\nu' L/\delta')$ iterations. Here $\nu' > 0$ is a parameter in the definition (5.11) of the potential function f'.

In any case, each iteration takes $O(n'^3) = O(n^3)$ arithmetic operations and we can compute an exact solution $(\boldsymbol{x}'^*, \boldsymbol{y}'^*) = (\boldsymbol{x}^*, \tilde{\boldsymbol{x}}^*, \boldsymbol{y}^*, \tilde{\boldsymbol{y}}^*)$ of the LCP′ in $O(n'^3) = O(n^3)$ arithmetic operations from the final iterate of the UIP method. Furthermore, according to $\tilde{\boldsymbol{x}}^* = \boldsymbol{0}$ or $\tilde{\boldsymbol{x}}^* \neq \boldsymbol{0}$, we either obtain a solution $(\boldsymbol{x}^*, \boldsymbol{y}^*)$ of the LCP or know that the LCP is infeasible, i.e., $S_+ = \emptyset$.

6. A Class of Potential Reduction Algorithms

This section presents a class of globally convergent potential reduction algorithms in a unified way as special cases of the UIP method. An algorithm in this class chooses a direction parameter $\beta \in [0,1]$ at each iteration, computes a search direction (dx, dy) solving the system (2.8) (or (4.27)) of Newton equations, and then searches a new point $(x, y) + \theta(dx, dy)$ which minimizes the potential function f of the form (2.2) with a parameter $\nu > 0$ along the direction (dx, dy) over a neighborhood of the path of centers S_{cen}. We may take S_{++} itself as the neighborhood of the path of centers. In that case, the algorithm works as a "usual" potential reduction algorithm, while it works as a path-following algorithm if we take a narrow neighborhood. Thus we may regard an algorithm in the class as an extension of both potential reduction and path-following algorithms.

To avoid the computation of the exact minimizer of the potential function along the direction (dx, dy) in a neighborhood of S_{cen} and to ensure the global and/or polynomial-time convergence, we will utilize the quadratic upper bounds given in Section 4.4 for the potential function $f = \nu f_{cp} + f_{cen}$ and their component functions f_{cp}, f_{cen}.

In Section 6.1, we describe in detail the class of potential reduction algorithms. Section 6.2 presents some global and/or polynomial-time convergence results. Their proofs will be given in Section 7.

6.1. Specialization of Steps 3 and 4 of the UIP Method for Potential Reduction Algorithms

Lot α_{bd} be either a positive number or $+\infty$. As an admissible region in which we generate a sequence $\{(x^k, y^k)\}$, we consider a neighborhood of the path of centers S_{cen}:

$$\begin{aligned} N_{cen}(\alpha_{bd}) &= \{(x, y) \in S_{++} : f_{cen}(x, y) \leq \alpha_{bd}\} \quad \text{if } \alpha_{bd} < +\infty, \\ N_{cen}(\alpha_{bd}) &= S_{++} \quad \text{if } \alpha_{bd} = +\infty. \end{aligned}$$

For the time being, we assume that $\alpha_{bd} < +\infty$. Suppose that a current point $(x, y) = (x^k, y^k)$ lies in $N_{cen}(\alpha_{bd})$. We wish to find a new point $(\bar{x}, \bar{y}) = (x, y) + \theta(dx, dy) \in N_{cen}(\alpha_{bd})$ at which we get a sufficient potential reduction to attain the global convergence. For this purpose, we use different strategies of choosing the direction parameter β depending on whether the current point (x, y) is close to the boundary of $N_{cen}(\alpha_{bd})$ or not. When (x, y) is close to the boundary of the neighborhood $N_{cen}(\alpha_{bd})$, we take a larger $\beta \in [0,1]$ so that the search direction (dx, dy) points toward the path of centers S_{cen} and that the new point $(\bar{x}, \bar{y})$ will be apart from the boundary of $N_{cen}(\alpha_{bd})$. When (x, y) is close to S_{cen} or far from the boundary of $N_{cen}(\alpha_{bd})$, we take a smaller $\beta \in [0,1]$ to gain more reduction in $x^T y$. These strategies were employed in the paper

Barnes, Chopra and Jensen [4]. To embody this idea in the UIP method, we introduce parameters α_{cen}, α_1, α_{bd}, β_{cen} and β_{bd} satisfying the following condition.

Condition 6.1.

$$0 < \alpha_{cen} \leq \alpha_1 < \alpha_{bd} < +\infty \text{ or}$$
$$0 < \alpha_{cen} \leq \alpha_1 \leq \alpha_{bd} = +\infty.$$
$$0 \leq \beta_{cen} < 1, \quad 0 < \beta_{bd} \leq 1.$$

Representative choices of the parameters α_{cen}, α_1 and α_{bd} satisfying the condition above are:

(a) $0 < \alpha_{cen} \leq \alpha_1 < \alpha_{bd} < +\infty$. See Figure 9 on page 22.
(b) $0 < \alpha_{cen} \leq \alpha_1 < \alpha_{bd} = +\infty$. See Figure 10 on page 22.
(c) $0 < \alpha_{cen} \leq \alpha_1 = \alpha_{bd} = +\infty$. See Figure 11 on page 23.

In the case (a) with a small positive $\alpha_{bd} < +\infty$, the algorithm described below may be regarded as a path-following algorithm, while we will have usual potential reduction algorithms in the cases (b) and (c). We replace Step 3 of the UIP method described in Section 2.2 by

Step 3′: Take

$$\beta = \beta_k \in \begin{cases} [0, \beta_{cen}] & \text{if } f_{cen}(\boldsymbol{x}, \boldsymbol{y}) < \alpha_{cen}, \\ [0, 1] & \text{if } \alpha_{cen} \leq f_{cen}(\boldsymbol{x}, \boldsymbol{y}) \leq \alpha_1, \\ [\beta_{bd}, 1] & \text{otherwise.} \end{cases} \tag{6.1}$$

Solve the system (2.8) of Newton equations to get the search direction $(d\boldsymbol{x}, d\boldsymbol{y})$.

We now explain how to choose a step size parameter θ. Define

$$\bar{\eta}(n, \nu) = \max\left\{1, \frac{\nu}{n}\right\} \tag{6.2}$$

for every positive integer n and positive number ν. The following lemma will lead to a choice of a step size parameter θ which implies sufficient reduction in the potential function so as to ensure the global convergence.

Lemma 6.2. *Let* $\nu > 0$, $(\boldsymbol{x}, \boldsymbol{y}) \in N_{cen}(\alpha_{bd})$ *for some* $\alpha_{bd} > 0$ *or* $= +\infty$, $\beta \in [0, 1]$ *and* $\beta \neq 1$ *if* $(\boldsymbol{x}, \boldsymbol{y}) \in S_{cen}$. *Let* $(d\boldsymbol{x}, d\boldsymbol{y})$ *be the solution of the system (2.8) of Newton equations. Define*

$$\bar{\tau} = \min\left\{\frac{1}{2}, \frac{g(\nu, \beta)}{2\bar{\eta}(n, \nu)}, \frac{g_{cen}(\beta) + \sqrt{g_{cen}(\beta)^2 + 5(\alpha_{bd} - f_{cen}(\boldsymbol{x}, \boldsymbol{y}))}}{(5/2)}\right\}, \tag{6.3}$$

$$\bar{\theta} = \frac{v_{min}\bar{\tau}}{\sqrt{1 + 2\Delta(\beta)\|\boldsymbol{h}(\beta)\|}}.$$

Then the new point $(\bar{x}, \bar{y}) = (x, y) + \bar{\theta}(dx, dy)$ *satisfies*

$$f(\bar{x}, \bar{y}) - f(x, y) \leq -\frac{\bar{\eta}(n, \nu)\bar{\tau}^2}{2}, \tag{6.4}$$

$$f_{cen}(\bar{x}, \bar{y}) \leq \alpha_{bd}. \tag{6.5}$$

See (4.8), (4.26), (4.32) and (4.33) for the definitions of functions v_{min}, $h(\beta)$, $\Delta(\beta)$, $g_{cp}(\beta)$, $g_{cen}(\beta)$ *and* $g(\nu, \beta)$ *in* $(x, y) \in S_{++}$.

Proof: By the definition, we see $\bar{\tau} \leq 1/2$. Hence, by Theorem 4.18, we obtain $(\bar{x}, \bar{y}) \in S_{++}$. Furthermore, we see that

$$-g(\nu, \beta)\bar{\tau} \leq -2\bar{\eta}(n, \nu)\bar{\tau}^2,$$

$$\left\{\frac{\nu}{4n} + \frac{1}{4} + \frac{1}{2(1-\bar{\tau})}\right\}\bar{\tau}^2 \leq \left(\frac{\bar{\eta}(n, \nu)}{4} + \frac{1}{4} + 1\right)\bar{\tau}^2 \leq \frac{3}{2}\bar{\eta}(n, \nu)\bar{\tau}^2.$$

Thus the inequality (6.4) follows from (4.36) of Theorem 4.18. If $\alpha_{bd} = +\infty$ the inequality (6.5) apparently holds. Assume that $\alpha_{bd} < +\infty$. By Theorem 4.18, if $0 \leq \tau \leq 1/2$ then

$$\begin{aligned} f_{cen}(\bar{x}, \bar{y}) &\leq f_{cen}(x, y) - g_{cen}(\beta)\tau + \left\{\frac{1}{4} + \frac{1}{2(1-\tau)}\right\}\tau^2 \\ &\leq f_{cen}(x, y) - g_{cen}(\beta)\tau + \frac{5}{4}\tau^2. \end{aligned}$$

Finally, noting that $\bar{\tau}$ has been chosen so that the quadratic function in τ above is not greater than α_{bd} whenever $0 \leq \tau \leq \bar{\tau}$, we obtain the inequality (6.5). ∎

We are ready to specialize Step 4 of the UIP method by:

Step 4′: Choose a step size parameter $\theta = \theta_k \geq 0$ such that the new point $(x, y) + \theta(dx, dy)$ satisfies

$$(x, y) + \theta(dx, dy) \in N_{cen}(\alpha_{bd}) \cup S_{cp},$$

$$f((x, y) + \theta(dx, dy)) \leq f(x, y) - \frac{\bar{\eta}(n, \nu)\bar{\tau}^2}{2}.$$

Here $\bar{\tau}$ is given by (6.3). Define the new point $(\bar{x}, \bar{y})$ by

$$(\bar{x}, \bar{y}) = (x, y) + \theta(dx, dy).$$

We will call the UIP method with Steps 3′ and 4′ replacing Steps 3 and 4 a potential reduction algorithm, which still involves the neighborhood parameters α_{cen}, α_1, α_{bd}, the potential function parameter $\nu > 0$ and the search direction parameter $\beta \in [0, 1]$ satisfying (6.1) to be specified besides the step size parameter θ. Thus it actually yields a class of potential reduction algorithms.

Lemma 6.2 enables us to take the step size parameter

$$\theta = \bar{\theta} = \frac{v_{min}\bar{\tau}}{\sqrt{1 + 2\Delta(\beta)\|h(\beta)\|}}$$

in Step 4′, which will ensure the global convergence of potential reduction algorithms. See Corollary 6.4. Practically, however, the step size parameter $\bar{\theta}$ may be too small to gain a big reduction in the potential function. We can perform various line search methods, starting from $\bar{\theta}$, for the one-dimensional minimization problem:

$$\begin{array}{ll} \text{Minimize} & f((\boldsymbol{x}, \boldsymbol{y}) + \theta(d\boldsymbol{x}, d\boldsymbol{y})) \\ \text{subject to} & f_{cen}((\boldsymbol{x}, \boldsymbol{y}) + \theta(d\boldsymbol{x}, d\boldsymbol{y})) \leq \alpha_{bd}, \quad \theta \geq 0, \end{array}$$

which we want to solve. To get a better initial estimate for such line search methods, we can utilize the quadratic upper bounds given in Theorem 4.17 for $f((\boldsymbol{x}, \boldsymbol{y}) + \theta(d\boldsymbol{x}, d\boldsymbol{y}))$ and $f_{cen}((\boldsymbol{x}, \boldsymbol{y}) + \theta(d\boldsymbol{x}, d\boldsymbol{y}))$ ($0 \leq \theta \leq \Theta(\tau)$, $0 \leq \tau < 1$). See also Theorem 4.18. In fact, the step size parameter $\hat{\theta}$ which solves the one-dimensional convex quadratic minimization problem:

$$\begin{array}{ll} \text{Minimize} & f(\boldsymbol{x}, \boldsymbol{y}) - G^{\bar{\tau}}(\theta) \\ \text{subject to} & f_{cen}(\boldsymbol{x}, \boldsymbol{y}) - G^{\bar{\tau}}_{cen}(\theta) \leq \alpha_{bd}, \quad 0 \leq \theta \leq \Theta(\bar{\tau}) \end{array}$$

fulfills the requirement of Step 4′ and serves as an initial estimate for line search methods.

6.2. Global and/or Polynomial-Time Convergence

This section shows some global and/or polynomial-time convergence results, Corollaries 6.4, 6.7, 6.9 and 6.10, of the potential reduction algorithms. All of the corollaries will be derived from Theorems 6.3, 6.6 and 6.8 described below. The proofs of the theorems will be given in the next section, Section 7. The first theorem leads to Corollary 6.4 which is a quite general global convergence result.

Theorem 6.3. *Suppose that the LCP (1.1) satisfies Condition 2.1. Let the parameters* α_{cen}, α_1, α_{bd}, β_{cen} *and* β_{bd} *satisfy Condition 6.1. Let* $\nu > 0$ *and* $\epsilon > 0$. *Then there exists a positive number* δ, *depending upon the parameters* α_{cen}, α_1, α_{bd}, β_{cen}, β_{bd}, ν, ϵ *and a given initial point* $(\boldsymbol{x}^1, \boldsymbol{y}^1)$ *such that whenever* $f_{cen}(\boldsymbol{x}, \boldsymbol{y}) \leq \alpha_{bd}$ *(i.e.,*$(\boldsymbol{x}, \boldsymbol{y}) \in N_{cen}(\alpha_{bd})$*),* $f(\boldsymbol{x}, \boldsymbol{y}) \leq f(\boldsymbol{x}^1, \boldsymbol{y}^1)$ *and* $\boldsymbol{x}^T\boldsymbol{y} \geq \epsilon$, *the new point* $(\bar{\boldsymbol{x}}, \bar{\boldsymbol{y}})$ *determined by Steps 3′ and 4′ satisfies*

$$f(\bar{\boldsymbol{x}}, \bar{\boldsymbol{y}}) \leq f(\boldsymbol{x}, \boldsymbol{y}) - \delta.$$

Corollary 6.4.

(i) *Suppose that the LCP (1.1) satisfies Condition 2.1. Let the parameters* α_{cen}, α_1, α_{bd}, β_{cen} *and* β_{bd} *satisfy Condition 6.1 and the inequality* $f_{cen}(\boldsymbol{x}^1, \boldsymbol{y}^1) \leq \alpha_{bd}$. *Let*

$\nu > 0$ and employ the inequality (5.27) with an arbitrary $\epsilon > 0$ as the stopping criterion. Then the potential reduction algorithm stops in a finite number of iterations. Furthermore, we can compute an exact solution $(\boldsymbol{x}^*, \boldsymbol{y}^*)$ of the LCP in $O(n^3)$ arithmetic operations if ϵ satisfies the inequality (5.31).

(ii) *Suppose that the LCP (1.1) satisfies Condition 5.5. Construct the LCP′ (5.1) with the dimension $n' = 2n$ by using (5.2) and (5.4). Take an initial point $(\boldsymbol{x}'^1, \boldsymbol{y}'^1) = (\boldsymbol{x}^1, \tilde{\boldsymbol{x}}^1, \boldsymbol{y}^1, \tilde{\boldsymbol{y}}^1)$ such that the inequalities (5.9) and (5.10) hold. Let the parameters α_{cen}, α_1, α_{bd}, β_{cen} and β_{bd} satisfy Condition 6.1 and the inequality $f'_{cen}(\boldsymbol{x}'^1, \boldsymbol{y}'^1) \leq \alpha_{bd}$. Let $\nu' > 0$ be the potential function parameter associated with the LCP′ as in (5.11), and employ the inequality (5.34) as the stopping criterion. Then the potential reduction algorithm applied to the LCP′ solves the LCP. More precisely, the algorithm stops in a finite number of iterations at an approximate solution $(\hat{\boldsymbol{x}}', \hat{\boldsymbol{y}}')$ of the LCP′ satisfying the stopping criterion (5.34). Furthermore, we can compute an exact solution $(\boldsymbol{x}'^*, \boldsymbol{y}'^*)$ of the LCP′ in $O(n^3)$ arithmetic operations. If $x_i'^* = 0$ $(i = n+1, n+2, \ldots, 2n)$ then $(\boldsymbol{x}^*, \boldsymbol{y}^*) = (x_1'^*, x_2'^*, \ldots, x_n'^*, y_1'^*, y_2'^*, \ldots, y_n'^*)$ is a solution of the LCP. Otherwise the LCP has no solution.*

Proof: From Theorem 6.3 and the inequality (2.5), we obtain a point $(\boldsymbol{x}^k, \boldsymbol{y}^k) \in S_+$ such that ${\boldsymbol{x}^k}^T \boldsymbol{y}^k \leq \epsilon$ in a finite number of iterations for any given $\epsilon > 0$. Hence the assertion (i) follows from Lemma 5.9. On the other hand, the constructed LCP′ satisfies Condition 2.1 by Lemma 5.7. Hence the assertion (ii) follows from (i) and Lemma 5.4. ∎

In the remainder of Section 6.2, assuming that the matrix M belongs to the class $P_*(\kappa)$ for some $\kappa \geq 0$, we evaluate the theoretical computational complexity of potential reduction algorithms with some special choices of the direction parameter β. Let $(\boldsymbol{x}, \boldsymbol{y}) \in S_{++}$. Define

$$\left.\begin{aligned} \bar{g}_{cp}(\beta) &= \bar{g}_{cp}(\beta, \boldsymbol{x}, \boldsymbol{y}) = \frac{(1-\beta)\pi}{\sqrt{(1+2\kappa)\{(1-\beta)^2 n\pi + \beta^2\omega^2\}}}, \\ \bar{g}_{cen}(\beta) &= \bar{g}_{cen}(\beta, \boldsymbol{x}, \boldsymbol{y}) = \frac{\beta\omega^2}{\sqrt{(1+2\kappa)\{(1-\beta)^2 n\pi + \beta^2\omega^2\}}}, \\ \bar{g}(\nu, \beta) &= \bar{g}(\nu, \beta, \boldsymbol{x}, \boldsymbol{y}) = \frac{\nu(1-\beta)\pi + \beta\omega^2}{\sqrt{(1+2\kappa)\{(1-\beta)^2 n\pi + \beta^2\omega^2\}}}. \end{aligned}\right\} \tag{6.6}$$

In view of (4.33) of Theorem 4.18 and Lemma 4.19, we then see that

$$\bar{g}_{cp}(\beta) \leq g_{cp}(\beta), \quad \bar{g}_{cen}(\beta) \leq g_{cen}(\beta) \quad \text{and} \quad \bar{g}(\nu, \beta) \leq g(\nu, \beta), \tag{6.7}$$

and that the new point $(\bar{\boldsymbol{x}}, \bar{\boldsymbol{y}}) = (\boldsymbol{x}, \boldsymbol{y}) + \theta(d\boldsymbol{x}, d\boldsymbol{y})$ given in Theorem 4.18 satisfies

$$f_{cp}(\bar{\boldsymbol{x}}, \bar{\boldsymbol{y}}) - f_{cp}(\boldsymbol{x}, \boldsymbol{y}) \leq -\bar{g}_{cp}(\beta)\tau + \frac{\tau^2}{4n},$$

$$f_{cen}(\bar{\boldsymbol{x}}, \bar{\boldsymbol{y}}) - f_{cen}(\boldsymbol{x}, \boldsymbol{y}) \leq -\bar{g}_{cen}(\beta)\tau + \left\{\frac{1}{4} + \frac{1}{2(1-\tau)}\right\}\tau^2,$$

$$f(\bar{\boldsymbol{x}}, \bar{\boldsymbol{y}}) - f(\boldsymbol{x}, \boldsymbol{y}) \leq -\bar{g}(\nu, \beta)\tau + \left\{\frac{\nu}{4n} + \frac{1}{4} + \frac{1}{2(1-\tau)}\right\}\tau^2.$$

Thus it is interesting to investigate values of β at which the coefficients $-\bar{g}_{cp}(\beta)$, $-\bar{g}_{cen}(\beta)$ and $-\bar{g}(\nu,\beta)$ of the linear terms in τ on the right-hand side of the above inequalities attain their minimum over the interval $[0,1]$. For a given $\nu > 0$, the following lemma shows that if $(\boldsymbol{x},\boldsymbol{y}) \in S_{++} \setminus S_{cen}$ then the functions $\bar{g}_{cp}(\beta)$, $\bar{g}_{cen}(\beta)$ and $\bar{g}(\nu,\beta)$ attain their maximum at $\beta = 0,\ 1,\ n/(n+\nu)$ over $[0,1]$, respectively, and that if $(\boldsymbol{x},\boldsymbol{y}) \in S_{cen}$ then the functions are constant over $[0,1)$.

Lemma 6.5. *Suppose that $\nu > 0$ and $(\boldsymbol{x},\boldsymbol{y}) \in S_{++}$. Then the functions $\bar{g}_{cp}(\beta)$, $\bar{g}_{cen}(\beta)$ and $\bar{g}(\nu,\beta)$ defined by (6.6) behave as follows:*

(i) (a) *If $(\boldsymbol{x},\boldsymbol{y}) \in S_{++} \setminus S_{cen}$ and $0 < \beta_1 < \beta_2 < 1$ then*

$$\frac{\sqrt{\pi}}{\sqrt{(1+2\kappa)n}} = \bar{g}_{cp}(0) > \bar{g}_{cp}(\beta_1) > \bar{g}_{cp}(\beta_2) > \bar{g}_{cp}(1) = 0.$$

(b) *If $(\boldsymbol{x},\boldsymbol{y}) \in S_{cen}$ and $0 \le \beta < 1$ then*

$$\bar{g}_{cp}(\beta) = \frac{1}{\sqrt{(1+2\kappa)n}}.$$

(ii) (a) *If $(\boldsymbol{x},\boldsymbol{y}) \in S_{++} \setminus S_{cen}$ and $0 < \beta_1 < \beta_2 < 1$ then*

$$0 = \bar{g}_{cen}(0) < \bar{g}_{cen}(\beta_1) < \bar{g}_{cen}(\beta_2) < \bar{g}_{cen}(1) = \frac{\omega}{\sqrt{1+2\kappa}}.$$

(b) *If $(\boldsymbol{x},\boldsymbol{y}) \in S_{cen}$ and $0 \le \beta < 1$ then*

$$\bar{g}_{cen}(\beta) = 0.$$

(iii) (a) *If $(\boldsymbol{x},\boldsymbol{y}) \in S_{++} \setminus S_{cen}$ and $0 < \beta_1 < \beta_2 < n/(n+\nu) < \beta_3 < \beta_4 < 1$ then*

$$\frac{\nu\sqrt{\pi}}{\sqrt{(1+2\kappa)n}} = \bar{g}(\nu,0) < \bar{g}(\nu,\beta_1) < \bar{g}(\nu,\beta_2) < \bar{g}\left(\nu,\frac{n}{n+\nu}\right) = \frac{\sqrt{(\nu^2/n)\pi+\omega^2}}{\sqrt{1+2\kappa}},$$

$$\bar{g}\left(\nu,\frac{n}{n+\nu}\right) = \frac{\sqrt{(\nu^2/n)\pi+\omega^2}}{\sqrt{1+2\kappa}} > \bar{g}(\nu,\beta_3) > \bar{g}(\nu,\beta_4) > \bar{g}(\nu,1) = \frac{\omega}{\sqrt{1+2\kappa}}.$$

(b) *If $(\boldsymbol{x},\boldsymbol{y}) \in S_{cen}$ and $0 \le \beta < 1$ then*

$$\bar{g}(\nu,\beta) = \frac{\nu}{\sqrt{(1+2\kappa)n}}.$$

See Figures 14 and 15.

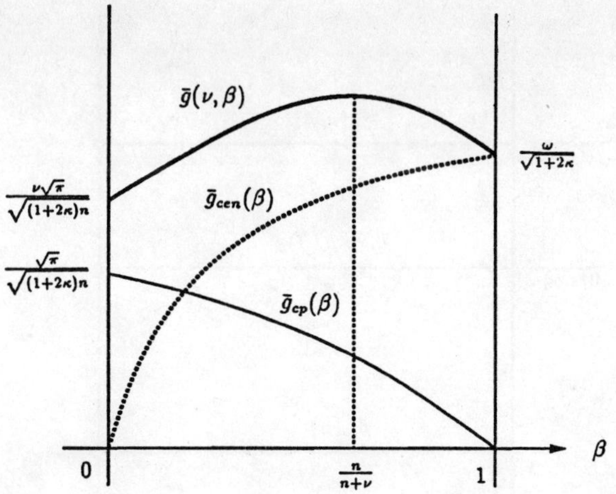

Figure 14: $\bar{g}_{cp}(\beta)$, $\bar{g}_{cen}(\beta)$ and $\bar{g}(\nu,\beta)$ in the case $(\boldsymbol{x},\boldsymbol{y}) \in S_{++} \setminus S_{cen}$.

Proof: If $(\boldsymbol{x},\boldsymbol{y}) \in S_{cen}$ then $\pi = 1$ and $\omega = 0$. Hence the equalities (i)-(b), (ii)-(b) and (iii)-(b) follow directly from the definitions of $\bar{g}_{cp}(\beta)$, $\bar{g}_{cen}(\beta)$ and $\bar{g}(\nu,\beta)$ in (6.6). If $(\boldsymbol{x},\boldsymbol{y}) \in S_{++} \setminus S_{cen}$, we have

$$\frac{\partial \bar{g}_{cp}(\beta)}{\partial \beta} = -\frac{\beta\pi\omega^2}{\sqrt{1+2\kappa}\,\{(1-\beta)^2 n\pi + \beta^2\omega^2\}^{3/2}},$$
$$\frac{\partial \bar{g}_{cen}(\beta)}{\partial \beta} = \frac{n(1-\beta)\pi\omega^2}{\sqrt{1+2\kappa}\,\{(1-\beta)^2 n\pi + \beta^2\omega^2\}^{3/2}},$$
$$\frac{\partial \bar{g}(\nu,\beta)}{\partial \beta} = \frac{\{n-(n+\nu)\beta\}\pi\omega^2}{\sqrt{1+2\kappa}\,\{(1-\beta)^2 n\pi + \beta^2\omega^2\}^{3/2}},$$

from which (i)-(a), (ii)-(a) and (iii)-(a) follow. ∎

By the inequalities in (6.7) and the definition (6.3) of $\bar{\tau}$ in Lemma 6.2 we obtain that

$$\bar{\tau} \;\geq\; \min\left\{\frac{1}{2}, \frac{\bar{g}(\nu,\beta)}{2\bar{\eta}(n,\nu)}, \frac{\bar{g}_{cen}(\beta) + \sqrt{\bar{g}_{cen}(\beta)^2 + 5(\alpha_{bd} - f_{cen}(\boldsymbol{x},\boldsymbol{y}))}}{(5/2)}\right\}. \tag{6.8}$$

This inequality will be used in Section 7 where Theorems 6.6 and 6.8 below are proved.

We will restrict ourselves, under Conditions 2.3 and 6.1, to the following three cases:

(A1) $0 < \alpha_{cen} \leq \alpha_1 < \alpha_{bd} < +\infty$, $\beta_{cen} = \beta_{bd} = n/(n+\nu)$.
(A2) $0 < \alpha_{cen} \leq \alpha_1 < \alpha_{bd} = +\infty$, $\beta_{cen} = \beta_{bd} = n/(n+\nu)$.

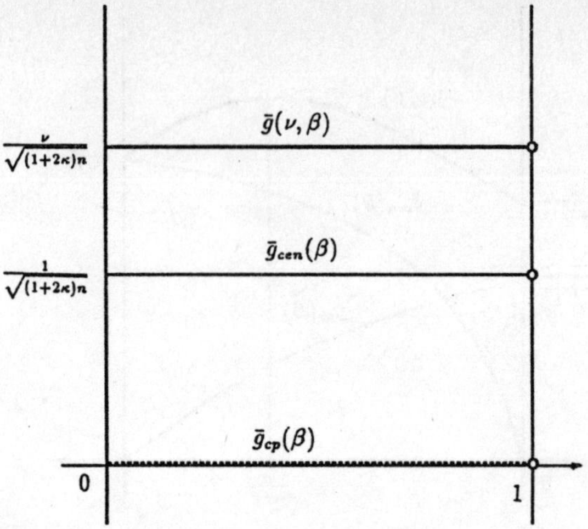

Figure 15: $\bar{g}_{cp}(\beta)$, $\bar{g}_{cen}(\beta)$ and $\bar{g}(\nu, \beta)$ in the case $(\boldsymbol{x}, \boldsymbol{y}) \in S_{cen}$.

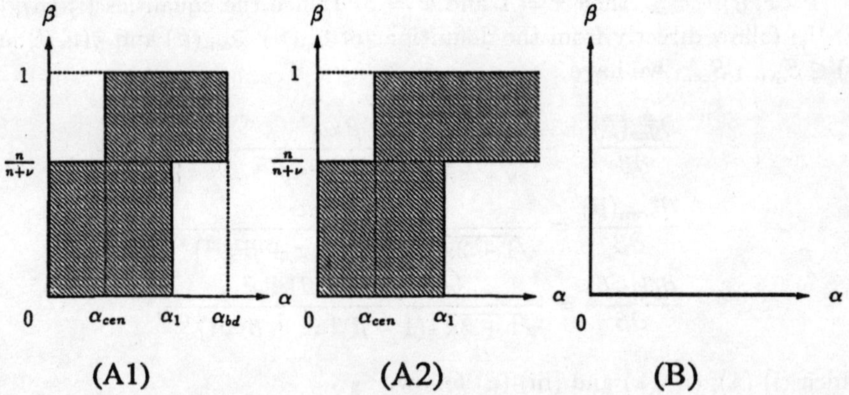

Figure 16: The cases (A1), (A2) and (B).

(B) $\alpha_{cen} = \alpha_1 = \alpha_{bd} = +\infty, \; \beta_{cen} = 0.$

See Figure 16. We will deal with the cases (A1) and (A2) in Theorem 6.6 and the case (B) in Theorem 6.8.

To present the theorem below, we need the following notation. For every α_{cen}, α_1, α_{bd} satisfying $0 < \alpha_{cen} \leq \alpha_1 \leq \alpha_{bd} \leq +\infty$, define

$$\psi_\infty(\alpha_{cen}, \alpha_1) = \frac{1}{4} \min\left\{\exp(-\alpha_1 - 1),\ \bar{\omega}(\alpha_{cen})^2\right\},$$

$$\psi_{bd}(\alpha_1, \alpha_{bd}) = \min\left\{\frac{4(\alpha_{bd} - \alpha_1)}{5},\ \frac{16\bar{\omega}(\alpha_1)^4}{25(1+\bar{\omega}(\alpha_1)^2)}\right\},$$

$$\psi(\alpha_{cen}, \alpha_1, \alpha_{bd}) = \min\left\{\psi_\infty(\alpha_{cen}, \alpha_1),\ \psi_{bd}(\alpha_1, \alpha_{bd})\right\}.$$

Here

$$\bar{\omega}(\alpha) = \frac{\sqrt{\alpha^2 + 2\alpha} - \alpha}{\sqrt{\alpha^2 + 2\alpha} - \alpha + 1} \quad \text{for every } \alpha \geq 0. \tag{6.9}$$

It should be noted that the quantities $\psi_\infty(\alpha_{cen}, \alpha_1)$, $\psi_{bd}(\alpha_1, \alpha_{bd})$ and $\psi(\alpha_{cen}, \alpha_1, \alpha_{bd})$ defined above are positive whenever α_{cen}, α_1 and α_{bd} are chosen as in the case (A1) or (A2). For every positive integer n and positive number ν, define

$$\eta(n, \nu) = \begin{cases} n/\nu^2 & \text{if } 0 < \nu \leq \sqrt{n}, \\ \nu^2/n & \text{if } \sqrt{n} < \nu \leq n, \\ \nu & \text{if } n < \nu, \end{cases}$$

$$\eta_\infty(n, \nu) = \begin{cases} n/\nu^2 & \text{if } 0 < \nu \leq \sqrt{n}, \\ 1 & \text{if } \sqrt{n} < \nu \leq n, \\ \nu/n & \text{if } n < \nu. \end{cases}$$

Theorem 6.6. *Suppose $M \in P_*(\kappa)$ for some $\kappa \geq 0$. Let the parameters α_{cen}, α_1, α_{bd}, β_{cen} and β_{bd} be as in the case (A1) or (A2). Let $\nu > 0$, $(x, y) \in N_{cen}(\alpha_{bd})$, and let $(\bar{x}, \bar{y}) = (x, y) + \theta(dx, dy)$ be a new point determined by Steps 3' and 4'. In the case (A1) the new point satisfies*

$$f(\bar{x}, \bar{y}) \leq f(x, y) - \frac{\psi(\alpha_{cen}, \alpha_1, \alpha_{bd})}{2\eta(n, \nu)(1 + 2\kappa)},$$

and in the case (A2) it satisfies

$$f(\bar{x}, \bar{y}) \leq f(x, y) - \frac{\psi_\infty(\alpha_{cen}, \alpha_1)}{2\eta_\infty(n, \nu)(1 + 2\kappa)}.$$

The theorem will be proved in Section 7.2. As a direct consequence of the theorem and Theorem 5.11, we have:

Corollary 6.7. *Suppose that the LCP (1.1) satisfies Condition 2.3. Let the parameters α_{cen}, α_1, α_{bd}, β_{cen} and β_{bd} be as in the case (A1) or (A2). Suppose that $f_{cen}(x^1, y^1) \leq \alpha_{bd}$ and $\nu > 0$. Apply the potential reduction algorithm to the LCP, with the initial point $(x^1, y^1) \in S_{++}$ given in Condition 2.3 and the stopping criterion (5.33). In the case (A1) the algorithm solves the LCP in $O(\nu\eta(n, \nu)(1 + \kappa)L)$ iterations, and in the case (A2) it solves the LCP in $O(\nu\eta_\infty(n, \nu)(1 + \kappa)L)$ iterations. See Figure 16 for the cases (A1) and (A2). Furthermore, in each of the cases, we can compute an exact solution (x^*, y^*) of the LCP in $O(n^3)$ arithmetic operations from the final iterate of the algorithm.*

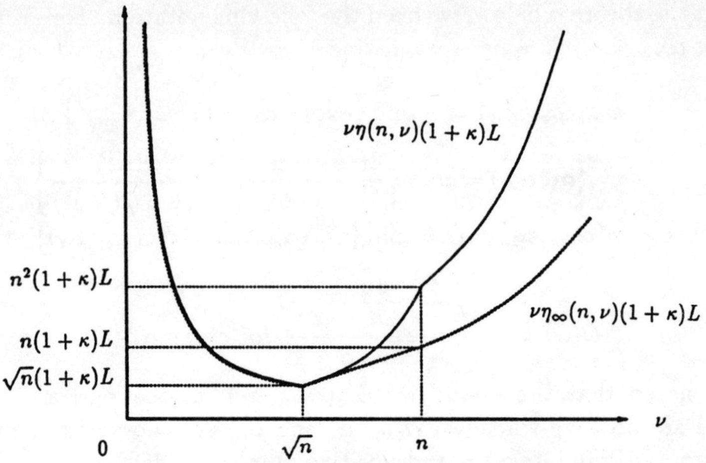

Figure 17: $O(\nu\eta(n,\nu)(1+\kappa)L)$ and $O(\nu\eta_\infty(n,\nu)(1+\kappa)L)$.

Figure 17 illustrates change of $O(\nu\eta(n,\nu)(1+\kappa)L)$ and $O(\nu\eta_\infty(n,\nu)(1+\kappa)L)$ with respect to the potential function parameter ν. We see from the figure that the minimum $O(\sqrt{n}(1+\kappa)L)$ is attained at $\nu = \sqrt{n}$ in both of the cases. This result is comparable with the one in the paper [18] where Freund showed that Ye's potential reduction algorithm [77] for linear programs attains the best theoretical computational complexity when the potential function parameter ν is taken such that $\nu = \sqrt{n}$. Suppose that $\nu = \sqrt{n}$ in Corollary 6.7. If we take $\alpha_{bd} = +\infty$ and $\beta_k = \beta_{cen} = \beta_{bd} = n/(n+\nu)$ $(k = 1, 2, \dots)$ then our potential reduction algorithm coincides with the one proposed by Kojima, Mizuno and Yoshise [36]. Note that we could take any α_{cen} and α_1 in this case, but their values would be redundant. On the other hand, it behaves like a path-following algorithm (Ding and Li [13], Kojima, Mizuno and Yoshise [35], Monteiro and Adler [53, 54], etc.) if we take $\alpha_{bd} < +\infty$.

Now we consider the case (B) which requires us to take the direction parameter $\beta_k = 0$ throughout the iterations. As we stated in Section 2.4, the potential reduction algorithm in this case may be regarded not only as a direct application of the damped Newton method to the system of equations

$$y = Mx + q, \quad x_i y_i = 0 \ (i \in N)$$

associated with the LCP, but also as an affine scaling interior point algorithm for the LCP.

For every positive integer n and positive number ν, define

$$\eta_0(n,\nu) = \begin{cases} n^{3/2}/\nu^2 & \text{if } 0 < \nu \le \sqrt{n}, \\ \nu & \text{if } \sqrt{n} < \nu \le n, \\ \nu^2/n & \text{if } n < \nu. \end{cases}$$

Theorem 6.8. *Suppose that $M \in P_*(\kappa)$ for some $\kappa \ge 0$ and that an initial point $(\boldsymbol{x}^1, \boldsymbol{y}^1) \in S_{++}$ is known. Let the parameters α_{cen}, α_1, α_{bd} and β_{cen} be as in the case (B). Let $\nu > 0$. Then the sequence $\{(\boldsymbol{x}^k, \boldsymbol{y}^k)\}$ generated by the potential reduction algorithm satisfies*

$$f_{cp}(\boldsymbol{x}^k, \boldsymbol{y}^k) \le f_{cp}(\boldsymbol{x}^1, \boldsymbol{y}^1) - \frac{\exp(-f_{cen}(\boldsymbol{x}^1, \boldsymbol{y}^1) - 1)}{40\eta_0(n,\nu)(1+2\kappa)} \log k$$

for $k = 1, 2, \ldots$.

In the above inequality, the value $\exp(-f_{cen}(\boldsymbol{x}^1, \boldsymbol{y}^1) - 1)$ in the coefficient of $\log k$ can be replaced by the constant $\exp(-\alpha - 1)$ when the LCP (1.1) satisfies Condition 2.3. Hence, as a direct consequence of Theorems 5.11 and 6.8, we have:

Corollary 6.9. *Suppose that the LCP (1.1) satisfies Condition 2.3. Let the parameters α_{cen}, α_1, α_{bd} and β_{cen} be as in the case (B). Let $\nu > 0$. Apply the potential reduction algorithm to the LCP, with the initial point $(\boldsymbol{x}^1, \boldsymbol{y}^1) \in S_{++}$ given in Condition 2.3 and the stopping criterion (5.33). Then the algorithm solves the LCP in $O(\exp\{\eta_0(n,\nu)(1+\kappa)L\})$ iterations. Furthermore, we can compute an exact solution $(\boldsymbol{x}^*, \boldsymbol{y}^*)$ of the LCP in $O(n^3)$ arithmetic operations from the final iterate of the algorithm.*

We conclude the section by stating the computational complexity of the potential reduction algorithms under Condition 5.6.

Corollary 6.10. *Let $n \ge 2$. Suppose that the LCP (1.1) satisfies Condition 5.6. Construct the LCP′ (5.1) with the dimension $n' = 2n$ by using (5.2) and (5.8). Let $(\boldsymbol{x}'^1, \boldsymbol{y}'^1)$ be the initial point given in Lemma 5.1. Let the parameters α_{cen}, α_1, α_{bd}, β_{cen} and β_{bd} satisfy Condition 6.1 and the inequality $f'_{cen}(\boldsymbol{x}'^1, \boldsymbol{y}'^1) \le \alpha_{bd}$. Let $\nu' > 0$ be the potential function parameter associated with the LCP′ as in (5.11). Apply the potential reduction algorithm to the LCP′ with the stopping criterion (5.36). We consider the three cases:*

(A1)′ $0 < \alpha_{cen} \le \alpha_1 < \alpha_{bd} < +\infty$, $\beta_{cen} = \beta_{bd} = 2n/(2n + \nu')$.
(A2)′ $0 < \alpha_{cen} \le \alpha_1 < \alpha_{bd} = +\infty$, $\beta_{cen} = \beta_{bd} = 2n/(2n + \nu')$.
(B) $\alpha_{cen} = \alpha_1 = \alpha_{bd} = +\infty$, $\beta_{cen} = 0$.

Then in the case (A1)′ the algorithm stops in $O(\nu'\eta(2n,\nu')(1+\kappa)L)$ iterations, in the case (A2)′ it stops in $O(\nu'\eta_\infty(2n,\nu')(1+\kappa)L)$ iterations, and in the case (B) it stops $O(\exp\{\eta_0(2n,\nu')(1+\kappa)L\})$ iterations. In any of the cases, from the generated approximate solution $(\hat{\boldsymbol{x}}', \hat{\boldsymbol{y}}')$ of the LCP′, we can compute an exact solution $(\boldsymbol{x}'^*, \boldsymbol{y}'^*)$ of the LCP′ in $O(n^3)$ arithmetic operations. If $x_i'^* = 0$ $(i = n+1, n+2, \ldots, 2n)$ then $(\boldsymbol{x}^*, \boldsymbol{y}^*) = (x_1'^*, x_2'^*, \ldots, x_n'^*, y_1'^*, y_2'^*, \ldots, y_n'^*)$ is a solution of the LCP, and otherwise the LCP does not have any feasible solution.

Proof: The corollary follows from Lemma 5.7, Theorems 5.12, 6.6 and 6.8. ∎

7. Proofs of Convergence Theorems

7.1. Proof of Theorem 6.3

Define

$$\begin{aligned}
B &= \{(\beta,\boldsymbol{x},\boldsymbol{y}) \in [0,1]\times S_{++} : f(\boldsymbol{x},\boldsymbol{y}) \le f(\boldsymbol{x}^1,\boldsymbol{y}^1),\ \boldsymbol{x}^T\boldsymbol{y} \ge \epsilon\},\\
B_{cen} &= \{(\beta,\boldsymbol{x},\boldsymbol{y}) \in B : \beta \in [0,\beta_{cen}],\ f_{cen}(\boldsymbol{x},\boldsymbol{y}) \le \alpha_{cen}\},\\
B_1 &= \{(\beta,\boldsymbol{x},\boldsymbol{y}) \in B : \alpha_{cen} \le f_{cen}(\boldsymbol{x},\boldsymbol{y}) \le \alpha_1\},\\
B_{bd} &= \{(\beta,\boldsymbol{x},\boldsymbol{y}) \in B : \beta \in [\beta_{bd},1],\ \alpha_1 \le f_{cen}(\boldsymbol{x},\boldsymbol{y}) \le \alpha_{bd}\}.
\end{aligned}$$

If $(\boldsymbol{x},\boldsymbol{y}) \in N_{cen}(\alpha_{bd})$, $f(\boldsymbol{x},\boldsymbol{y}) \le f(\boldsymbol{x}^1,\boldsymbol{y}^1)$, $\boldsymbol{x}^T\boldsymbol{y} \ge \epsilon$, and if β is determined in Step 3′, then $(\beta,\boldsymbol{x},\boldsymbol{y}) \in B_{cen} \cup B_1 \cup B_{bd}$. We also see by the definition (4.33) of $g_{cen}(\beta,\boldsymbol{x},\boldsymbol{y})$ in Theorem 4.18 that $g_{cen}(\beta,\boldsymbol{x},\boldsymbol{y})$ is nonnegative for any $(\beta,\boldsymbol{x},\boldsymbol{y}) \in B$. Hence, in view of (6.3), it suffices to show the existence of positive numbers γ_1 and γ_2 such that if $(\beta,\boldsymbol{x},\boldsymbol{y}) \in B_{cen} \cup B_1 \cup B_{bd}$ then

$$\gamma_1 \le g(\nu,\beta,\boldsymbol{x},\boldsymbol{y}), \tag{7.1}$$

$$\gamma_2 \le g_{cen}(\beta,\boldsymbol{x},\boldsymbol{y})^2 + 5(\alpha_{bd} - f_{cen}(\boldsymbol{x},\boldsymbol{y})). \tag{7.2}$$

For this purpose, we first show that all the sets B, B_{cen}, B_1 and B_{bd} are compact. By (iii) of Condition 2.1, the set B' consisting of all the points $(\boldsymbol{x},\boldsymbol{y})$ such that

$$(\boldsymbol{x},\boldsymbol{y}) \in S_{++} \quad \text{and} \quad \boldsymbol{x}^T\boldsymbol{y} \le \exp(f(\boldsymbol{x}^1,\boldsymbol{y}^1)/\nu)$$

is bounded. But we know from the inequality (2.5), i.e.,

$$\nu f_{cp}(\boldsymbol{x},\boldsymbol{y}) = \nu \log \boldsymbol{x}^T\boldsymbol{y} \le f(\boldsymbol{x},\boldsymbol{y}) \quad \text{for every} \quad (\boldsymbol{x},\boldsymbol{y}) \in S_{++}$$

that $(\boldsymbol{x},\boldsymbol{y})$ is contained in the set B' if $(\beta,\boldsymbol{x},\boldsymbol{y}) \in B$. Hence there is a positive number σ such that

$$0 < x_i \le \sigma \ (i \in N) \ \text{and} \ 0 < y_i \le \sigma \ (i \in N) \qquad \text{for every } (\beta,\boldsymbol{x},\boldsymbol{y}) \in B. \tag{7.3}$$

By the definition of the set B, we also see

$$\begin{aligned}
f(\boldsymbol{x},\boldsymbol{y}) &= (n+\nu)\log \boldsymbol{x}^T\boldsymbol{y} - \sum_{i\in N} \log x_i y_i - n\log n \le f(\boldsymbol{x}^1,\boldsymbol{y}^1),\\
\boldsymbol{x}^T\boldsymbol{y} &\ge \epsilon
\end{aligned}$$

for every $(\beta,\boldsymbol{x},\boldsymbol{y}) \in B$. This implies that

$$\sum_{i\in N} \log x_i y_i \ \ge\ -f(\boldsymbol{x}^1,\boldsymbol{y}^1) + (n+\nu)\log\epsilon - n\log n$$

for every $(\beta, \boldsymbol{x}, \boldsymbol{y}) \in B$. The inequality above and the inequality (7.3) ensure the existence of a positive number $\bar{\epsilon}$ such that

$$\bar{\epsilon} \leq x_i \ \ (i \in N) \ \text{ and } \ \bar{\epsilon} \leq y_i \ \ (i \in N) \ \text{ for every } (\beta, \boldsymbol{x}, \boldsymbol{y}) \in B.$$

Thus we have shown that

$$B \subset \{(\beta, \boldsymbol{x}, \boldsymbol{y}) \in [0,1] \times S_{++} : (\boldsymbol{x}, \boldsymbol{y}) \in [\bar{\epsilon}, \sigma]^n\}.$$

Obviously, the set on the right-hand side is compact, and their subsets B, B_{cen}, B_1 and B_{bd} are closed with respect to the set. Therefore all the subsets are compact.

To show the existence of positive numbers γ_1 and γ_2 such that (7.1) and (7.2) hold for every $(\beta, \boldsymbol{x}, \boldsymbol{y}) \in B_{cen} \cup B_1 \cup B_{bd}$, we will evaluate the quantities $\Delta(\beta)$, π and ω, which appeared in the definitions of $g(\nu, \beta, \boldsymbol{x}, \boldsymbol{y})$ and $g_{cp}(\beta, \boldsymbol{x}, \boldsymbol{y})$ (see Theorem 4.18), on the set B. It follows from (4.32) and (4.8) that for every $(\beta, \boldsymbol{x}, \boldsymbol{y}) \in B$

$$\begin{aligned} &\Delta(\beta) \geq 0, \quad \pi > 0, \\ &\omega \geq 0 \ \text{ and } \ \omega = 0 \ \text{ if and only if } \ (\boldsymbol{x}, \boldsymbol{y}) \in S_{cen} \ \textit{i.e.}, \ f_{cen}(\boldsymbol{x}, \boldsymbol{y}) = 0. \end{aligned}$$

Using these inequalities, we can easily verify that

$$\begin{aligned} &g(\nu, \beta, \boldsymbol{x}, \boldsymbol{y}) > 0 \ \text{ for every } (\beta, \boldsymbol{x}, \boldsymbol{y}) \in B_{cen} \cup B_1 \cup B_{bd}, \\ &g_{cen}(\beta, \boldsymbol{x}, \boldsymbol{y})^2 + 5(\alpha_{bd} - f_{cen}(\boldsymbol{x}, \boldsymbol{y})) > 0 \ \text{ for every } (\beta, \boldsymbol{x}, \boldsymbol{y}) \in B_{cen} \cup B_1 \cup B_{bd}. \end{aligned}$$

Since $g(\nu, \beta, \boldsymbol{x}, \boldsymbol{y})$ and $g_{cen}(\beta, \boldsymbol{x}, \boldsymbol{y})^2 + 5(\alpha_{bd} - f_{cen}(\boldsymbol{x}, \boldsymbol{y}))$ are continuous on $B_{cen} \cup B_1 \cup B_{bd}$, there exist positive numbers γ_1 and γ_2 such that the inequalities (7.1) and (7.2) hold for every $(\beta, \boldsymbol{x}, \boldsymbol{y}) \in B_{cen} \cup B_1 \cup B_{bd}$. This completes the proof of Theorem 6.3.

7.2. Proof of Theorem 6.6

If $(\boldsymbol{x}, \boldsymbol{y})$ lies in $N_{cen}(\alpha_{bd})$ and β is determined by Step 3′, then $(\beta, \boldsymbol{x}, \boldsymbol{y})$ belongs to one of the sets

$$\begin{aligned} \tilde{B}_{cen} &= \{(\beta, \boldsymbol{x}, \boldsymbol{y}) \in [0, n/(n+\nu)] \times S_{++} : f_{cen}(\boldsymbol{x}, \boldsymbol{y}) \leq \alpha_{cen}\}, \\ \tilde{B}_1 &= \{(\beta, \boldsymbol{x}, \boldsymbol{y}) \in [0,1] \times S_{++} : \alpha_{cen} \leq f_{cen}(\boldsymbol{x}, \boldsymbol{y}) \leq \alpha_1\}, \\ \tilde{B}_{bd} &= \{(\beta, \boldsymbol{x}, \boldsymbol{y}) \in [n/(n+\nu), 1] \times S_{++} : \alpha_1 \leq f_{cen}(\boldsymbol{x}, \boldsymbol{y}) \leq \alpha_{bd}\}. \end{aligned}$$

For each $(\beta, \boldsymbol{x}, \boldsymbol{y}) \in \tilde{B}_{cen} \cup \tilde{B}_1 \cup \tilde{B}_{bd}$ we make an estimate of the value $\bar{\tau}$ given in Lemma 6.2 according to the inequality (6.8).

We first consider the case that $(\beta, \boldsymbol{x}, \boldsymbol{y}) \in \tilde{B}_{cen}$. By Lemma 6.5, we have

$$\bar{g}(\nu, \beta) \geq \frac{\nu\sqrt{\pi}}{\sqrt{(1+2\kappa)n}}.$$

On the other hand, by (v) of Theorem 4.9, we have

$$\pi \geq \exp(-\alpha_{cen} - 1).$$

Hence, by the definition (6.2) of $\bar{\eta}(n, \nu)$,

$$\begin{aligned}
\bar{\tau} &\geq \min\left\{\frac{1}{2}, \frac{\nu\sqrt{\exp(-\alpha_{cen} - 1)}}{2\bar{\eta}(n,\nu)\sqrt{(1+2\kappa)n}}, \frac{2\sqrt{\alpha_{bd} - \alpha_{cen}}}{\sqrt{5}}\right\} \\
&\geq \left(\min\left\{1, \frac{n}{\nu}\right\}\right)\left(\min\left\{1, \frac{\nu}{\sqrt{n}}\right\}\right)\left(\frac{1}{\sqrt{1+2\kappa}}\right) \\
&\quad \left(\min\left\{\frac{\sqrt{\exp(-\alpha_{cen} - 1)}}{2}, \frac{2\sqrt{\alpha_{bd} - \alpha_{cen}}}{\sqrt{5}}\right\}\right) \quad \text{if } (\beta, \boldsymbol{x}, \boldsymbol{y}) \in \tilde{B}_{cen}. \qquad (7.4)
\end{aligned}$$

Second we consider the case $(\beta, \boldsymbol{x}, \boldsymbol{y}) \in \tilde{B}_1$. By Lemma 6.5, we have that

$$\bar{g}(\nu, \beta) \geq \min\left\{\frac{\nu\sqrt{\pi}}{\sqrt{(1+2\kappa)n}}, \frac{\omega}{\sqrt{1+2\kappa}}\right\}.$$

By (v) and (vi) of Theorem 4.9, we also see that

$$\pi \geq \exp(-\alpha_1 - 1) \text{ and } \omega \geq \bar{\omega}(\alpha_{cen})$$

since the function $\bar{\omega}$ defined in Theorem 4.9 or (6.9) is monotone increasing. Hence

$$\begin{aligned}
\bar{\tau} &\geq \min\left\{\frac{1}{2}, \frac{\nu\sqrt{\exp(-\alpha_1 - 1)}}{2\bar{\eta}(n,\nu)\sqrt{(1+2\kappa)n}}, \frac{\bar{\omega}(\alpha_{cen})}{2\bar{\eta}(n,\nu)\sqrt{1+2\kappa}}, \frac{2\sqrt{\alpha_{bd} - \alpha_1}}{\sqrt{5}}\right\} \\
&\geq \left(\min\left\{1, \frac{n}{\nu}\right\}\right)\left(\min\left\{1, \frac{\nu}{\sqrt{n}}\right\}\right)\left(\frac{1}{\sqrt{1+2\kappa}}\right) \\
&\quad \left(\min\left\{\frac{\sqrt{\exp(-\alpha_1 - 1)}}{2}, \frac{\bar{\omega}(\alpha_{cen})}{2}, \frac{2\sqrt{\alpha_{bd} - \alpha_1}}{\sqrt{5}}\right\}\right) \quad \text{if } (\beta, \boldsymbol{x}, \boldsymbol{y}) \in \tilde{B}_1. \qquad (7.5)
\end{aligned}$$

Now we consider the case $(\beta, \boldsymbol{x}, \boldsymbol{y}) \in \tilde{B}_{bd}$. By Lemma 6.5, we have that

$$\begin{aligned}
\bar{g}(\nu, \beta) &\geq \frac{\omega}{\sqrt{1+2\kappa}}, \\
\bar{g}_{cen}(\beta) &\geq \bar{g}_{cen}\left(\frac{n}{n+\nu}\right) \\
&= \frac{\omega^2}{\sqrt{(1+2\kappa)\{(\nu^2/n)\pi + \omega^2\}}} \\
&\geq \frac{\omega^2}{\sqrt{(1+2\kappa)(\nu^2/n + \omega^2)}}. \qquad (7.6)
\end{aligned}$$

By (vi) of Theorem 4.9, we also have that $\omega \geq \bar{\omega}(\alpha_1)$. Since the right-hand side of the last inequality in (7.6) is monotone increasing with respect to ω, we see that

$$\bar{g}_{cen}(\beta) \;\geq\; \frac{\bar{\omega}(\alpha_1)^2}{\sqrt{(1+2\kappa)(\nu^2/n+\bar{\omega}(\alpha_1)^2)}}.$$

If $\alpha_{bd} < +\infty$ then

$$\begin{aligned}
&\frac{\bar{g}_{cen}(\beta)+\sqrt{\bar{g}_{cen}(\beta)^2+5(\alpha_{bd}-f_{cen}(\boldsymbol{x},\boldsymbol{y}))}}{(5/2)} \\
&\geq \frac{4\bar{g}_{cen}(\beta)}{5} \\
&\geq \frac{4\bar{\omega}(\alpha_1)^2}{5\sqrt{(1+2\kappa)(\nu^2/n+\bar{\omega}(\alpha_1)^2)}} \\
&\geq \left(\min\left\{1,\frac{\sqrt{n}}{\nu}\right\}\right)\left(\frac{4\bar{\omega}(\alpha_1)^2}{5\sqrt{(1+2\kappa)(1+\bar{\omega}(\alpha_1)^2)}}\right)
\end{aligned}$$

and otherwise

$$\frac{\bar{g}_{cen}(\beta)+\sqrt{\bar{g}_{cen}(\beta)^2+5(\alpha_{bd}-f_{cen}(\boldsymbol{x},\boldsymbol{y}))}}{(5/2)} = +\infty.$$

We see from (6.9) that $0 < \bar{\omega}(\alpha) \leq 1/2$ for every $\alpha > 0$. Hence if $\alpha_{bd} < +\infty$ then

$$\begin{aligned}
\bar{\tau} &\geq \min\left\{\frac{1}{2},\frac{\bar{\omega}(\alpha_1)}{2\bar{\eta}(n,\nu)\sqrt{1+2\kappa}},\left(\min\left\{1,\frac{\sqrt{n}}{\nu}\right\}\right)\left(\frac{4\bar{\omega}(\alpha_1)^2}{5\sqrt{(1+2\kappa)(1+\bar{\omega}(\alpha_1)^2)}}\right)\right\} \\
&\geq \left(\min\left\{1,\frac{n}{\nu},\frac{\sqrt{n}}{\nu}\right\}\right)\left(\frac{1}{\sqrt{1+2\kappa}}\right)\left(\min\left\{\frac{1}{2},\frac{\bar{\omega}(\alpha_1)}{2},\frac{4\bar{\omega}(\alpha_1)^2}{5\sqrt{1+\bar{\omega}(\alpha_1)^2}}\right\}\right) \\
&= \left(\min\left\{1,\frac{\sqrt{n}}{\nu}\right\}\right)\left(\frac{1}{\sqrt{1+2\kappa}}\right)\left(\min\left\{\frac{\bar{\omega}(\alpha_1)}{2},\frac{4\bar{\omega}(\alpha_1)^2}{5\sqrt{1+\bar{\omega}(\alpha_1)^2}}\right\}\right)
\end{aligned}$$

and otherwise

$$\begin{aligned}
\bar{\tau} &\geq \min\left\{\frac{1}{2},\frac{\bar{\omega}(\alpha_1)}{2\bar{\eta}(n,\nu)\sqrt{1+2\kappa}}\right\} \\
&= \left(\min\left\{1,\frac{n}{\nu}\right\}\right)\left(\frac{1}{\sqrt{1+2\kappa}}\right)\left(\frac{\bar{\omega}(\alpha_1)}{2}\right).
\end{aligned}$$

Therefore we obtain

$$\bar{\tau} \geq \left(\min\left\{1,\frac{\sqrt{n}}{\nu}\right\}\right)\left(\frac{1}{\sqrt{1+2\kappa}}\right)\left(\min\left\{\frac{\bar{\omega}(\alpha_1)}{2},\frac{4\bar{\omega}(\alpha_1)^2}{5\sqrt{1+\bar{\omega}(\alpha_1)^2}}\right\}\right)$$

$$\text{if } \alpha_{bd} < \infty \text{ and } (\beta,\boldsymbol{x},\boldsymbol{y}) \in \tilde{B}_{bd}, \qquad (7.7)$$

$$\bar{\tau} \geq \left(\min\left\{1,\frac{n}{\nu}\right\}\right)\left(\frac{1}{\sqrt{1+2\kappa}}\right)\left(\frac{\bar{\omega}(\alpha_1)}{2}\right)$$

$$\text{if } \alpha_{bd} = \infty \text{ and } (\beta,\boldsymbol{x},\boldsymbol{y}) \in \tilde{B}_{bd}. \qquad (7.8)$$

Taking account of all the inequalities (7.4), (7.5), (7.7), (7.8) and the choice of θ in Step 4′, we obtain that if $\alpha_{bd} < +\infty$ and $(\beta, \boldsymbol{x}, \boldsymbol{y}) \in \tilde{B}_{cen} \cup \tilde{B}_1 \cup \tilde{B}_{bd}$ then

$$\begin{aligned}
\bar{\tau} &\geq \left(\min\left\{1, \frac{\sqrt{n}}{\nu}\right\}\right) \left(\min\left\{1, \frac{\nu}{\sqrt{n}}\right\}\right) \left(\frac{1}{\sqrt{1+2\kappa}}\right) \\
&\quad \left(\min\left\{\frac{\sqrt{\exp(-\alpha_1 - 1)}}{2}, \frac{\bar{\omega}(\alpha_{cen})}{2}, \frac{2\sqrt{\alpha_{bd} - \alpha_1}}{\sqrt{5}}, \frac{4\bar{\omega}(\alpha_1)^2}{5\sqrt{1+\bar{\omega}(\alpha_1)^2}}\right\}\right), \\
\frac{\bar{\eta}(n,\nu)\bar{\tau}^2}{2} &\geq \left(\max\left\{1, \frac{\nu}{n}\right\}\right) \left(\min\left\{1, \frac{n}{\nu^2}\right\}\right) \left(\min\left\{1, \frac{\nu^2}{n}\right\}\right) \left(\frac{1}{2(1+2\kappa)}\right) \\
&\quad \left(\min\left\{\frac{\exp(-\alpha_1 - 1)}{4}, \frac{\bar{\omega}(\alpha_{cen})^2}{4}, \frac{4(\alpha_{bd} - \alpha_1)}{5}, \frac{16\bar{\omega}(\alpha_1)^4}{25(1+\bar{\omega}(\alpha_1)^2)}\right\}\right) \\
&= \frac{\psi(\alpha_{cen}, \alpha_1, \alpha_{bd})}{2\eta(n,\nu)(1+2\kappa)}, \\
f(\bar{\boldsymbol{x}}, \bar{\boldsymbol{y}}) &\leq f(\boldsymbol{x}, \boldsymbol{y}) - \frac{\psi(\alpha_{cen}, \alpha_1, \alpha_{bd})}{2\eta(n,\nu)(1+2\kappa)},
\end{aligned}$$

and that if $\alpha_{bd} = +\infty$ and $(\beta, \boldsymbol{x}, \boldsymbol{y}) \in \tilde{B}_{cen} \cup \tilde{B}_1 \cup \tilde{B}_{bd}$ then

$$\begin{aligned}
\bar{\tau} &\geq \left(\min\left\{1, \frac{n}{\nu}\right\}\right) \left(\min\left\{1, \frac{\nu}{\sqrt{n}}\right\}\right) \left(\frac{1}{\sqrt{1+2\kappa}}\right) \\
&\quad \left(\min\left\{\frac{\sqrt{\exp(-\alpha_1 - 1)}}{2}, \frac{\bar{\omega}(\alpha_{cen})}{2}\right\}\right), \\
\frac{\bar{\eta}(n,\nu)\bar{\tau}^2}{2} &\geq \left(\min\left\{1, \frac{n}{\nu}\right\}\right) \left(\min\left\{1, \frac{\nu^2}{n}\right\}\right) \left(\frac{1}{2(1+2\kappa)}\right) \\
&\quad \left(\min\left\{\frac{\exp(-\alpha_1 - 1)}{4}, \frac{\bar{\omega}(\alpha_{cen})^2}{4}\right\}\right) \\
&= \frac{\psi_\infty(\alpha_{cen}, \alpha_1)}{2\eta_\infty(n,\nu)(1+2\kappa)}, \\
f(\bar{\boldsymbol{x}}, \bar{\boldsymbol{y}}) &\leq f(\boldsymbol{x}, \boldsymbol{y}) - \frac{\psi_\infty(\alpha_{cen}, \alpha_1)}{2\eta_\infty(n,\nu)(1+2\kappa)}.
\end{aligned}$$

This completes the proof of Theorem 6.6.

7.3. Proof of Theorem 6.8

We need a series of lemmas to prove Theorem 6.8. Let

$$\phi(n,\nu) = \min\left\{1, \frac{\nu^2}{n}\right\} \text{ and } \bar{\eta}(n,\nu) = \max\left\{1, \frac{\nu}{n}\right\}.$$

Lemma 7.1. *Suppose that $M \in P_*(\kappa)$ for some $\kappa \geq 0$. Let $\nu > 0$, $(x, y) \in S_{++}$, $\beta = 0$, and let (dx, dy) be the solution of the system (2.8) of Newton equations.*

(i) *Assume that*

$$0 \leq \theta \leq \frac{v_{min}}{2(1+2\kappa)\|h(0)\|} = \frac{\sqrt{\pi}}{2(1+2\kappa)\sqrt{n}}. \tag{7.9}$$

Then the new point $(\bar{x}, \bar{y}) = (x, y) + \theta(dx, dy)$ satisfies

$$\begin{aligned} (\bar{x}, \bar{y}) &\in S_{++}, \\ f(\bar{x}, \bar{y}) &\geq f(x, y) - \frac{5\nu\theta}{\sqrt{\phi(n, \nu)}}. \end{aligned}$$

(ii) *Let $\theta \geq 0$ be such that*

$$(\bar{x}, \bar{y}) = (x, y) + \theta(dx, dy) \in S_{++}.$$

Then

$$f_{cp}(\bar{x}, \bar{y}) \leq f_{cp}(x, y) - \theta.$$

Proof: Since (dx, dy) satisfies the system (2.8) of Newton equations with $\beta = 0$, we have

$$Y dx + X dy = -Xy.$$

This implies that

$$y^T dx + x^T dy = -x^T y \text{ and } X^{-1} dx + Y^{-1} dy = -e. \tag{7.10}$$

(i) Since we see from (7.9) and Lemma 4.19 that

$$\theta \leq \frac{v_{min}\tau}{\sqrt{1 + 2\Delta(\beta)}\|h(\beta)\|}$$

where $\tau = 1/2$ and $\beta = 0$, the relation $(\bar{x}, \bar{y}) \in S_{++}$ follows from Theorem 4.18. By $\|h(0)\|^2 = \|v\|^2 = x^T y$, the definition (4.32) of $\Delta(\beta)$ in Theorem 4.18 and Lemma 4.19, we also have

$$-\frac{dx^T dy}{x^T y} = -\frac{dx^T dy}{\|h(0)\|^2} \leq \Delta(0) \leq \kappa. \tag{7.11}$$

It is easily verified from the assumption (7.9) that

$$\kappa\theta \leq \frac{1}{4\sqrt{n}},$$

$$1 + \kappa\theta \leq \frac{5}{4},$$

$$1 - (\theta + \kappa\theta^2) > \frac{3}{8}, \tag{7.12}$$

$$\kappa\theta + \frac{(1+\kappa\theta)^2\theta}{2\{1 - (\theta + \kappa\theta^2)\}} \leq \frac{2}{\sqrt{n}}. \tag{7.13}$$

Hence

$$\begin{aligned} f_{cp}(\bar{\boldsymbol{x}},\bar{\boldsymbol{y}}) - f_{cp}(\boldsymbol{x},\boldsymbol{y}) &= f_{cp}(\boldsymbol{x}+\theta d\boldsymbol{x}, \boldsymbol{y}+\theta d\boldsymbol{y}) - f_{cp}(\boldsymbol{x},\boldsymbol{y}) \\ &= \log\left(\boldsymbol{x}^T\boldsymbol{y} + \theta(\boldsymbol{y}^T d\boldsymbol{x} + \boldsymbol{x}^T d\boldsymbol{y}) + \theta^2 d\boldsymbol{x}^T d\boldsymbol{y}\right) - \log \boldsymbol{x}^T\boldsymbol{y} \\ &= \log\left\{1 + \frac{\theta(\boldsymbol{y}^T d\boldsymbol{x} + \boldsymbol{x}^T d\boldsymbol{y})}{\boldsymbol{x}^T\boldsymbol{y}} + \frac{\theta^2 d\boldsymbol{x}^T d\boldsymbol{y}}{\boldsymbol{x}^T\boldsymbol{y}}\right\} \\ &\geq \log\{1 - (\theta + \kappa\theta^2)\} \quad \text{(by (7.10) and (7.11))} \\ &\geq -\theta - \kappa\theta^2 - \frac{(1+\kappa\theta)^2\theta^2}{2\{1-(\theta+\kappa\theta^2)\}} \\ &\qquad \text{(by (7.12) and (ii) of Lemma 4.10)} \\ &\geq -\left(1 + \frac{2}{\sqrt{n}}\right)\theta \quad \text{(by (7.13))}, \end{aligned}$$

and

$$\begin{aligned} & f_{cen}(\bar{\boldsymbol{x}},\bar{\boldsymbol{y}}) - f_{cen}(\boldsymbol{x},\boldsymbol{y}) \\ = \ & f_{cen}(\boldsymbol{x}+\theta d\boldsymbol{x}, \boldsymbol{y}+\theta d\boldsymbol{y}) - f_{cen}(\boldsymbol{x},\boldsymbol{y}) \\ = \ & n(f_{cp}(\bar{\boldsymbol{x}},\bar{\boldsymbol{y}}) - f_{cp}(\boldsymbol{x},\boldsymbol{y})) \\ & - \sum_{i=1}^n \{\log(x_i + \theta dx_i) + \log(y_i + \theta dy_i)\} + \sum_{i=1}^n (\log x_i + \log y_i) \\ = \ & n(f_{cp}(\bar{\boldsymbol{x}},\bar{\boldsymbol{y}}) - f_{cp}(\boldsymbol{x},\boldsymbol{y})) - \sum_{i=1}^n \left\{\log\left(1 + \frac{\theta dx_i}{x_i}\right) + \log\left(1 + \frac{\theta dy_i}{y_i}\right)\right\} \\ \geq \ & n(f_{cp}(\bar{\boldsymbol{x}},\bar{\boldsymbol{y}}) - f_{cp}(\boldsymbol{x},\boldsymbol{y})) - \sum_{i=1}^n \left(\frac{\theta dx_i}{x_i} + \frac{\theta dy_i}{y_i}\right) \quad \text{(by (i) of Lemma 4.10)} \\ = \ & n(f_{cp}(\bar{\boldsymbol{x}},\bar{\boldsymbol{y}}) - f_{cp}(\boldsymbol{x},\boldsymbol{y})) + n\theta \quad \text{(by (7.10))}. \end{aligned}$$

Therefore we obtain

$$\begin{aligned} f(\bar{\boldsymbol{x}},\bar{\boldsymbol{y}}) - f(\boldsymbol{x},\boldsymbol{y}) &= \nu(f_{cp}(\bar{\boldsymbol{x}},\bar{\boldsymbol{y}}) - f_{cp}(\boldsymbol{x},\boldsymbol{y})) + (f_{cen}(\bar{\boldsymbol{x}},\bar{\boldsymbol{y}}) - f_{cen}(\boldsymbol{x},\boldsymbol{y})) \\ &\geq (\nu+n)(f_{cp}(\bar{\boldsymbol{x}},\bar{\boldsymbol{y}}) - f_{cp}(\boldsymbol{x},\boldsymbol{y})) + n\theta \\ &\geq -(\nu+n)\left(1 + \frac{2}{\sqrt{n}}\right)\theta + n\theta \\ &= -\nu\left(1 + \frac{2}{\sqrt{n}} + \frac{2\sqrt{n}}{\nu}\right)\theta \\ &\geq -\frac{5\nu\theta}{\sqrt{\phi(n,\nu)}} \\ &\qquad \left(\text{since } \frac{1}{\sqrt{n}} \leq 1 \leq \frac{1}{\sqrt{\phi(n,\nu)}} \text{ and } \frac{\sqrt{n}}{\nu} \leq \frac{1}{\sqrt{\phi(n,\nu)}}\right). \end{aligned}$$

(ii) By the definition (4.26) of $\boldsymbol{h}(\beta)$ and Lemma 4.20, we see that $d\boldsymbol{x}^T d\boldsymbol{y} \leq \|\boldsymbol{h}(0)\|^2/4 = \boldsymbol{x}^T\boldsymbol{y}/4$. Hence it follows from (7.10) that

$$f_{cp}(\bar{\boldsymbol{x}},\bar{\boldsymbol{y}}) - f_{cp}(\boldsymbol{x},\boldsymbol{y}) = f_{cp}(\boldsymbol{x}+\theta d\boldsymbol{x}, \boldsymbol{y}+\theta d\boldsymbol{y}) - f_{cp}(\boldsymbol{x},\boldsymbol{y})$$

$$
\begin{aligned}
&= \log\left\{x^T y + \theta(y^T dx + x^T dy) + \theta^2 dx^T dy\right\} - \log x^T y \\
&= \log\left\{1 + \frac{\theta(y^T dx + x^T dy)}{x^T y} + \frac{\theta^2 dx^T dy}{x^T y}\right\} \\
&\leq \log\left(1 - \theta + \frac{\theta^2}{4}\right) \\
&= 2\log\left(1 - \frac{\theta}{2}\right) \\
&\leq -\theta.
\end{aligned}
$$

∎

Lemma 7.2. *Suppose that $M \in P_*(\kappa)$ for some $\kappa \geq 0$. Let $\nu > 0$, $(x, y) \in S_{++}$ and assume the case (B) (i.e., $\alpha_{cen} = \alpha_1 = \alpha_{bd} = +\infty$ and $\beta_{cen} = 0$). Define*

$$\tilde{\theta} = \frac{\phi(n,\nu)^{3/2}\pi}{40\nu\bar{\eta}(n,\nu)(1+2\kappa)}.$$

Then the new point $(\bar{x}, \bar{y}) = (x, y) + \theta(dx, dy) \in S_{++}$ determined by Step 4′ satisfies

$$f(\bar{x}, \bar{y}) \leq f(x, y) - \frac{\phi(\nu, n)\pi}{8\bar{\eta}(n,\nu)(1+2\kappa)}, \tag{7.14}$$

$$\theta \geq \tilde{\theta},$$

$$f_{cp}(\bar{x}, \bar{y}) \leq f_{cp}(x, y) - \tilde{\theta}.$$

Proof: In view of the choice of θ in Step 4′, the inequality (6.8), $\alpha_{bd} = +\infty$ and $\beta = 0$, we have

$$
\begin{aligned}
f(\bar{x}, \bar{y}) &\leq f(x, y) - \frac{1}{2}\bar{\eta}(n,\nu)\left(\min\left\{\frac{1}{4}, \frac{\bar{g}(\nu,0)^2}{4\bar{\eta}(n,\nu)^2}\right\}\right) \\
&= f(x, y) - \frac{1}{2}\bar{\eta}(n,\nu)\left(\min\left\{\frac{1}{4}, \frac{(\nu^2/n)\pi}{4\bar{\eta}(n,\nu)^2(1+2\kappa)}\right\}\right) \\
&\leq f(x, y) - \frac{1}{2}\bar{\eta}(n,\nu)\left\{\frac{\phi(n,\nu)\pi}{4\bar{\eta}(n,\nu)^2(1+2\kappa)}\right\} \\
&= f(x, y) - \frac{\phi(n,\nu)\pi}{8\bar{\eta}(n,\nu)(1+2\kappa)}.
\end{aligned}
$$

Hence we have shown the first inequality (7.14) of the lemma. By a simple calculation, we have

$$
\begin{aligned}
\tilde{\theta} &\leq \frac{\phi(n,\nu)\sqrt{\pi}}{40\nu\bar{\eta}(n,\nu)(1+2\kappa)} \\
&= \frac{\min\{1, \nu^2/n\}\sqrt{\pi}}{40\nu\max\{1, \nu/n\}(1+2\kappa)} \\
&\leq \frac{\sqrt{\pi}}{2(1+2\kappa)\sqrt{n}}.
\end{aligned}
$$

If $\theta < \tilde{\theta}$, we would have, by Lemma 7.1,

$$\begin{aligned} f(\bar{x},\bar{y}) &> f(x,y) - \frac{5\nu}{\sqrt{\phi(n,\nu)}} \frac{\phi(n,\nu)^{3/2}\pi}{40\nu\bar{\eta}(n,\nu)(1+2\kappa)} \\ &= f(x,y) - \frac{\phi(n,\nu)\pi}{8\bar{\eta}(n,\nu)(1+2\kappa)}. \end{aligned}$$

This contradicts the inequality (7.14). Thus we have shown the second inequality of the lemma. The last inequality of the lemma also follows from Lemma 7.1. ∎

Lemma 7.3. *Let $\gamma \in (0, 0.6]$. Suppose that a sequence $\{a^k\}$ of real numbers satisfies*

$$a^{k+1} - a^k \le -\gamma \exp(a^k - a^1) \quad (k = 1, 2, \ldots).$$

Then

$$a^k - a^1 \le -\gamma \log k \quad (k = 1, 2, \ldots). \tag{7.15}$$

Proof: We show the inequality (7.15) by induction. The inequality (7.15) holds when $k = 1$ or $k = 2$ because

$$\begin{aligned} a^1 - a^1 &= -\gamma \log 1, \\ a^2 - a^1 &\le -\gamma \exp(a^1 - a^1) \le -\gamma \log 2. \end{aligned}$$

Assume that (7.15) holds for some $k = p \ge 2$. If $a^p - a^1 \le -\gamma \log(p+1)$ then

$$\begin{aligned} a^{p+1} - a^1 &= (a^{p+1} - a^p) + (a^p - a^1) \\ &\le -\gamma \exp(a^p - a^1) - \gamma \log(p+1) \\ &< -\gamma \log(p+1) \end{aligned}$$

since $-\gamma \exp(a^p - a^1) < 0$. Otherwise, $a^p - a^1 > -\gamma \log(p+1)$. It follows that

$$\begin{aligned} a^{p+1} - a^1 &= (a^{p+1} - a^p) + (a^p - a^1) \\ &\le -\gamma \exp(-\gamma \log(p+1)) - \gamma \log p \\ &< -\gamma \exp(-\log p) - \gamma \log p \\ &\quad \text{(since } p \ge 2 \text{ and } \gamma \in (0, 0.6]) \\ &= -\gamma \left(\frac{1}{p} + \log p \right) \\ &\le -\gamma \log(p+1). \end{aligned}$$

Here the last inequality follows from

$$\log(p+1) - \log p = \log\left(1 + \frac{1}{p}\right) \le \frac{1}{p}.$$

Thus we have shown the inequality (7.15) for $k = p + 1$. ∎

Now we are ready to prove Theorem 6.8. It follows from $f(\mathbf{x}^k, \mathbf{y}^k) \le f(\mathbf{x}^1, \mathbf{y}^1)$ that

$$-f_{cen}(\mathbf{x}^k, \mathbf{y}^k) \ge \nu f_{cp}(\mathbf{x}^k, \mathbf{y}^k) - \nu f_{cp}(\mathbf{x}^1, \mathbf{y}^1) - f_{cen}(\mathbf{x}^1, \mathbf{y}^1) \quad (k = 1, 2, \ldots).$$

Hence, by (v) of Theorem 4.9, we have for $k = 1, 2, \ldots,$

$$\begin{aligned} \pi(\mathbf{x}^k, \mathbf{y}^k) &\ge \exp(-f_{cen}(\mathbf{x}^k, \mathbf{y}^k) - 1) \\ &\ge \exp(\nu f_{cp}(\mathbf{x}^k, \mathbf{y}^k) - \nu f_{cp}(\mathbf{x}^1, \mathbf{y}^1) - f_{cen}(\mathbf{x}^1, \mathbf{y}^1) - 1) \\ &= \exp(-f_{cen}(\mathbf{x}^1, \mathbf{y}^1) - 1) \exp(\nu f_{cp}(\mathbf{x}^k, \mathbf{y}^k) - \nu f_{cp}(\mathbf{x}^1, \mathbf{y}^1)). \end{aligned}$$

Let

$$\gamma = \frac{\phi(\nu, n)^{3/2} \exp(-f_{cen}(\mathbf{x}^1, \mathbf{y}^1) - 1)}{40\bar{\eta}(n, \nu)(1 + 2\kappa)}.$$

Applying Lemma 7.2 to the pair of $(\mathbf{x}, \mathbf{y}) = (\mathbf{x}^k, \mathbf{y}^k)$ and $(\bar{\mathbf{x}}, \bar{\mathbf{y}}) = (\mathbf{x}^{k+1}, \mathbf{y}^{k+1})$, we obtain

$$\begin{aligned} \nu f_{cp}(\mathbf{x}^{k+1}, \mathbf{y}^{k+1}) - \nu f_{cp}(\mathbf{x}^k, \mathbf{y}^k) &\le -\frac{\phi(n, \nu)^{3/2} \pi(\mathbf{x}^k, \mathbf{y}^k)}{40\bar{\eta}(n, \nu)(1 + 2\kappa)} \\ &\le -\gamma \exp(\nu f_{cp}(\mathbf{x}^k, \mathbf{y}^k) - \nu f_{cp}(\mathbf{x}^1, \mathbf{y}^1)). \end{aligned}$$

Obviously, $0 < \gamma \le 1/40$. Hence, applying Lemma 7.3 to the sequence $\{a^k = \nu f_{cp}(\mathbf{x}^k, \mathbf{y}^k)\}$, we obtain for $k = 1, 2, \ldots,$

$$\begin{aligned} \nu f_{cp}(\mathbf{x}^k, \mathbf{y}^k) - \nu f_{cp}(\mathbf{x}^1, \mathbf{y}^1) &\le -\frac{\phi(\nu, n)^{3/2} \exp(-f_{cen}(\mathbf{x}^1, \mathbf{y}^1) - 1)}{40\bar{\eta}(n, \nu)(1 + 2\kappa)} \log k, \\ f_{cp}(\mathbf{x}^k, \mathbf{y}^k) - f_{cp}(\mathbf{x}^1, \mathbf{y}^1) &\le -\frac{\phi(\nu, n)^{3/2} \exp(-f_{cen}(\mathbf{x}^1, \mathbf{y}^1) - 1)}{40\nu\bar{\eta}(n, \nu)(1 + 2\kappa)} \log k \\ &= -\left\{\frac{\exp(-f_{cen}(\mathbf{x}^1, \mathbf{y}^1) - 1)}{40(1 + 2\kappa)}\right\} \left\{\frac{(\min\{1, \nu^2/n\})^{3/2}}{\nu \max\{1, \nu/n\}}\right\} \log k \\ &= -\frac{\exp(-f_{cen}(\mathbf{x}^1, \mathbf{y}^1) - 1)}{40\eta_0(n, \nu)(1 + 2\kappa)} \log k. \end{aligned}$$

This completes the proof of Theorem 6.8.

Appendix: List of Symbols

R^n: the n-dimensional Euclidean space.
$R^n_+ = \{x \in R^n : x \geq 0\}$: the nonnegative orthant of R^n.
$R^n_{++} = \{x \in R^n : x > 0\}$: the positive orthant of R^n.
e: the n-dimensional vector of ones.
$N = \{1, 2, \ldots, n\}$.

I: the identity matrix.
O: the zero matrix.
$X = \text{diag } x$: the $n \times n$ diagonal matrix with the coordinates of a vector $x \in R^n$.
$Y = \text{diag } y$: the $n \times n$ diagonal matrix with the coordinates of a vector $y \in R^n$.

$S_+ = \{(x, y) \in R^{2n}_+ : y = Mx + q\}$: the feasible region of the LCP.
$S_{++} = \{(x, y) \in R^{2n}_{++} : y = Mx + q\}$: the interior of the feasible region of the LCP.
$S_{cp} = \{(x, y) \in S_+ : x_i y_i = 0 \ (i \in N)\}$: the solution set of the LCP.
$S^t_+ = \{(x, y) \in S_+ : x^T y \leq t\}$.
$S_{cen} = \{(x, y) \in S_{++} : Xy = te \text{ for some } t > 0\}$: the path of centers.

For every $\alpha \geq 0$:
$N_{cen}(\alpha) = \{(x, y) \in S_{++} : f_{cen}(x, y) \leq \alpha\}$,
$N_{\chi}(\alpha) = \{(x, y) \in S_{++} : \chi(x, y) \leq \alpha\}$,
$N_{\omega}(\alpha) = \{(x, y) \in S_{++} : \omega(x, y) \leq \alpha\}$,
$N_{\pi}(\alpha) = \{(x, y) \in S_{++} : 1 - \pi(x, y) \leq \alpha\}$.

SS: the class of skew-symmetric matrices, i.e., matrices M satisfying $\xi^T M \xi = 0$ for every $\xi \in R^n$.
PSD: the class of positive semi-definite matrices, i.e., matrices M satisfying $\xi^T M \xi \geq 0$ for every $\xi \in R^n$.
P: the class of matrices with all the principal minors positive.
$P_*(\kappa)$: the class of matrices M satisfying

$$(1 + 4\kappa) \sum_{i \in I_+(\xi)} \xi_i [M\xi]_i + \sum_{i \in I_-(\xi)} \xi_i [M\xi]_i \geq 0 \quad \text{for every } \xi \in R^n,$$

where $[M\xi]_i$ denotes the i-th component of the vector $M\xi$,

$$I_+(\xi) = \{i \in N : \xi_i [M\xi]_i > 0\}, \quad I_-(\xi) = \{i \in N : \xi_i [M\xi]_i < 0\},$$

and κ is a nonnegative number.

P_*: the union of all the $P_*(\kappa)$ $(\kappa \geq 0)$.
CS: the class of column sufficient matrices, i.e., matrices $\boldsymbol{M}$ such that $\xi_i[\boldsymbol{M\xi}]_i \leq 0$ $(i \in N)$ always implies $\xi_i[\boldsymbol{M\xi}]_i = 0$ $(i \in N)$.
P_0: the class of matrices with all the principal minors nonnegative.

$\lambda_{min}(\boldsymbol{M}) = \min_{\|\xi\|=1} \boldsymbol{\xi}^T\boldsymbol{M}\boldsymbol{\xi}$ for every matrix $\boldsymbol{M}$.

$\gamma(\boldsymbol{M}) = \min_{\|\xi\|=1} \max_{i \in N} \xi_i[\boldsymbol{M\xi}]_i$ for every $n \times n$ matrix $\boldsymbol{M}$.

$\bar{\gamma}(\boldsymbol{M}) = \sqrt{\gamma(\boldsymbol{M})\gamma(\boldsymbol{M}^{-1})}$ for every P-matrix $\boldsymbol{M}$.

For every $(\boldsymbol{x}, \boldsymbol{y}) \in S_{++}$:

$$f(\boldsymbol{x}, \boldsymbol{y}) = (n + \nu) \log \boldsymbol{x}^T\boldsymbol{y} - \sum_{i=1}^{n} \log x_i y_i - n \log n$$
$$= \nu f_{cp}(\boldsymbol{x}, \boldsymbol{y}) + f_{cen}(\boldsymbol{x}, \boldsymbol{y}): \text{ the potential function,}$$
$$f_{cp}(\boldsymbol{x}, \boldsymbol{y}) = \log \boldsymbol{x}^T\boldsymbol{y},$$
$$f_{cen}(\boldsymbol{x}, \boldsymbol{y}) = n \log \boldsymbol{x}^T\boldsymbol{y} - \sum_{i=1}^{n} \log x_i y_i - n \log n.$$

For every $(\boldsymbol{x}, \boldsymbol{y}) \in R^{2n}_{++}$:

$$\boldsymbol{u} = \boldsymbol{u}(\boldsymbol{x}, \boldsymbol{y}) = (x_1y_1, x_2y_2, \ldots, x_ny_n)^T,$$
$$\boldsymbol{v} = \boldsymbol{v}(\boldsymbol{x}, \boldsymbol{y}) = (\sqrt{x_1y_1}, \sqrt{x_2y_2}, \ldots, \sqrt{x_ny_n})^T,$$
$$\boldsymbol{V} = \boldsymbol{V}(\boldsymbol{x}, \boldsymbol{y}) = \text{diag } \boldsymbol{v}(\boldsymbol{x}, \boldsymbol{y}),$$
$$v_{min} = v_{min}(\boldsymbol{x}, \boldsymbol{y}) = \min_{i \in N} \sqrt{x_iy_i} = \min_{i \in N} v_i(\boldsymbol{x}, \boldsymbol{y}),$$
$$\mu = \mu(\boldsymbol{x}, \boldsymbol{y}) = \frac{\boldsymbol{x}^T\boldsymbol{y}}{n} = \frac{\|\boldsymbol{v}(\boldsymbol{x}, \boldsymbol{y})\|^2}{n},$$
$$\chi = \chi(\boldsymbol{x}, \boldsymbol{y}) = \left\| \frac{\boldsymbol{u}(\boldsymbol{x}, \boldsymbol{y})}{\mu(\boldsymbol{x}, \boldsymbol{y})} - \boldsymbol{e} \right\|,$$
$$\omega = \omega(\boldsymbol{x}, \boldsymbol{y}) = v_{min}(\boldsymbol{x}, \boldsymbol{y}) \left\| \frac{\boldsymbol{v}(\boldsymbol{x}, \boldsymbol{y})}{\mu(\boldsymbol{x}, \boldsymbol{y})} - \boldsymbol{V}(\boldsymbol{x}, \boldsymbol{y})^{-1}\boldsymbol{e} \right\|$$
$$= v_{min}(\boldsymbol{x}, \boldsymbol{y}) \left\| \frac{n\boldsymbol{v}(\boldsymbol{x}, \boldsymbol{y})}{\|\boldsymbol{v}(\boldsymbol{x}, \boldsymbol{y})\|^2} - \boldsymbol{V}(\boldsymbol{x}, \boldsymbol{y})^{-1}\boldsymbol{e} \right\|,$$
$$\pi = \pi(\boldsymbol{x}, \boldsymbol{y}) = \frac{v_{min}(\boldsymbol{x}, \boldsymbol{y})^2}{\mu(\boldsymbol{x}, \boldsymbol{y})} = \frac{nv_{min}(\boldsymbol{x}, \boldsymbol{y})^2}{\|\boldsymbol{v}(\boldsymbol{x}, \boldsymbol{y})\|^2}.$$

$$h_{cp} = h_{cp}(x, y) = \frac{v}{\|v\|^2}.$$

$$h_{cen} = h_{cen}(x, y) = \frac{nv}{\|v\|^2} - V^{-1}e = \frac{v}{\mu} - V^{-1}e.$$

$$h(\beta) = h(\beta, x, y) = V^{-1}(\beta\mu e - Xy) = \beta\mu V^{-1}e - v.$$

ρ_{max}: the maximum value of the ratios Δ_1/Δ_2 for all minors Δ_1 of order n of the matrix $(-M \;\; I \;\; q)$ and all nonzero minors Δ_2 of order n of the matrix $(-M \;\; I)$.

ρ_{min}: the positive minimum value of the ratios Δ_1/Δ_2 for all minors Δ_1 of order n of the matrix $(-M \;\; I \;\; q)$ and all nonzero minors Δ_2 of order n of the matrix $(-M \;\; I)$.

$$\bar{L} = \sum_{i=1}^{n}\sum_{j=1}^{n} \log_2(|m_{ij}| + 1) + \sum_{i=1}^{n} \log_2(|q_i| + 1) + 2\log_2 n.$$

$L = \sum_{i=1}^{n}\sum_{j=1}^{n} \lceil \log_2(|m_{ij}| + 1)\rceil + \sum_{i=1}^{n} \lceil \log_2(|q_i| + 1)\rceil + 2\lceil \log_2(n+1)\rceil + n(n+1)$: the size of the LCP.

$(dx, dy) \in R^{2n}$: the solution of the system

$$\begin{pmatrix} Y & X \\ -M & I \end{pmatrix} \begin{pmatrix} dx \\ dy \end{pmatrix} = \begin{pmatrix} \beta \frac{x^T y}{n} e - Xy \\ 0 \end{pmatrix}$$

for every $0 \leq \beta \leq 1$ and $(x, y) \in S_{++}$.

$(dx^a, dy^a) \in R^{2n}$: the solution of the system

$$\begin{pmatrix} Y & X \\ -M & I \end{pmatrix} \begin{pmatrix} dx \\ dy \end{pmatrix} = \begin{pmatrix} -Xy \\ 0 \end{pmatrix}$$

for every $(x, y) \in S_{++}$.

$(dx^c, dy^c) \in R^{2n}$: the solution of the system

$$\begin{pmatrix} Y & X \\ -M & I \end{pmatrix} \begin{pmatrix} dx \\ dy \end{pmatrix} = \begin{pmatrix} \frac{x^T y}{n} e - Xy \\ 0 \end{pmatrix}$$

for every $(x, y) \in S_{++}$.

$$\Theta(\tau) = \sup\{\theta \geq 0 : \theta dx \geq -\tau x, \;\; \theta dy \geq -\tau y\}.$$

$$\Delta(\beta) = \max\left\{0, -\frac{dx^T dy}{\|h(\beta)\|^2}\right\}.$$

$$g_{cp}(\beta) = g_{cp}(\beta, \boldsymbol{x}, \boldsymbol{y}) = \frac{(1-\beta)\pi}{\sqrt{(1+2\Delta(\beta))\{(1-\beta)^2 n\pi + \beta^2\omega^2\}}}.$$

$$g_{cen}(\beta) = g_{cen}(\beta, \boldsymbol{x}, \boldsymbol{y}) = \frac{\beta\omega^2}{\sqrt{(1+2\Delta(\beta))\{(1-\beta)^2 n\pi + \beta^2\omega^2\}}}.$$

$$g(\nu, \beta) = g(\nu, \beta, \boldsymbol{x}, \boldsymbol{y}) = \frac{\nu(1-\beta)\pi + \beta\omega^2}{\sqrt{(1+2\Delta(\beta))\{(1-\beta)^2 n\pi + \beta^2\omega^2\}}}.$$

$$\bar{g}_{cp}(\beta) = \bar{g}_{cp}(\beta, \boldsymbol{x}, \boldsymbol{y}) = \frac{(1-\beta)\pi}{\sqrt{(1+2\kappa)\{(1-\beta)^2 n\pi + \beta^2\omega^2\}}}.$$

$$\bar{g}_{cen}(\beta) = \bar{g}_{cen}(\beta, \boldsymbol{x}, \boldsymbol{y}) = \frac{\beta\omega^2}{\sqrt{(1+2\kappa)\{(1-\beta)^2 n\pi + \beta^2\omega^2\}}}.$$

$$\bar{g}(\nu, \beta) = \bar{g}(\nu, \beta, \boldsymbol{x}, \boldsymbol{y}) = \frac{\nu(1-\beta)\pi + \beta\omega^2}{\sqrt{(1+2\kappa)\{(1-\beta)^2 n\pi + \beta^2\omega^2\}}}.$$

$$\bar{\tau} = \min\left\{\frac{1}{2}, \frac{g(\nu,\beta)}{2\bar{\eta}(n,\nu)}, \frac{g_{cen}(\beta) + \sqrt{g_{cen}(\beta)^2 + 5(\alpha_{bd} - f_{cen}(\boldsymbol{x}, \boldsymbol{y}))}}{(5/2)}\right\}.$$

$$\bar{\theta} = \frac{v_{min}\bar{\tau}}{\sqrt{1 + 2\Delta(\beta)\|\boldsymbol{h}(\beta)\|}}.$$

$$\bar{\omega}(\alpha) = \frac{\sqrt{\alpha^2 + 2\alpha} - \alpha}{\sqrt{\alpha^2 + 2\alpha} - \alpha + 1} \quad \text{for every } \alpha \geq 0.$$

For every $0 < \alpha_{cen} \leq \alpha_1 \leq \alpha_{bd}$:

$$\psi_\infty(\alpha_{cen}, \alpha_1) = \frac{1}{4}\min\left\{\exp(-\alpha_1 - 1),\ \bar{\omega}(\alpha_{cen})^2\right\},$$

$$\psi_{bd}(\alpha_1, \alpha_{bd}) = \min\left\{\frac{4(\alpha_{bd} - \alpha_1)}{5},\ \frac{16\bar{\omega}(\alpha_1)^4}{25(1 + \bar{\omega}(\alpha_1)^2)}\right\},$$

$$\psi(\alpha_{cen}, \alpha_1, \alpha_{bd}) = \min\{\psi_\infty(\alpha_{cen}, \alpha_1),\ \psi_{bd}(\alpha_1, \alpha_{bd})\}.$$

For every positive integer n and positive number ν:

$$\bar{\eta}(n, \nu) = \max\left\{1, \frac{\nu}{n}\right\},$$

$$\eta(n, \nu) = \begin{cases} n/\nu^2 & \text{if } 0 < \nu \leq \sqrt{n}, \\ \nu^2/n & \text{if } \sqrt{n} < \nu \leq n, \\ \nu & \text{if } n < \nu, \end{cases}$$

$$\eta_\infty(n,\nu) = \begin{cases} n/\nu^2 & \text{if } 0 < \nu \le \sqrt{n}, \\ 1 & \text{if } \sqrt{n} < \nu \le n, \\ \nu/n & \text{if } n < \nu, \end{cases}$$

$$\eta_0(n,\nu) = \begin{cases} n^{3/2}/\nu^2 & \text{if } 0 < \nu \le \sqrt{n}, \\ \nu & \text{if } \sqrt{n} < \nu \le n, \\ \nu^2/n & \text{if } n < \nu, \end{cases}$$

$$\phi(n,\nu) = \min\left\{1,\ \frac{\nu^2}{n}\right\}.$$

References

[1] I. Adler, M. G. C. Resende, G. Veiga and N. Karmarkar. An implementation of Karmarkar's algorithm for linear programming. *Mathematical Programming*, 44:297–335, 1989.

[2] M. Aganagić and R. W. Cottle. A constructive characterization of Q_0-matrices with nonnegative principal minors. *Mathematical Programming*, 37:223–231, 1987.

[3] E. R. Barnes. A variation on Karmarkar's algorithm for solving linear programming problems. *Mathematical Programming*, 36:174–182, 1986.

[4] E. R. Barnes, S. Chopra and D. L. Jensen. A polynomial time version of the affine algorithm. Technical report, IBM Thomas J. Watson Research Center, Yorktown Heights, New York 10598, 1988.

[5] D. A. Bayer and J. C. Lagarias. The nonlinear geometry of linear programming I. Affine and projective scaling trajectories. *Transactions of the American Mathematical Society*, 314:499–526, 1989.

[6] D. A. Bayer and J. C. Lagarias. The nonlinear geometry of linear programming II. Legendre transform coordinates and central trajectories. *Transactions of the American Mathematical Society*, 314:527–581, 1989.

[7] W. J. Carolan, J. E. Hill, J. L. Kennington, S. Niemi and S. J. Wichmann. An empirical evaluation of the KORBX algorithms for military airlift applications. *The Journal of the Operations Research Society of America*, 38:240–248, 1990.

[8] S. J. Chung. A note on the complexity of the LCP: the LCP is strongly NP-complete. Technical Report 792, Department of Industrial and Operations Engineering, The University of Michigan, Ann Arbor, MI 48109-2117, 1979.

[9] R. W. Cottle, J.-S. Pang and V. Venkateswaran. Sufficient matrices and the linear complementarity problem. *Linear Algebra and Its Applications*, 114/115:231–249, 1989.

[10] D. den Hertog, C. Roos and T. Terlaky. A potential reduction variant of Renegar's short-step path-following method for linear programming. Technical Report, Faculty of Technical Mathematics and Informatics, Delft University of Technology, P. O. Box 356, 2600 AJ Delft, The Netherlands, 1990.

[11] I. I. Dikin. Iterative solution of problems of linear and quadratic programming. *Soviet Mathematics Doklady*, 8:674–675, 1967.

[12] I. I. Dikin. On the speed of an iterative process. *Upravlyaemye Sistemi*, 12:54–60, 1974.

[13] J. Ding and T.-Y. Li. A polynomial-time predictor-corrector algorithm for linear complementarity problems. Technical report, Department of Mathematics, Michigan State University, East Lansing, MI 48824, 1989.

[14] A. V. Fiacco and G. P. McCormick. *Nonlinear Programming: Sequential Unconstrained Minimization Technique.* John Wiley, New York, 1968.

[15] M. Fiedler and V. Pták. On matrices with non-positive off-diagonal elements and positive principal minors. *Czechoslovak Mathematical Journal*, 12:382–400, 1962.

[16] M. Fiedler and V. Pták. Some generalizations of positive definiteness and monotonicity. *Numerische Mathematik*, 9:163–172, 1966.

[17] B. A. Freedman, S. C. Puthenpura and L. P. Sinha. A new affine scaling based algorithm for optimizing convex, nonlinear functions with linear constraints. AT&T Bell Laboratories, Holmdel, NJ, 1990.

[18] R. M. Freund. Polynomial-time algorithms for linear programming based only on primal scaling and projected gradients of a potential function. OR 182-88, Sloan School of Management, Massachusetts Institute of Technology, Cambridge, Massachusetts 02139, 1988.

[19] K. R. Frish. The logarithmic potential method of convex programming. Technical report, University Institute of Economics, Oslo, Norway, 1955.

[20] D. Goldfarb and S. Liu. An $O(n^3L)$ primal interior point algorithm for convex quadratic programming. Technical report, Department of Industrial Engineering and Operations Research, Columbia University, New York, New York 10027, 1988.

[21] D. Goldfarb and M. J. Todd. Linear Programming. In G. L. Nemhauser, A. H. G. Rinnooy Kan and M. J. Todd, editor, *Handbooks in Operations Research and Management Science, Volume 1, Optimization*, pages 73-170, North-Holland, Amsterdam, 1989,

[22] C. C. Gonzaga. An algorithm for solving linear programming programs in $O(n^3L)$ operations. In N. Megiddo, editor, *Progress in Mathematical Programming, Interior Point and Related Methods*, pages 1–28, Springer-Verlag, New York, 1989.

[23] C. C. Gonzaga. Polynomial affine algorithms for linear programming. ES-139/88, Dept. of Systems Engineering and Computer Sciences, COPPE-Federal University of Rio de Janeiro, Cx. Postal 68511, 21941 Rio de Janeiro, RJ, Brazil, 1988.

[24] C. C. Gonzaga. Newton barrier function algorithms for following the central trajectory in linear programming problems. Presented at the 13th Mathematical Programming Symposium, Tokyo, Dept. of Systems Engineering and Computer Sciences, COPPE-Federal University of Rio de Janeiro, Cx. Postal 68511, 21941 Rio de Janeiro, RJ, Brazil, 1988.

[25] H. Hironaka. Triangulation of algebraic sets. In R. Hartshorne, editor, *Proceedings of Symposia in Pure Mathematics Vol. 29*, pages 165–185, American Mathematical Society, Providence, Rhode Island, 1975.

[26] F. Jarre, G. Sonnevend and J. Stoer. On the numerical solution of generalized quadratic programs by following a central path. Technical report, Institut für Angewandte Mathematik und Statistik, Universität Würzburg, Am Hubland, 8700 Würzburg, West-Germany, 1987.

[27] S. Kapoor and P. M. Vaidya. An extension of Karmarkar's interior point method to convex quadratic programming. Technical report, Department of Computer Science, University of Illinois at Urbana-Champaign, Urbana, IL 61801, 1988.

[28] N. Karmarkar. A new polynomial-time algorithm for linear programming. *Combinatorica*, 4:373–395, 1984.

[29] M. Kojima, N. Megiddo and T. Noma. Homotopy continuation methods for complementarity problems. Research Report RJ 6638 (63949), IBM Research, Almaden Research Center, San Jose, CA 95120-6099, 1989.

[30] M. Kojima, N. Megiddo and T. Noma. Homotopy continuation methods for nonlinear complementarity problems. *Mathematics of Operations Research*, to appear.

[31] M. Kojima, N. Megiddo and Y. Ye. An interior point potential reduction algorithm for the linear complementarity problem. *Mathematical Programming*, to appear.

[32] M. Kojima, S. Mizuno and T. Noma. A new continuation method for complementarity problems with uniform P-functions. *Mathematical Programming*, 43:107–113, 1989.

[33] M. Kojima, S. Mizuno and T. Noma. Limiting behavior of trajectories generated by a continuation method for monotone complementarity problems. *Mathematics of Operations Research*, to appear.

[34] M. Kojima, S. Mizuno and A. Yoshise. A primal-dual interior point algorithm for linear programming. In N. Megiddo, editor, *Progress in Mathematical Programming, Interior-Point and Related Methods*, pages 29–47, Springer-Verlag, New York, 1989.

[35] M. Kojima, S. Mizuno and A. Yoshise. A polynomial-time algorithm for a class of linear complementary problems. *Mathematical Programming*, 44:1–26, 1989.

[36] M. Kojima, S. Mizuno and A. Yoshise. An $O(\sqrt{n}L)$ iteration potential reduction algorithm for linear complementarity problems. *Mathematical Programming*, to appear.

[37] I. J. Lustig. Private communication, Program in Statistics and Operations Research, Department of Civil Engineering and Operations Research, School of Engineering and Applied Science, Princeton University, Princeton, New Jersey 08544, 1989.

[38] R. Marsten, R. Subramanina, M. Saltzman, I. Lustig and D. Shanno. Interior point methods for linear programming: Just call Newton, Lagrange, and Fiacco and McCormick!. *Interface*, 20:105–116, 1990.

[39] H. Markowitz. *Portfolio Selection*. John Wiley & Sons, New York, 1959.

[40] L. McLinden. The complementarity problem for maximal monotone multifunctions. In R. W. Cottle, F. Giannessi and J. L. Lions, editors, *Variational Inequalities and Complementarity Problems*, pages 251–270, John Wiley, New York, 1980.

[41] K. A. McShane, C. L. Monma and D. F. Shanno. An implementation of a primal-dual interior point method for linear programming. *ORSA Journal on Computing*, 1:70–83, 1989.

[42] N. Megiddo. Pathways to the optimal set in linear programming. In N. Megiddo, editor, *Progress in Mathematical Programming, Interior-Point and Related Methods*, pages 131–158, Springer-Verlag, New York, 1989.

[43] N. Megiddo and M. Shub. Boundary behavior of interior point algorithms in linear programming. *Mathematics of Operations Research*, 14:97–146, 1989.

[44] S. Mehrotra. Implementations of affine scaling methods: Approximate solutions of systems of linear equations using preconditioned conjugate gradient methods. Technical Report 89-04, Department of Industrial Engineering and Management Sciences, Northwestern University, Evanston, IL 60208, 1989.

[45] S. Mehrotra. Implementations of affine scaling methods: Towards faster implementations with complete Cholesky factor in use. Technical Report 89-15, Department of Industrial Engineering and Management Sciences, Northwestern University, Evanston, IL 60208, 1989.

[46] S. Mehrotra and J. Sun. An algorithm for convex quadratic programming that requires $O(n^{3.5}L)$ arithmetic operations. *Mathematics of Operations Research*, 15:342–363, 1990.

[47] S. Mizuno. A new polynomial time method for a linear complementarity problem. Technical Report No. 16, Department of Industrial Engineering and Management, Tokyo Institute of Technology, Oh-Okayama, Meguro-ku, Tokyo 152, Japan, 1989.

[48] S. Mizuno. An $O(n^3L)$ algorithm using a sequence for linear complementarity problem. Technical Report No. 18, Department of Industrial Engineering and Management, Tokyo Institute of Technology, Oh-Okayama, Meguro-ku, Tokyo 152, Japan, 1989.

[49] S. Mizuno. $O(n^{\rho}L)$ iteration $O(n^3L)$ potential reduction algorithms for linear programming. Technical Report No. 22, Department of Industrial Engineering and Management, Tokyo Institute of Technology, Oh-Okayama, Meguro-ku, Tokyo 152, Japan, 1989.

[50] S. Mizuno and M. J. Todd. An $O(n^3L)$ long step path following algorithm for a linear complementarity problem. Technical Report No. 23, Department of Industrial Engineering and Management, Tokyo Institute of Technology, Oh-Okayama, Meguro-ku, Tokyo 152, Japan, 1989.

[51] S. Mizuno, A. Yoshise and T. Kikuchi. Practical polynomial time algorithms for linear complementarity problems. *J. Operations Research Soc. of Japan*, 32:75–92, 1989.

[52] C. L. Monma and A. J. Morton. Computational experience with a dual affine variant of Karmarkar's method for linear programming. Technical report, Bell Communications Research, Morristown, New Jersey 07960, 1986.

[53] R. D. C. Monteiro and I. Adler. Interior path following primal-dual algorithms. Part I: Linear programming. *Mathematical Programming*, 44:27–41, 1989.

[54] R. D. C. Monteiro and I. Adler. Interior path following primal-dual algorithms. Part II: Convex quadratic programming. *Mathematical Programming*, 44:43–66, 1989.

[55] J. E. Nesterov and A. S. Nemirovsky. Self-concordant functions and polynomial-time methods in convex programming, Central Economical and Mathematical Institute, USSR Acad. Sci., Moskow, USSR, 1989.

[56] J.-S. Pang. Iterative descent algorithms for a row sufficient linear complementarity problem. Technical report, Department of Mathematical Sciences, The Whiting School of Engineering, The Johns Hopkins University, Baltimore, MD 21218, 1989.

[57] J. Renegar. A polynomial-time algorithm based on Newton's method for linear programming. *Mathematical Programming*, 40:59–94, 1988.

[58] J. Renegar and M. Shub. Simplified complexity analysis for Newton LP methods. Technical Report No. 807, School of Operations Research and Industrial Engineering, College of Engineering, Cornell University, Ithaca, New York 14853-7501, 1988.

[59] C. Roos and J.-P. Vial. A polynomial method of approximate centers for linear programming. Report 88-68, Faculty of Technical Mathematics and Informatics, Delft University of Technology, P. O. Box 356, 2600 AJ Delft, The Netherlands, 1988.

[60] H. Samelson, R. Thrall and O. Wesler. A partition theorem for Euclidean n-space. In *Proceedings of American Mathematical Society, 9*, pages 805–807, 1958.

[61] A. Schrijver. *Theory of Linear and Integer Programming.* John-Wiley & Sons, New York, 1986.

[62] J. T. Schwartz. *Nonlinear Functional Analysis.* Gordon and Breach Science Publishers, New York, NY 10011, 1969.

[63] D. F. Shanno. Current state of primal-dual interior code. Presented at the Second Asilomar Workshop on Progress in Mathematical Programming, Department of Civil Engineering and Operations Research, Princeton University, Princeton, New Jersey, 1990.

[64] D. F. Shanno. Interior point methodsfor linear programming – state-of-the-art. Presented at SIAM Annual Meeting, Chicago, July, 1990.

[65] G. Sonnevend. An "analytical centre" for polyhedrons and new classes of global algorithms for linear (smooth, convex) programming. In *Lecture Notes in Control and Information Sciences 84*, pages 866–876, New York, 1985. Springer.

[66] G. Sonnevend. A new method for solving a set of linear (convex) inequalities and its applications. Technical report, Department of Numerical Analysis, Institute of Mathematics, L. Eötvös University, Budapest, 1088. Muzeum krt. 6-8. Hungary, 1985.

[67] K. Tanabe. Center flattening transformation and a centered Newton method for linear programming. Technical report, The Institute of Statistical Mathematics, 4-6-7 Minamiazabu, Minato-ku, Tokyo, Japan, 1987.

[68] K. Tanabe. Complementarity-enforcing centered Newton method for mathematical programming. In K. Tone, editor, *New Methods for Linear Programming*, pages 118–144, The Institute of Statistical Mathematics, 4-6-7 Minamiazabu, Minato-ku, Tokyo 106, Japan, 1987.

[69] K. Tanabe. Centered Newton method for mathematical programming. In M. Iri and K. Yajima, editors, *System Modelling and Optimization*, pages 197–206. Springer-Verlag, New York, 1988.

[70] M. J. Todd. Recent developments and new directions in linear programming, In N. Iri and K. Tanabe, editors, *Mathematical Programming, Recent Developments and Applications*, pages 109–157, Kluwer Academic Publishers, London, 1989,

[71] M. J. Todd and B. P. Burrell. An extension of Karmarkar's algorithm for linear programming using dual variables. *Algorithmica*, 1:409–424, 1986.

[72] M. J. Todd and Y. Ye. A centered projective algorithm for linear programming. *Mathematics of Operations Research*, 15:508–529, 1990.

[73] T. Tsuchiya. Global convergence property of the affine scaling methods for primal degenerate linear programming problems. Technical report, The Institute of Statistical Mathematics, Minami-Azabu, Minato-ku, Tokyo 106, Japan, 1989.

[74] P. M. Vaidya. An algorithm for linear programming which requires $O(((m+n)n^2 + (m+n)^{1.5}n)L)$ arithmetic operations. Technical report, AT&T Bell Laboratories, Murray Hill, New Jersey 07974, 1987.

[75] R. J. Vanderbei and J. C. Lagarias. I. I. Dikin's convergence result for the affine-scaling algorithm. Technical report, AT&T Bell Laboratories, Murray Hill, New Jersey 07974, 1988.

[76] R. J. Vanderbei, M. S. Meketon and B. A. Freedman. A modification of Karmarkar's linear programming algorithm. *Algorithmica*, 1:395–407, 1986.

[77] Y. Ye. A class of potential functions for linear programming. Technical report, Integrated Systems Inc., Santa Clara, CA and Department of Engineering-Economic Systems, Stanford University, Stanford, CA, 1988.

[78] Y. Ye. A further result on the potential reduction algorithm for the P-matrix linear complementarity problem. Technical report, Department of Management Sciences, The University of Iowa, Iowa City, Iowa 52242, 1988.

[79] Y. Ye. The potential algorithm for linear complementarity problems. Technical report, Department of Management Sciences, The University of Iowa, Iowa City, Iowa 52242, 1988.

[80] Y. Ye. Line search in potential reduction algorithms for linear programming. Technical report, Department of Management Sciences, The University of Iowa, Iowa City, Iowa 52242, 1989.

[81] Y. Ye. An $O(n^3L)$ potential reduction algorithm for linear programming. Technical report, Department of Management Sciences, The University of Iowa, Iowa City, Iowa 52242, 1989.

[82] Y. Ye and P. Pardalos. A class of linear complementarity problems solvable in polynomial time. Technical report, Department of Management Sciences, The University of Iowa, Iowa City, Iowa 52242, 1989.

Lecture Notes in Computer Science

For information about Vols. 1–454
please contact your bookseller or Springer-Verlag

Vol. 455: C.A. Floudas, P.M. Pardalos, A Collection of Test Problems for Constrained Global Optimization Algorithms. XIV, 180 pages. 1990.

Vol. 456: P. Deransart, J. Maluszyński (Eds.), Programming Language Implementation and Logic Programming. Proceedings, 1990. VIII, 401 pages. 1990.

Vol. 457: H. Burkhart (Ed.), CONPAR '90 – VAPP IV. Proceedings, 1990. XIV, 900 pages. 1990.

Vol. 458: J.C.M. Baeten, J.W. Klop (Eds.), CONCUR '90. Proceedings, 1990. VII, 537 pages. 1990.

Vol. 459: R. Studer (Ed.), Natural Language and Logic. Proceedings, 1989. VII, 252 pages. 1990. (Subseries LNAI).

Vol. 460: J. Uhl, H.A. Schmid, A Systematic Catalogue of Reusable Abstract Data Types. XII, 344 pages. 1990.

Vol. 461: P. Deransart, M. Jourdan (Eds.), Attribute Grammars and their Applications. Proceedings, 1990. VIII, 358 pages. 1990.

Vol. 462: G. Gottlob, W. Nejdl (Eds.), Expert Systems in Engineering. Proceedings, 1990. IX, 260 pages. 1990. (Subseries LNAI).

Vol. 463: H. Kirchner, W. Wechler (Eds.), Algebraic and Logic Programming. Proceedings, 1990. VII, 386 pages. 1990.

Vol. 464: J. Dassow, J. Kelemen (Eds.), Aspects and Prospects of Theoretical Computer Science. Proceedings, 1990. VI, 298 pages. 1990.

Vol. 465: A. Fuhrmann, M. Morreau (Eds.), The Logic of Theory Change. Proceedings, 1989. X, 334 pages. 1991. (Subseries LNAI).

Vol. 466: A. Blaser (Ed.), Database Systems of the 90s. Proceedings, 1990. VIII, 334 pages. 1990.

Vol. 467: F. Long (Ed.), Software Engineering Environments. Proceedings, 1989. VI, 313 pages. 1990.

Vol. 468: S.G. Akl, F. Fiala, W.W. Koczkodaj (Eds.), Advances in Computing and Information – ICCI '90. Proceedings, 1990. VII, 529 pages. 1990.

Vol. 469: I. Guessarian (Ed.), Semantics of Systems of Concurrent Processes. Proceedings, 1990. V, 456 pages. 1990.

Vol. 470: S. Abiteboul, P.C. Kanellakis (Eds.), ICDT '90. Proceedings, 1990. VII, 528 pages. 1990.

Vol. 471: B.C. Ooi, Efficient Query Processing in Geographic Information Systems. VIII, 208 pages. 1990.

Vol. 472: K.V. Nori, C.E. Veni Madhavan (Eds.), Foundations of Software Technology and Theoretical Computer Science. Proceedings, 1990. X, 420 pages. 1990.

Vol. 473: I.B. Damgård (Ed.), Advances in Cryptology – EUROCRYPT '90. Proceedings, 1990. VIII, 500 pages. 1991.

Vol. 474: D. Karagiannis (Ed.), Information Systems and Artificial Intelligence: Integration Aspects. Proceedings, 1990. X, 293 pages. 1991. (Subseries LNAI).

Vol. 475: P. Schroeder-Heister (Ed.), Extensions of Logic Programming. Proceedings, 1989. VIII, 364 pages. 1991. (Subseries LNAI).

Vol. 476: M. Filgueiras, L. Damas, N. Moreira, A.P. Tomás (Eds.), Natural Language Processing. Proceedings, 1990. VII, 253 pages. 1991. (Subseries LNAI).

Vol. 477: D. Hammer (Ed.), Compiler Compilers. Proceedings, 1990. VI, 227 pages. 1991.

Vol. 478: J. van Eijck (Ed.), Logics in AI. Proceedings, 1990. IX, 562 pages. 1991. (Subseries in LNAI).

Vol. 479: H. Schmidt, Meta-Level Control for Deductive Database Systems. VI, 155 pages. 1991.

Vol. 480: C. Choffrut, M. Jantzen (Eds.), STACS 91. Proceedings, 1991. X, 549 pages. 1991.

Vol. 481: E. Lang, K.-U. Carstensen, G. Simmons, Modelling Spatial Knowledge on a Linguistic Basis. IX, 138 pages. 1991. (Subseries LNAI).

Vol. 482: Y. Kodratoff (Ed.), Machine Learning – EWSL-91. Proceedings, 1991. XI, 537 pages. 1991. (Subseries LNAI).

Vol. 483: G. Rozenberg (Ed.), Advances in Petri Nets 1990. VI, 515 pages. 1991.

Vol. 484: R. H. Möhring (Ed.), Graph-Theoretic Concepts in Computer Science. Proceedings, 1990. IX, 360 pages. 1991.

Vol. 485: K. Furukawa, H. Tanaka, T. Fuijsaki (Eds.), Logic Programming '89. Proceedings, 1989. IX, 183 pages. 1991. (Subseries LNAI).

Vol. 486: J. van Leeuwen, N. Santoro (Eds.), Distributed Algorithms. Proceedings, 1990. VI, 433 pages. 1991.

Vol. 487: A. Bode (Ed.), Distributed Memory Computing. Proceedings, 1991. XI, 506 pages. 1991.

Vol. 488: R. V. Book (Ed.), Rewriting Techniques and Applications. Proceedings, 1991. VII, 458 pages. 1991.

Vol. 489: J. W. de Bakker, W. P. de Roever, G. Rozenberg (Eds.), Foundations of Object-Oriented Languages. Proceedings, 1990. VIII, 442 pages. 1991.

Vol. 490: J. A. Bergstra, L. M. G. Feijs (Eds.), Algebraic Methods II: Theory, Tools and Applicatlons. VI, 434 pages. 1991.

Vol. 491: A. Yonezawa, T. Ito (Eds.), Concurrency: Theory, Language, and Architecture. Proceedings, 1989. VIII, 339 pages. 1991.

Vol. 492: D. Sriram, R. Logcher, S. Fukuda (Eds.), Computer-Aided Cooperative Product Development. Proceedings, 1989 VII, 630 pages. 1991.

Vol. 493: S. Abramsky, T. S. E. Maibaum (Eds.), TAPSOFT '91. Volume 1. Proceedings, 1991. VIII, 455 pages. 1991.

Vol. 494: S. Abramsky, T. S. E. Maibaum (Eds.), TAPSOFT '91. Volume 2. Proceedings, 1991. VIII, 482 pages. 1991.

Vol. 495: 9. Thalheim, J. Demetrovics, H.-D. Gerhardt (Eds.), MFDBS '91. Proceedings, 1991. VI, 395 pages. 1991.

Vol. 496: H.-P. Schwefel, R. Männer (Eds.), Parallel Problem Solving from Nature. Proceedings, 1990. XI, 485 pages. 1991.

Vol. 497: F. Dehne, F. Fiala. W.W. Koczkodaj (Eds.), Advances in Computing and Information - ICCI '91. Proceedings, 1991. VIII, 745 pages. 1991.

Vol. 498: R. Andersen, J. A. Bubenko jr., A. Sølvberg (Eds.), Advanced Information Systems Engineering. Proceedings, 1991. VI, 579 pages. 1991.

Vol. 499: D. Christodoulakis (Ed.), Ada: The Choice for '92. Proceedings, 1991. VI, 411 pages. 1991.

Vol. 500: M. Held, On the Computational Geometry of Pocket Machining. XII, 179 pages. 1991.

Vol. 501: M. Bidoit, H.-J. Kreowski, P. Lescanne, F. Orejas, D. Sannella (Eds.), Algebraic System Specification and Development. VIII, 98 pages. 1991.

Vol. 502: J. Bārzdiņž, D. Bjørner (Eds.), Baltic Computer Science. X, 619 pages. 1991.

Vol. 503: P. America (Ed.), Parallel Database Systems. Proceedings, 1990. VIII, 433 pages. 1991.

Vol. 504: J. W. Schmidt, A. A. Stogny (Eds.), Next Generation Information System Technology. Proceedings, 1990. IX, 450 pages. 1991.

Vol. 505: E. H. L. Aarts, J. van Leeuwen, M. Rem (Eds.), PARLE '91. Parallel Architectures and Languages Europe, Volume I. Proceedings, 1991. XV, 423 pages. 1991.

Vol. 506: E. H. L. Aarts, J. van Leeuwen, M. Rem (Eds.), PARLE '91. Parallel Architectures and Languages Europe, Volume II. Proceedings, 1991. XV, 489 pages. 1991.

Vol. 507: N. A. Sherwani, E. de Doncker, J. A. Kapenga (Eds.), Computing in the 90's. Proceedings, 1989. XIII, 441 pages. 1991.

Vol. 508: S. Sakata (Ed.), Applied Algebra, Algebraic Algorithms and Error-Correcting Codes. Proceedings, 1990. IX, 390 pages. 1991.

Vol. 509: A. Endres, H. Weber (Eds.), Software Development Environments and CASE Technology. Proceedings, 1991. VIII, 286 pages. 1991.

Vol. 510: J. Leach Albert, B. Monien, M. Rodríguez (Eds.), Automata, Languages and Programming. Proceedings, 1991. XII, 763 pages. 1991.

Vol. 511: A. C. F. Colchester, D.J. Hawkes (Eds.), Information Processing in Medical Imaging. Proceedings, 1991. XI, 512 pages. 1991.

Vol. 512: P. America (Ed.), ECOOP '91. European Conference on Object-Oriented Programming. Proceedings, 1991. X, 396 pages. 1991.

Vol. 513: N. M. Mattos, An Approach to Knowledge Base Management. IX, 247 pages. 1991. (Subseries LNAI).

Vol. 514: G. Cohen, P. Charpin (Eds.), EUROCODE '90. Proceedings, 1990. XI, 392 pages. 1991.

Vol. 515: J. P. Martins, M. Reinfrank (Eds.), Truth Maintenance Systems. Proceedings, 1990. VII, 177 pages. 1991. (Subseries LNAI).

Vol. 516: S. Kaplan, M. Okada (Eds.), Conditional and Typed Rewriting Systems. Proceedings, 1990. IX, 461 pages. 1991.

Vol. 517: K. Nökel, Temporally Distributed Symptoms in Technical Diagnosis. IX, 164 pages. 1991. (Subseries LNAI).

Vol. 518: J. G. Williams, Instantiation Theory. VIII, 133 pages. 1991. (Subseries LNAI).

Vol. 519: F. Dehne, J.-R. Sack, N. Santoro (Eds.), Algorithms and Data Structures. Proceedings, 1991. X, 496 pages. 1991.

Vol. 520: A. Tarlecki (Ed.), Mathematical Foundations of Computer Science 1991. Proceedings, 1991. XI, 435 pages. 1991.

Vol. 521: B. Bouchon-Meunier, R. R. Yager, L. A. Zadek (Eds.), Uncertainty in Knowledge-Bases. Proceedings, 1990. X, 609 pages. 1991.

Vol. 522: J. Hertzberg (Ed.), European Workshop on Planning. Proceedings, 1991. VII, 121 pages. 1991. (Subseries LNAI).

Vol. 523: J. Hughes (Ed.), Functional Programming Languages and Computer Architecture. Proceedings, 1991. VIII, 666 pages. 1991.

Vol. 524: G. Rozenberg (Ed.), Advances in Petri Nets 1991. VIII, 572 pages. 1991.

Vol. 525: O. Günther, H.-J. Schek (Eds.), Advances in Spatial Databases. Proceedings, 1991. XI, 471 pages. 1991.

Vol. 526: T. Ito, A. R. Meyer (Eds.), Theoretical Aspects of Computer Software. Proceedings, 1991. X, 772 pages. 1991.

Vol. 527: J.C.M. Baeten, J. F. Groote (Eds.), CONCUR '91. Proceedings, 1991. VIII, 541 pages. 1991.

Vol. 528: J. Maluszynski, M. Wirsing (Eds.), Programming Language Implementation and Logic Programming. Proceedings, 1991. XI, 433 pages. 1991.

Vol. 529: L. Budach (Ed.), Fundamentals of Computation Theory. Proceedings, 1991. XII, 426 pages. 1991.

Vol. 530: D. H. Pitt, P.-L. Curien, S. Abramsky, A. M. Pitts, A. Poigné, D. E. Rydeheard (Eds.), Category Theory and Computer Science. Proceedings, 1991. VII, 301 pages. 1991.

Vol. 531: E. M. Clarke, R. P. Kurshan (Eds.), Computer-Aided Verification. Proceedings, 1990. XIII, 372 pages. 1991.

Vol. 532: H. Ehrig, H.-J. Kreowski, G. Rozenberg (Eds.), Graph Grammars and Their Application to Computer Science. Proceedings, 1990. X, 703 pages. 1991.

Vol. 533: E. Börger, H. Kleine Büning, M. M. Richter, W. Schönfeld (Eds.), Computer Science Logic. Proceedings, 1990. VIII, 399 pages. 1991.

Vol. 534: H. Ehrig, K. P. Jantke, F. Orejas, H. Reichel (Eds.), Recent Trends in Data Type Specification. Proceedings, 1990. VIII, 379 pages. 1991.

Vol. 535: P. Jorrand, J. Kelemen (Eds.), Fundamentals of Artificial Intelligence Research. Proceedings, 1991. VIII, 255 pages. 1991. (Subseries LNAI).

Vol. 536: J. E. Tomayko, Software Engineering Education. Proceedings, 1991. VIII, 296 pages. 1991.

Vol. 537: A. J. Menezes, S. A. Vanstone (Eds.), Advances in Cryptology – CRYPTO '90. Proceedings. XIII, 644 pages. 1991.

Vol. 538: M. Kojima, N. Megiddo, T. Noma, A. Yoshise, A Unified Approach to Interior Point Algorithms for Linear Complementarity Problems. VIII, 108 pages. 1991.